RECORD OF
GRANCREST
WAR

3

Original Story by **Ryo Mizuno**
Story & Art by **Makoto Yotsuba**
Character Design by **Miyuu**

PREVIOUSLY...

Story

Previously...
In a world where chaos is the most powerful force, the people are terrified of the threat it poses. They live under the protection of Lords, who are the only ones capable of wielding crests that can quell chaos.

However, the Lords use their crests to fight each other in petty battles over territory, and the continent has been plunged into a war-torn era.

Siluca Meletes, a mage, voids her contract with the Lustful Earl, Villar Constance, in order to enter a contract with a wandering Lord named Theo. Together, they defeat a feudal Lord, making Theo the Lord of that territory. Hearing that an unknown Lord had claimed the land, their ambitious neighbor and rival Lord, Lassic David, and his mage, Moreno, attack. However, with the help of Siluca's foster sister, the Artist Aishela, Siluca and Theo win the battle.

With Lassic David now serving him, Theo manages to defeat more Lords and expand his domain. He then takes the family name of Cornaro—after a legendary hero—and makes a vow to save the oppressed people of his homeland Sistina. In Theo, Siluca sees the ideal Lord—one who has great intuition and, more importantly, a sense of responsibility for his people.

In the meantime, the King of Sievis is making a move...

Key

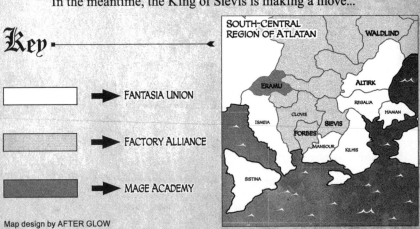

- FANTASIA UNION
- FACTORY ALLIANCE
- MAGE ACADEMY

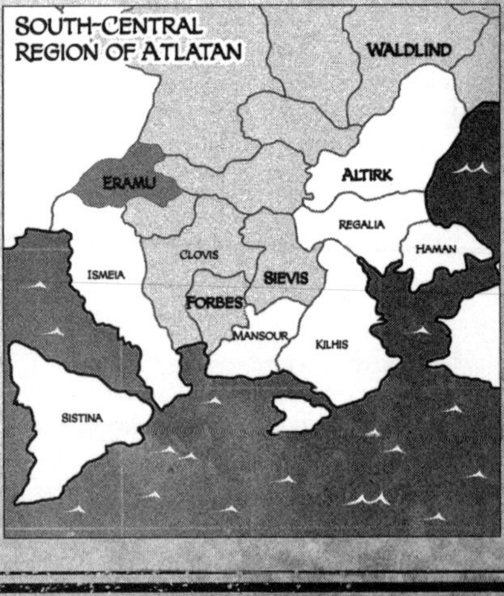
SOUTH-CENTRAL
REGION OF ATLATAN
WALDLIND
ERAMU
ALTIRK
REGALIA
HAMAN
ISMEIA
CLOVIS
SIEVIS
FORBES
MANSOUR
KILHIS
SISTINA

Map design by AFTER GLOW

Characters

Theo

A wandering Lord who hopes one day to free his homeland from tyranny. He enters into a contract with Siluca. He cares about his people and has great instincts.

Siluca Meletes

A mage thought to be a genius at school. She believes that Theo could be an ideal Lord and decides to serve him.

Irvin

A brilliant artist who used to serve an Archduke. Seeing potential in Siluca due to her ability to "treat him roughly," he chooses to serve her.

Aishela

A warrior and artist who loves Siluca. She is distrustful of Theo. Skilled with pole weapons, in battle she is both beautiful and deadly.

Lassic David

The ambitious Lord of Sievis. He sees potential in Theo and decides to serve him in hopes of one day fulfilling his own ambition.

Moreno Dortous

A mage who serves Lassic. He believes Lassic to have the makings of an emperor and advises him with that in mind.

Contents

RECORD OF
GRANCREST
WAR

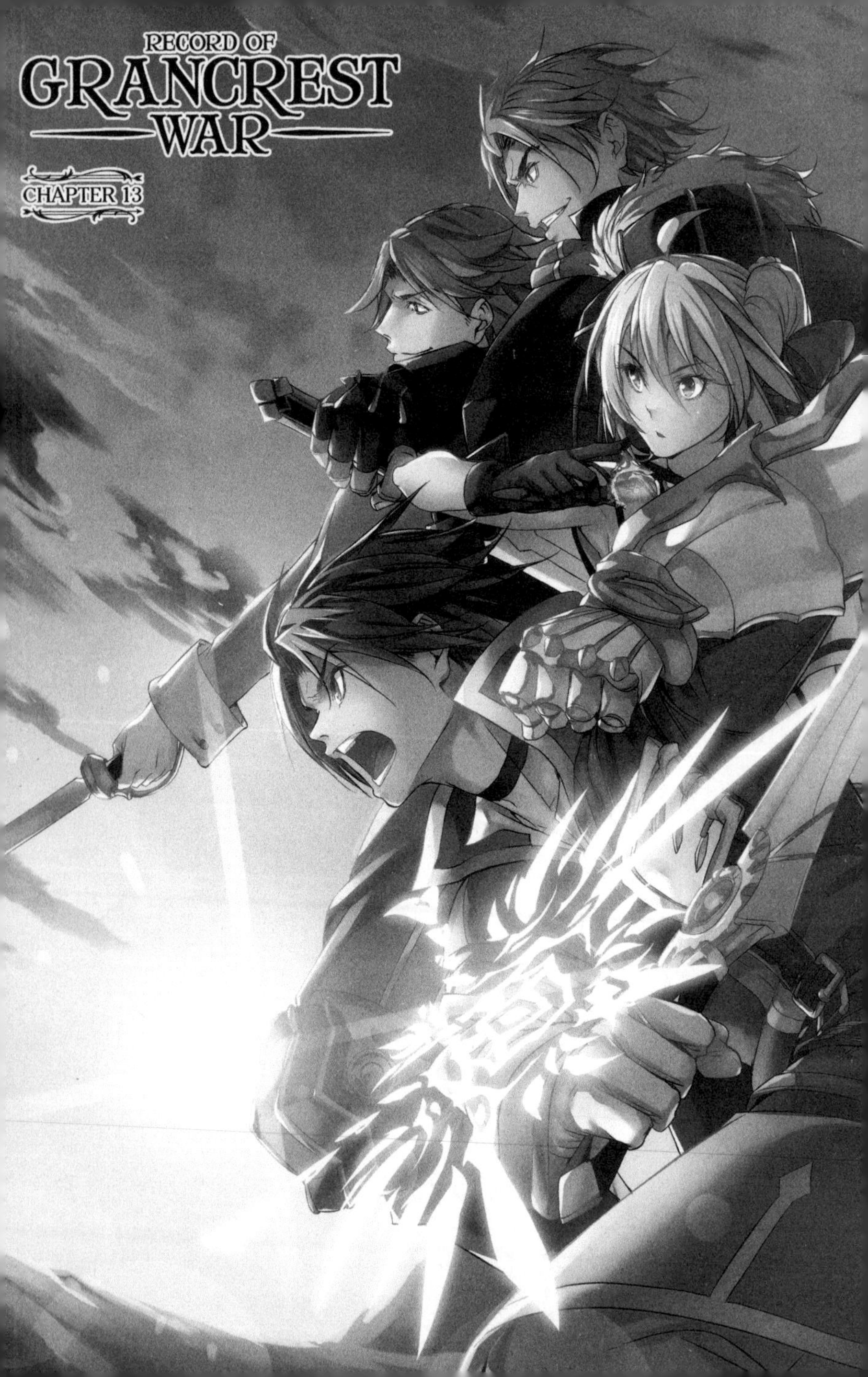
RECORD OF
GRANCREST
WAR
CHAPTER 13

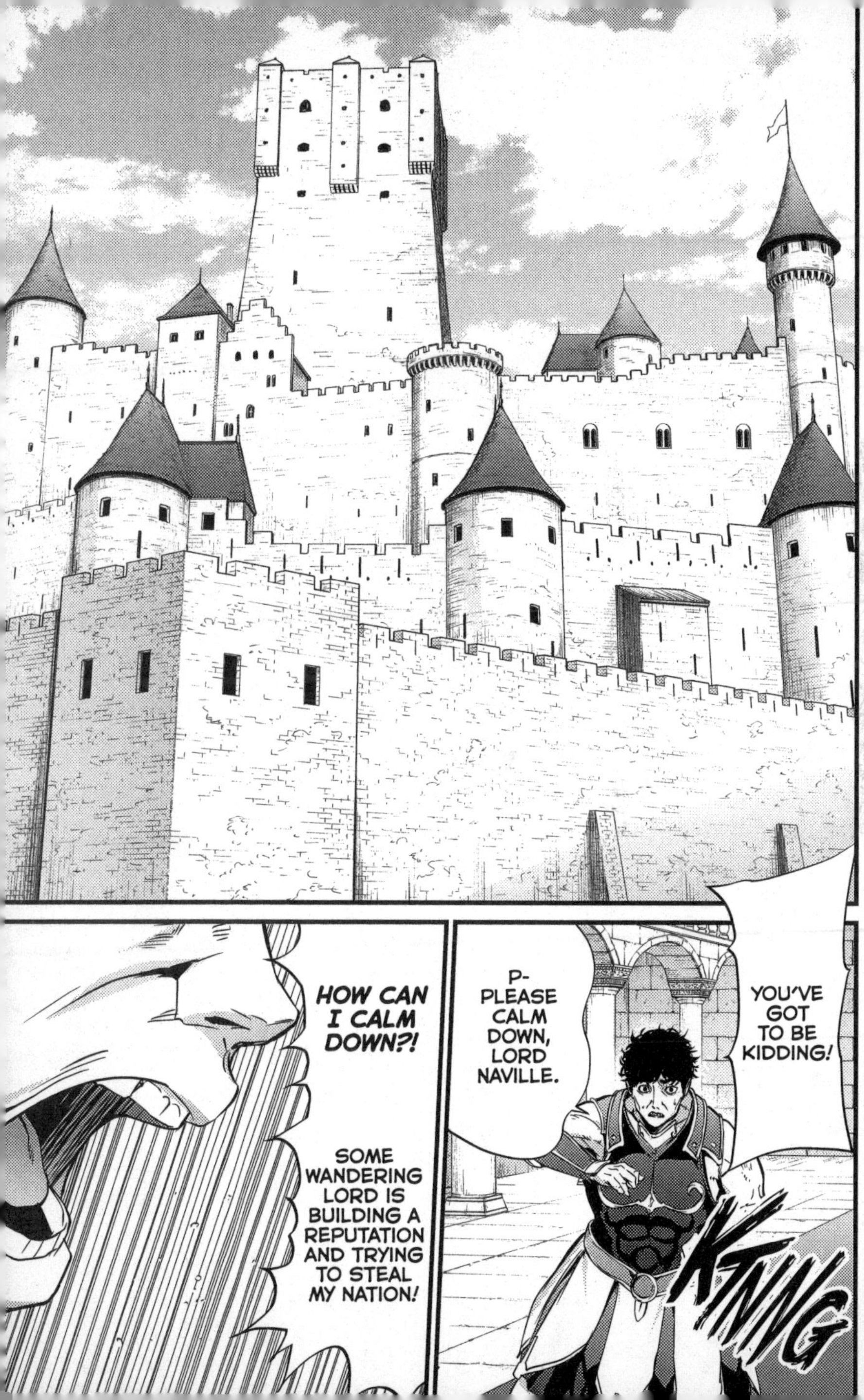
YOU'VE GOT TO BE KIDDING!
P-PLEASE CALM DOWN, LORD NAVILLE.
HOW CAN I CALM DOWN?!
SOME WANDERING LORD IS BUILDING A REPUTATION AND TRYING TO STEAL MY NATION!

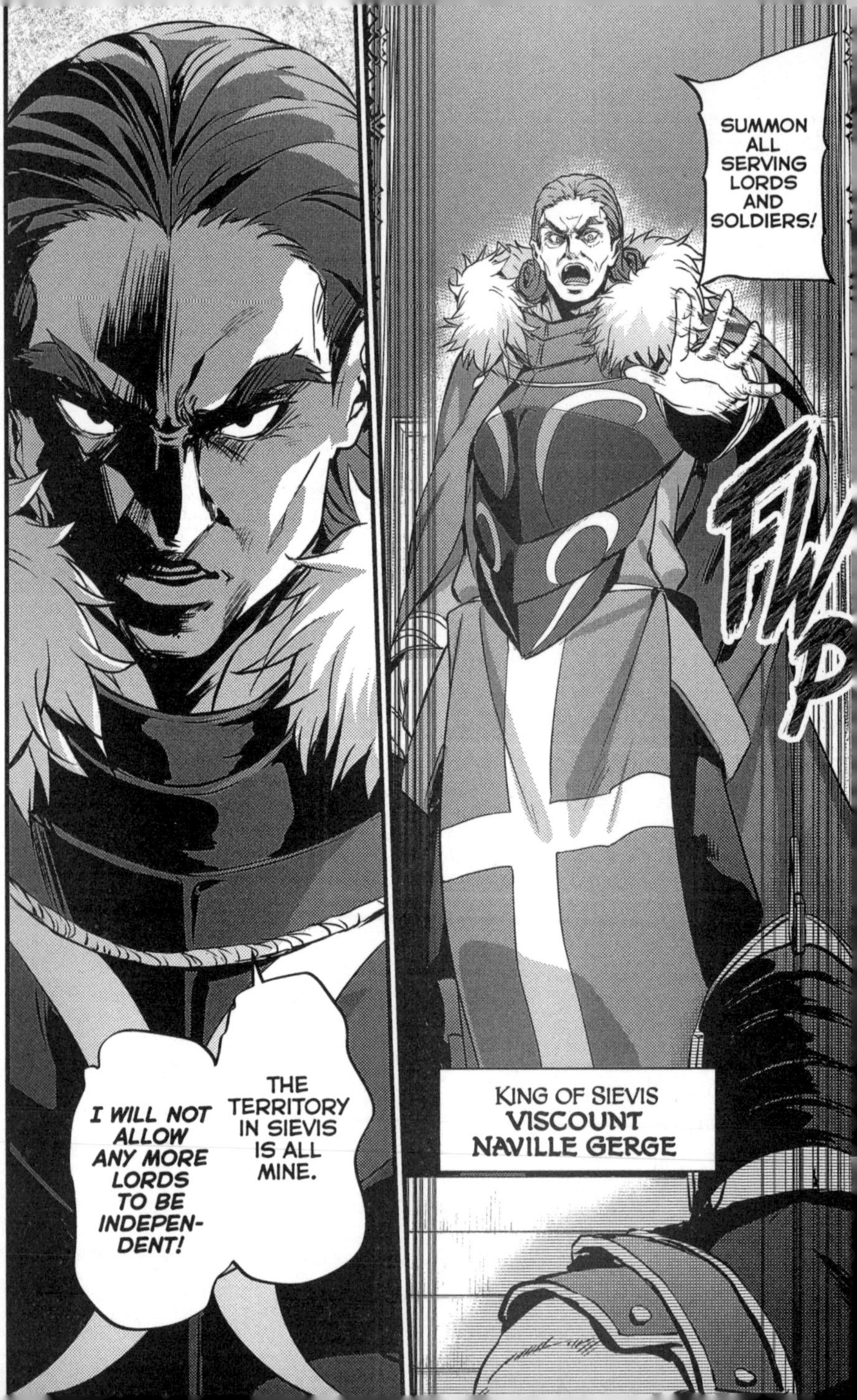
SUMMON ALL SERVING LORDS AND SOLDIERS!
FWAP
KING OF SIEVIS
VISCOUNT NAVILLE GERGE
THE TERRITORY IN SIEVIS IS ALL MINE.
I WILL NOT ALLOW ANY MORE LORDS TO BE INDEPENDENT!

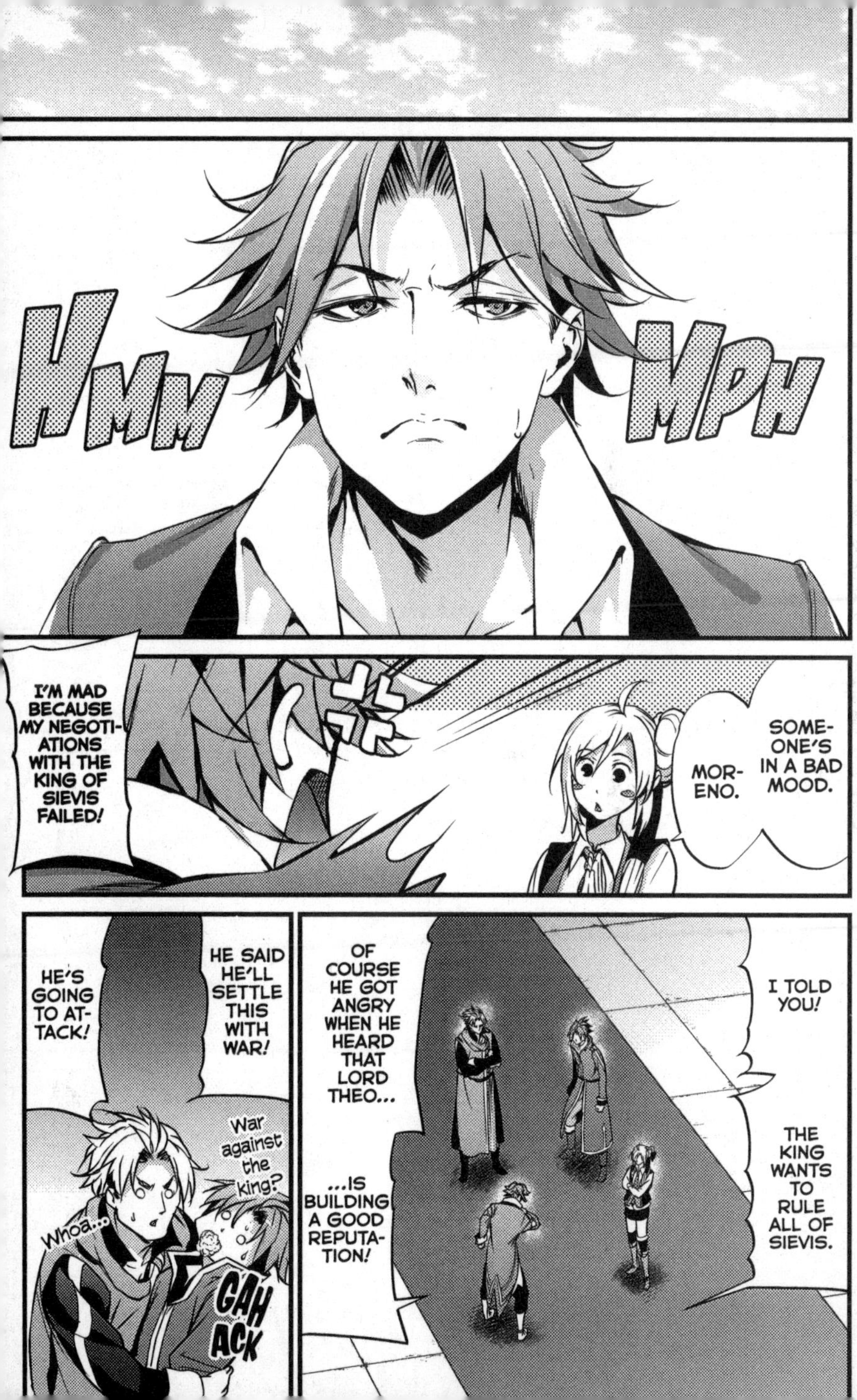
HMM MPH
SOME-ONE'S IN A BAD MOOD.
MOR-ENO.
I'M MAD BECAUSE MY NEGOTI-ATIONS WITH THE KING OF SIEVIS FAILED!
I TOLD YOU!
THE KING WANTS TO RULE ALL OF SIEVIS.
OF COURSE HE GOT ANGRY WHEN HE HEARD THAT LORD THEO...
...IS BUILDING A GOOD REPUTA-TION!
HE SAID HE'LL SETTLE THIS WITH WAR!
HE'S GOING TO AT-TACK!
War against the king?
Whoa...
GAH ACK

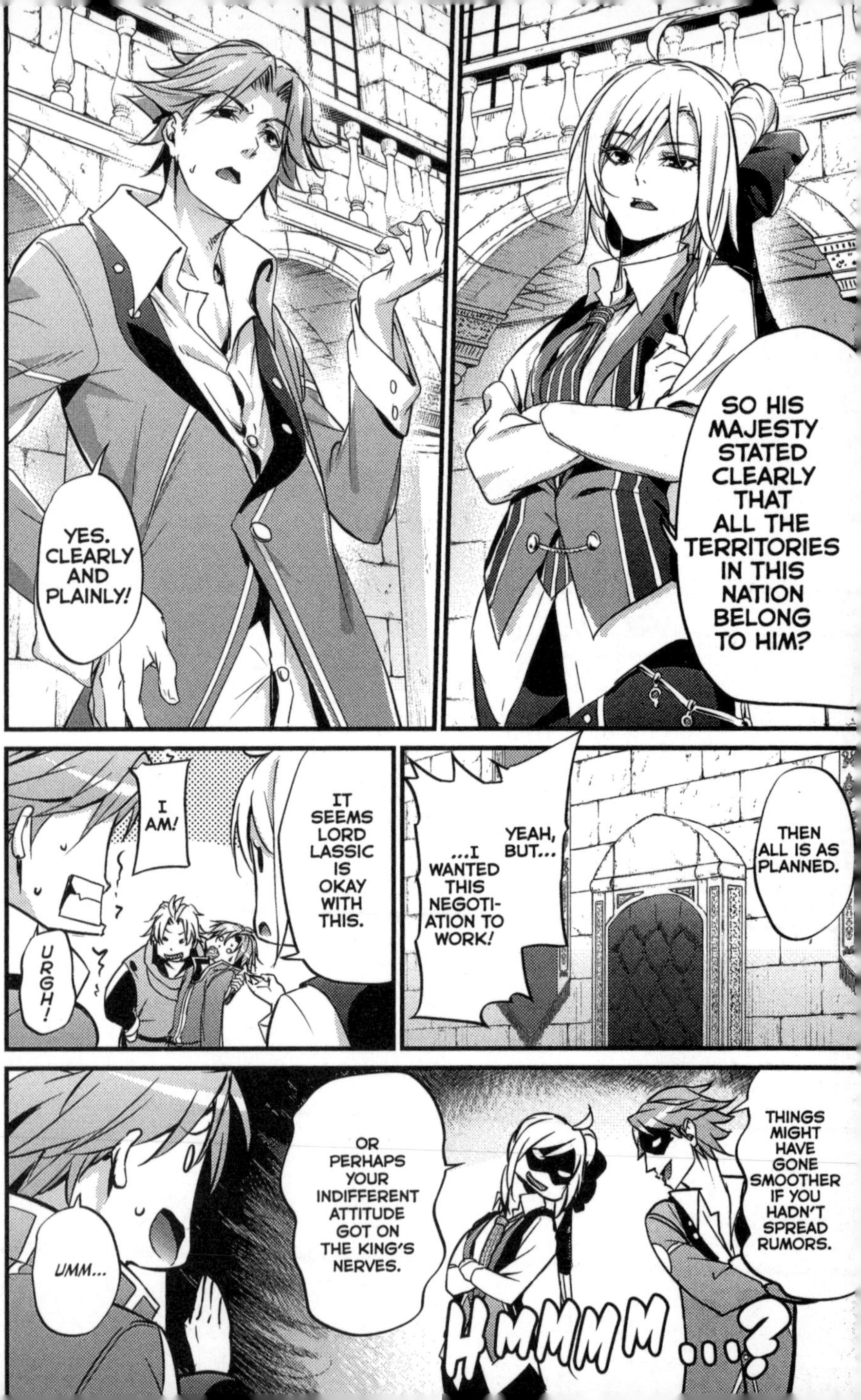
SO HIS MAJESTY STATED CLEARLY THAT ALL THE TERRITORIES IN THIS NATION BELONG TO HIM?
YES. CLEARLY AND PLAINLY!
THEN ALL IS AS PLANNED.
YEAH, BUT...
...I WANTED THIS NEGOTI-ATION TO WORK!
IT SEEMS LORD LASSIC IS OKAY WITH THIS.
I AM!
URGH!
THINGS MIGHT HAVE GONE SMOOTHER IF YOU HADN'T SPREAD RUMORS.
OR PERHAPS YOUR INDIFFERENT ATTITUDE GOT ON THE KING'S NERVES.
HMMMM...?
UMM...

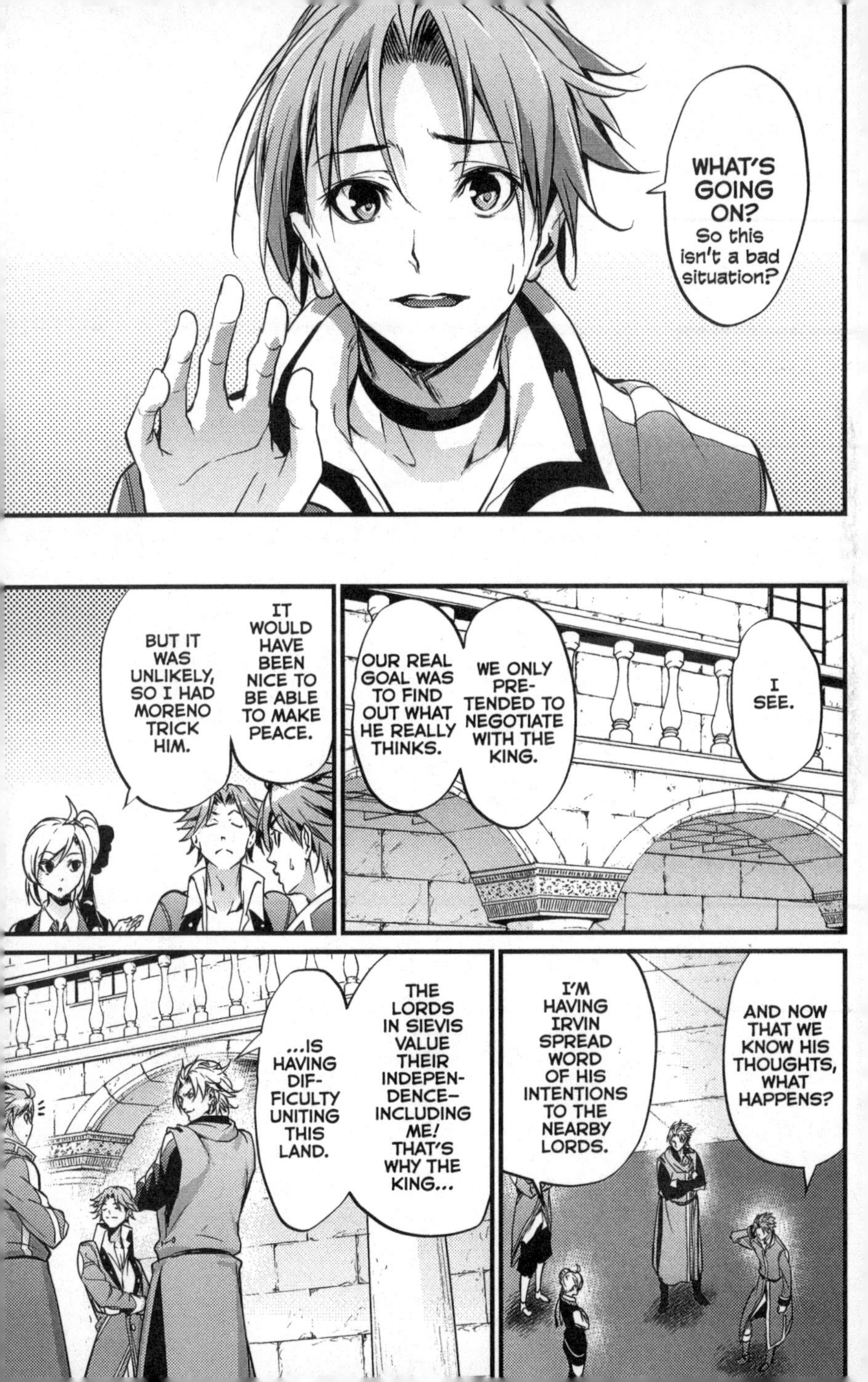
WHAT'S GOING ON?
So this isn't a bad situation?
I SEE.
WE ONLY PRETENDED TO NEGOTIATE WITH THE KING.
OUR REAL GOAL WAS TO FIND OUT WHAT HE REALLY THINKS.
IT WOULD HAVE BEEN NICE TO BE ABLE TO MAKE PEACE.
BUT IT WAS UNLIKELY, SO I HAD MORENO TRICK HIM.
AND NOW THAT WE KNOW HIS THOUGHTS, WHAT HAPPENS?
I'M HAVING IRVIN SPREAD WORD OF HIS INTENTIONS TO THE NEARBY LORDS.
THE LORDS IN SIEVIS VALUE THEIR INDEPENDENCE—INCLUDING ME! THAT'S WHY THE KING...
...IS HAVING DIFFICULTY UNITING THIS LAND.

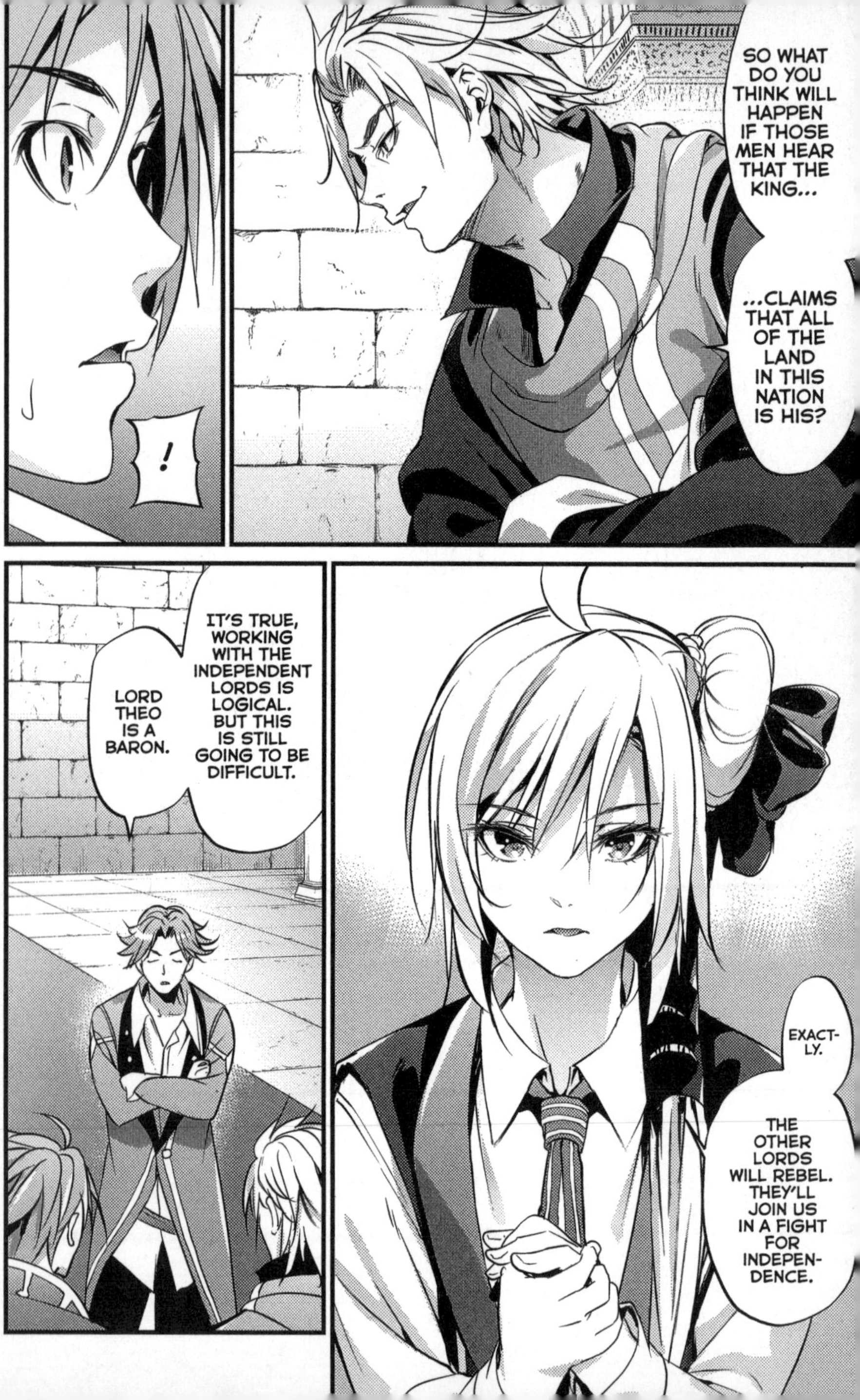
SO WHAT DO YOU THINK WILL HAPPEN IF THOSE MEN HEAR THAT THE KING...
...CLAIMS THAT ALL OF THE LAND IN THIS NATION IS HIS?
!
EXACT-LY.
THE OTHER LORDS WILL REBEL. THEY'LL JOIN US IN A FIGHT FOR INDEPEN-DENCE.
IT'S TRUE, WORKING WITH THE INDEPENDENT LORDS IS LOGICAL. BUT THIS IS STILL GOING TO BE DIFFICULT.
LORD THEO IS A BARON.

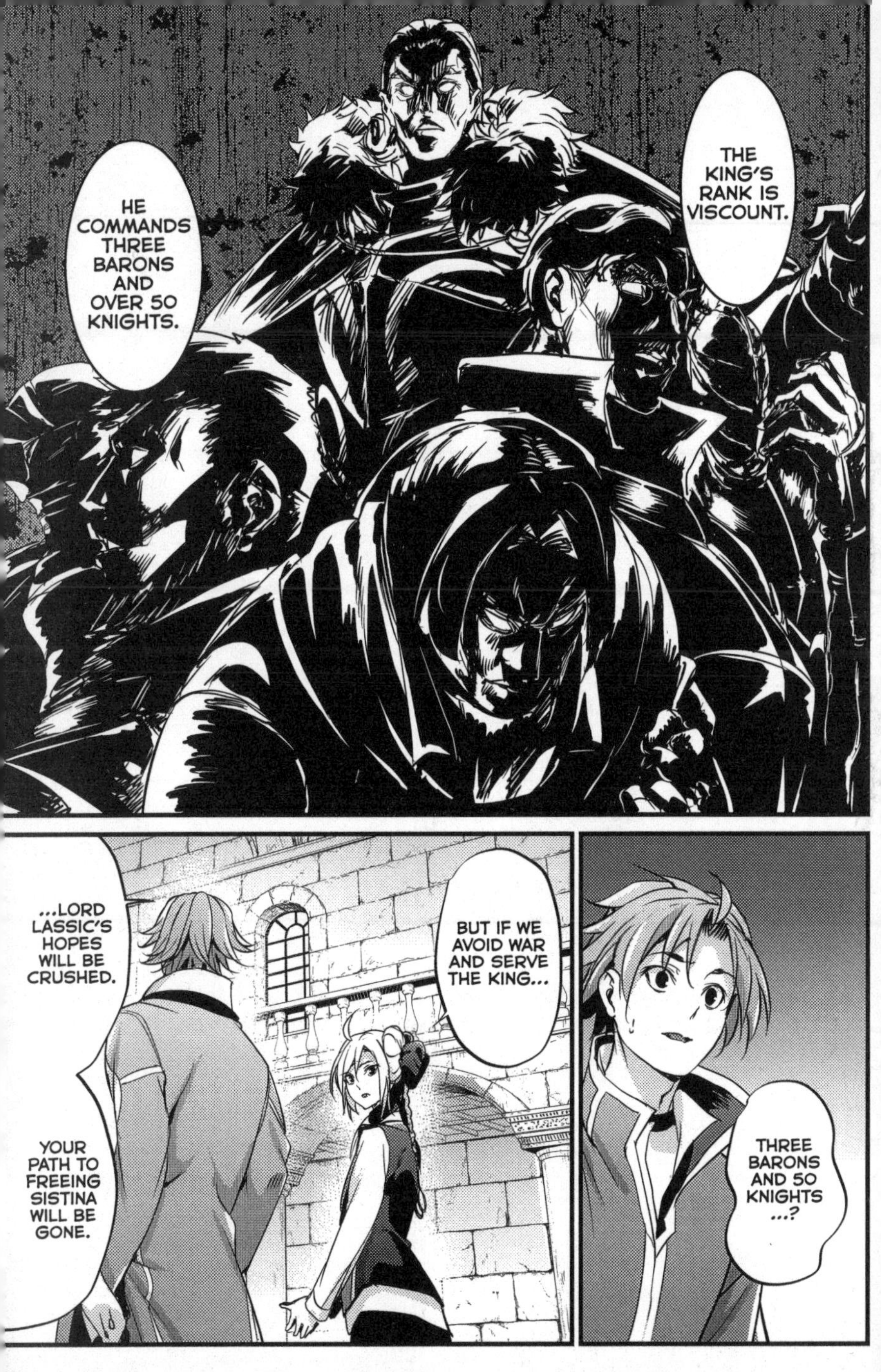
THE KING'S RANK IS VISCOUNT.
HE COMMANDS THREE BARONS AND OVER 50 KNIGHTS.
THREE BARONS AND 50 KNIGHTS ...?
BUT IF WE AVOID WAR AND SERVE THE KING...
...LORD LASSIC'S HOPES WILL BE CRUSHED.
YOUR PATH TO FREEING SISTINA WILL BE GONE.

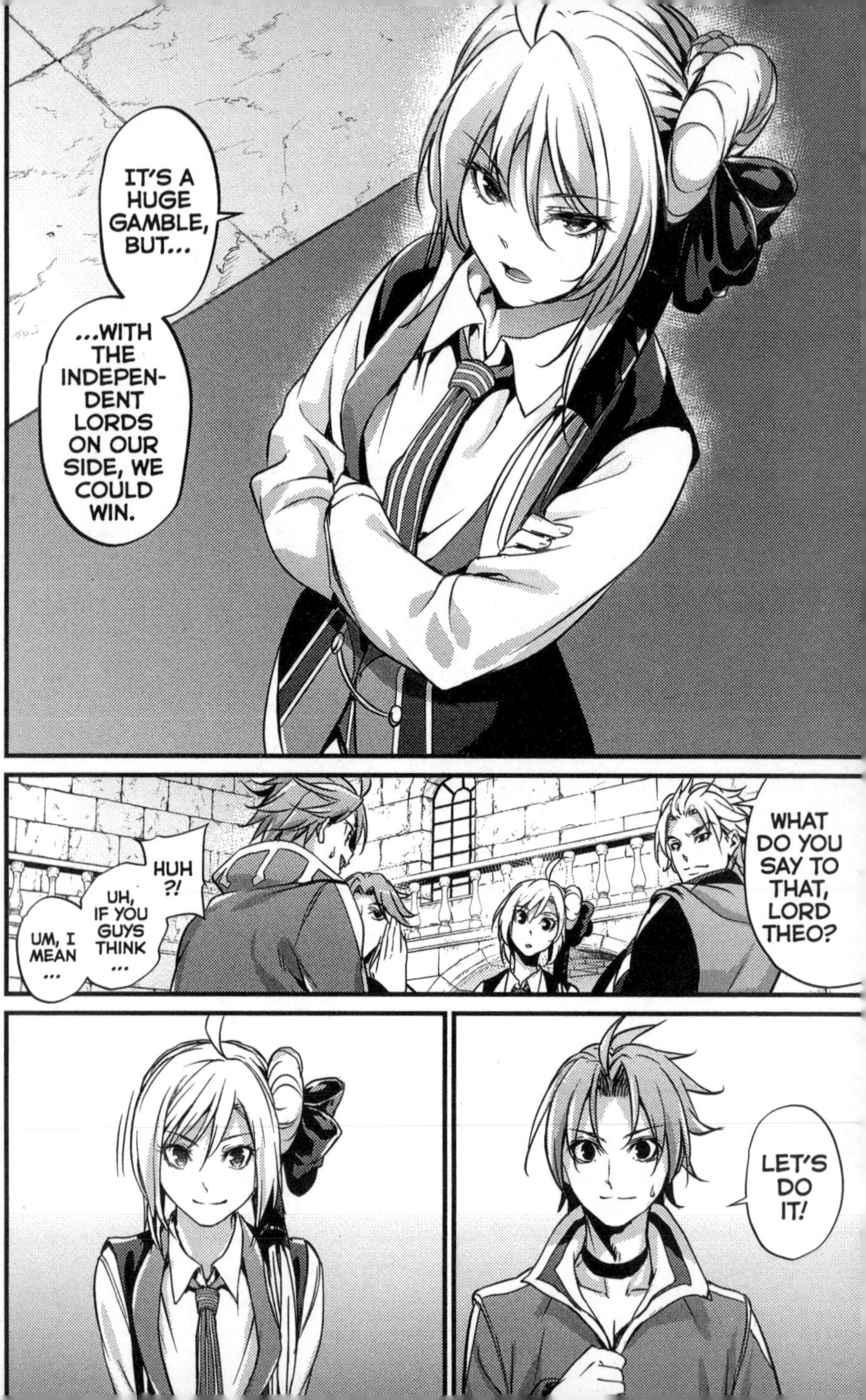
IT'S A HUGE GAMBLE, BUT...
...WITH THE INDEPEN-DENT LORDS ON OUR SIDE, WE COULD WIN.
WHAT DO YOU SAY TO THAT, LORD THEO?
HUH?!
UH, IF YOU GUYS THINK...
UM, I MEAN...
LET'S DO IT!

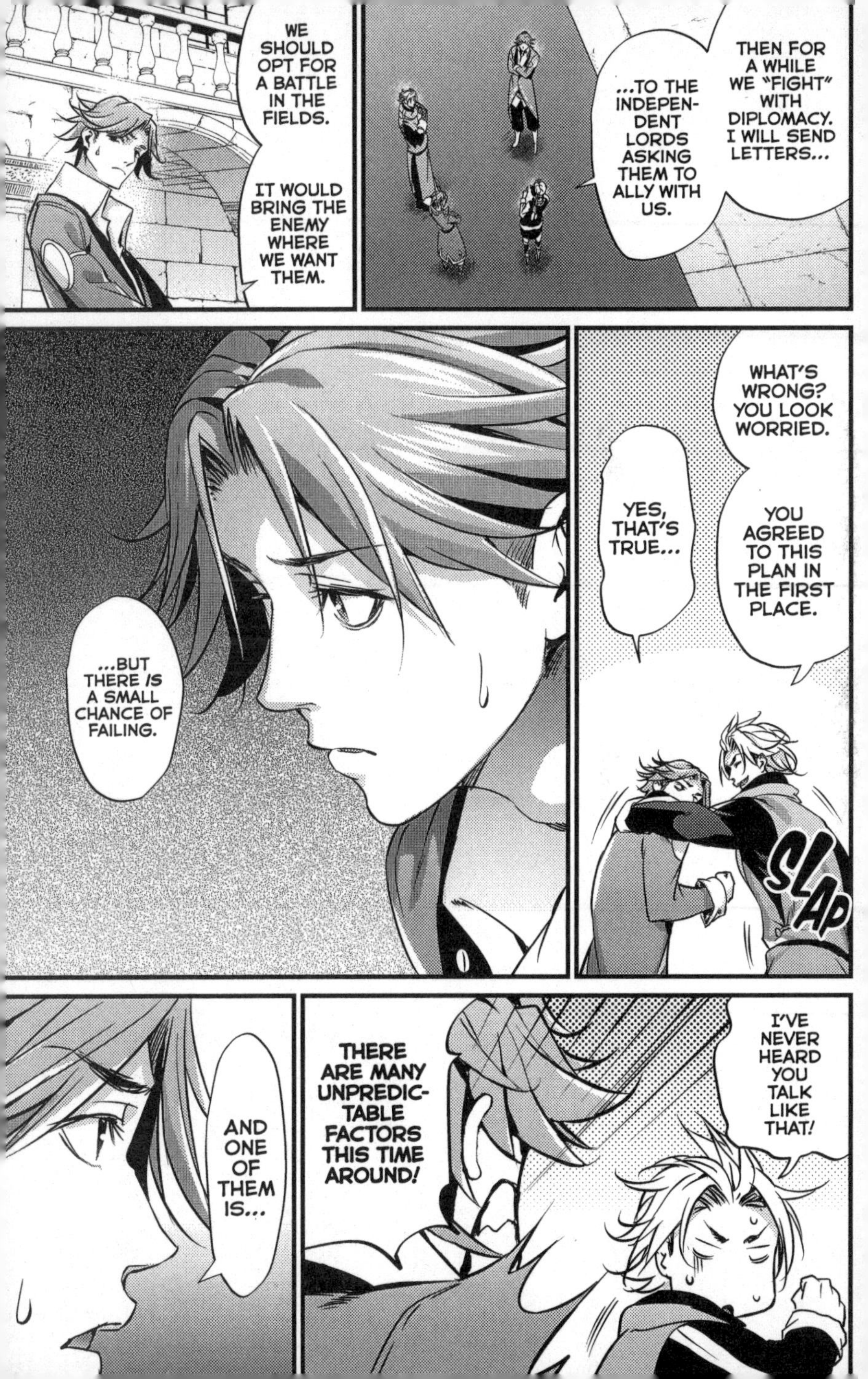
THEN FOR A WHILE WE "FIGHT" WITH DIPLOMACY. I WILL SEND LETTERS...
...TO THE INDEPEN-DENT LORDS ASKING THEM TO ALLY WITH US.
WE SHOULD OPT FOR A BATTLE IN THE FIELDS.
IT WOULD BRING THE ENEMY WHERE WE WANT THEM.
WHAT'S WRONG? YOU LOOK WORRIED.
YOU AGREED TO THIS PLAN IN THE FIRST PLACE.
YES, THAT'S TRUE...
SLAP
...BUT THERE *IS* A SMALL CHANCE OF FAILING.
I'VE NEVER HEARD YOU TALK LIKE THAT!
THERE ARE MANY UNPREDIC-TABLE FACTORS THIS TIME AROUND!
AND ONE OF THEM IS...

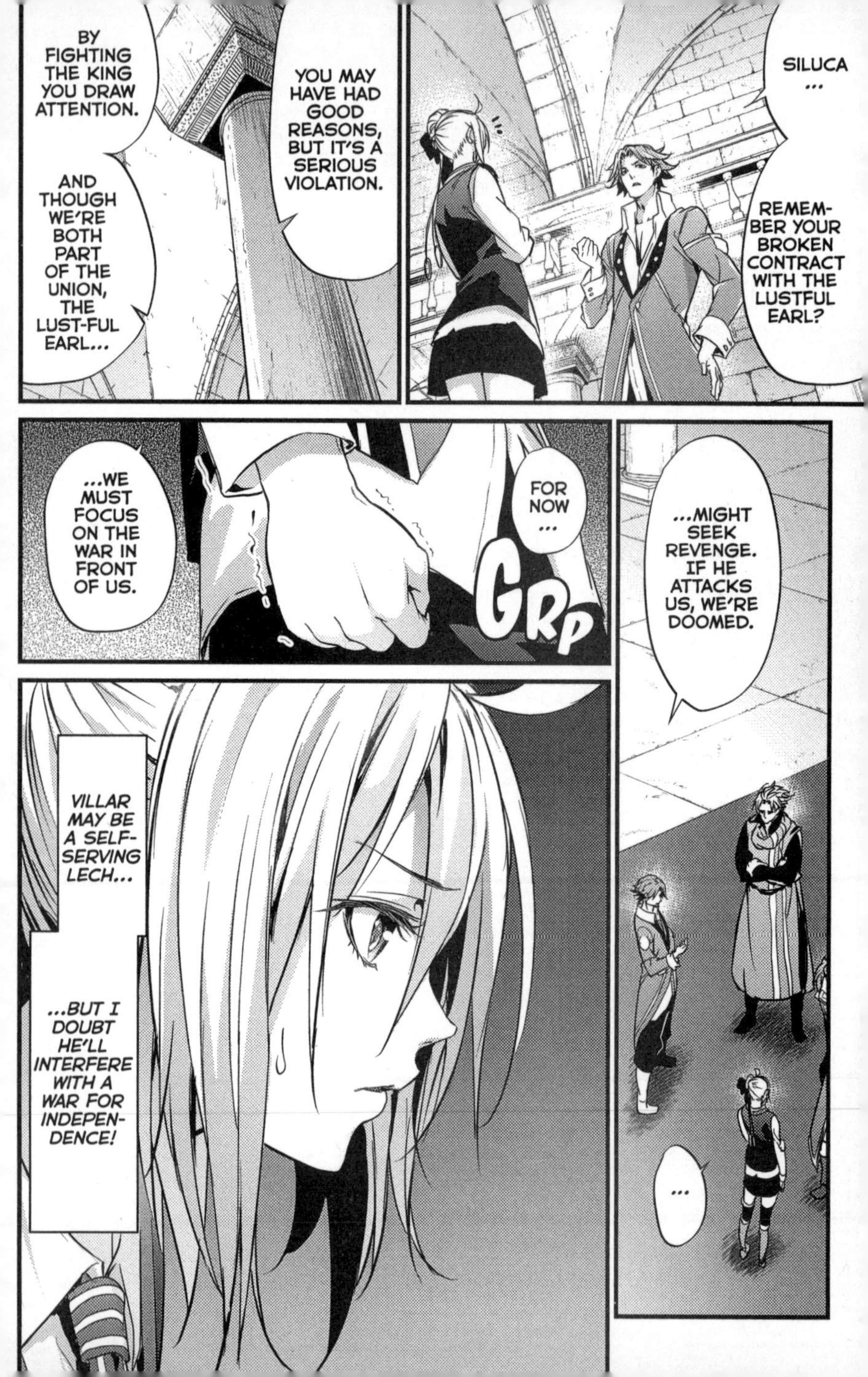
SILUCA ...
REMEMBER YOUR BROKEN CONTRACT WITH THE LUSTFUL EARL?
YOU MAY HAVE HAD GOOD REASONS, BUT IT'S A SERIOUS VIOLATION.
BY FIGHTING THE KING YOU DRAW ATTENTION.
AND THOUGH WE'RE BOTH PART OF THE UNION, THE LUST-FUL EARL...
...MIGHT SEEK REVENGE. IF HE ATTACKS US, WE'RE DOOMED.
...
FOR NOW ...
...WE MUST FOCUS ON THE WAR IN FRONT OF US.
GRP
VILLAR MAY BE A SELF-SERVING LECH...
...BUT I DOUBT HE'LL INTERFERE WITH A WAR FOR INDEPEN-DENCE!

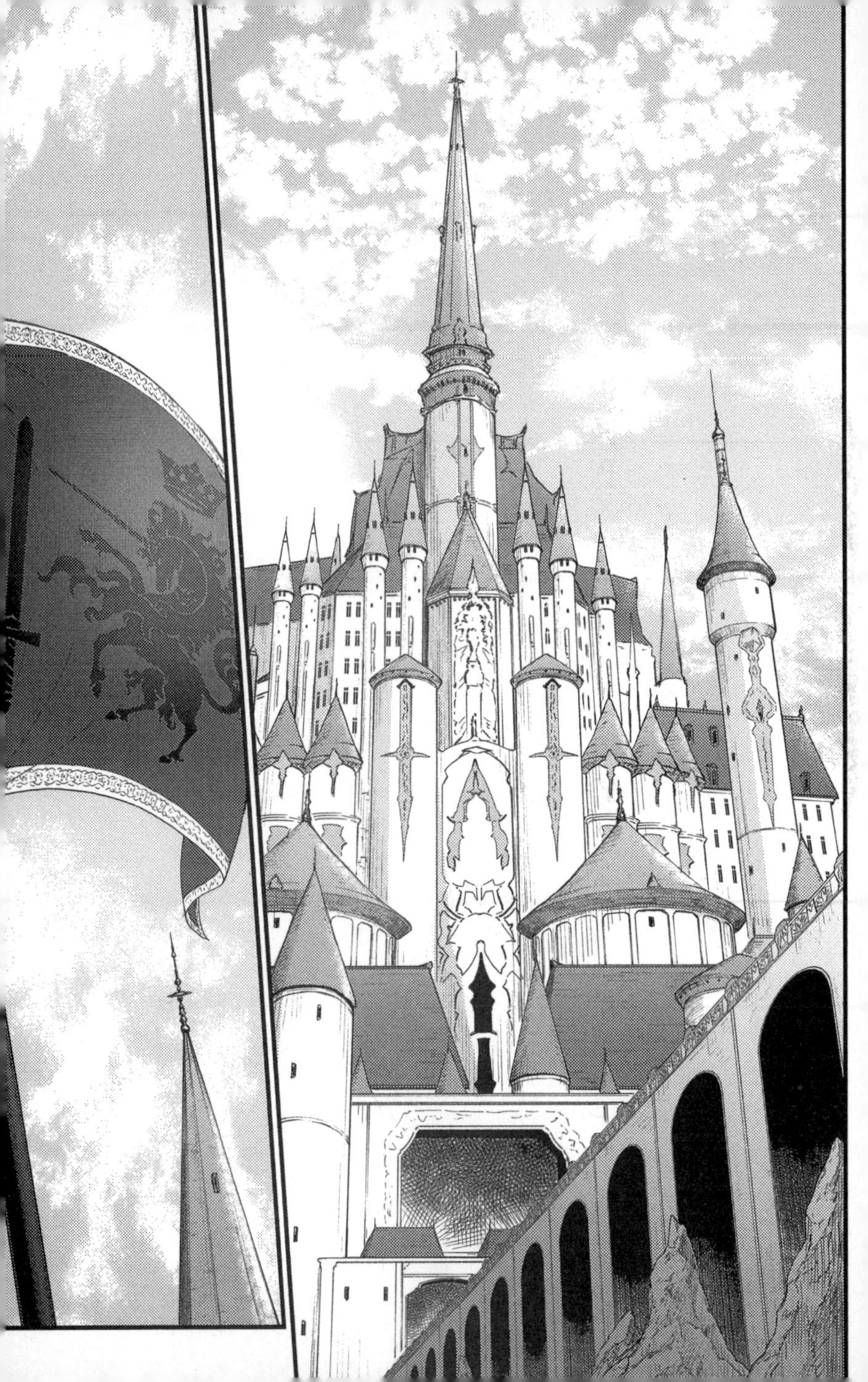

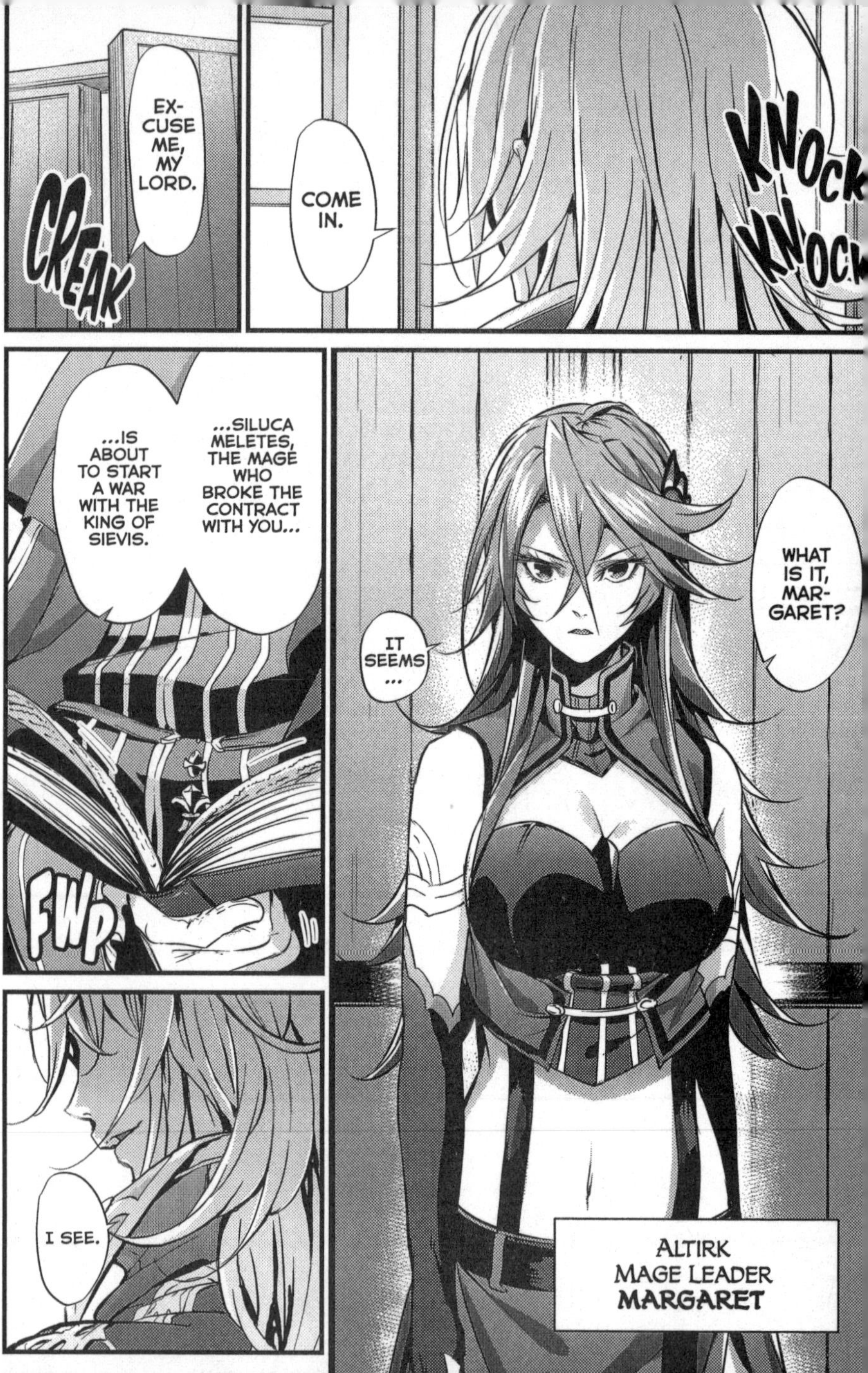
KNOCK KNOCK
COME IN.
EX-CUSE ME, MY LORD.
CREAK
WHAT IS IT, MAR-GARET?
IT SEEMS...
ALTIRK MAGE LEADER MARGARET
...SILUCA MELETES, THE MAGE WHO BROKE THE CONTRACT WITH YOU...
...IS ABOUT TO START A WAR WITH THE KING OF SIEVIS.
FWP
I SEE.

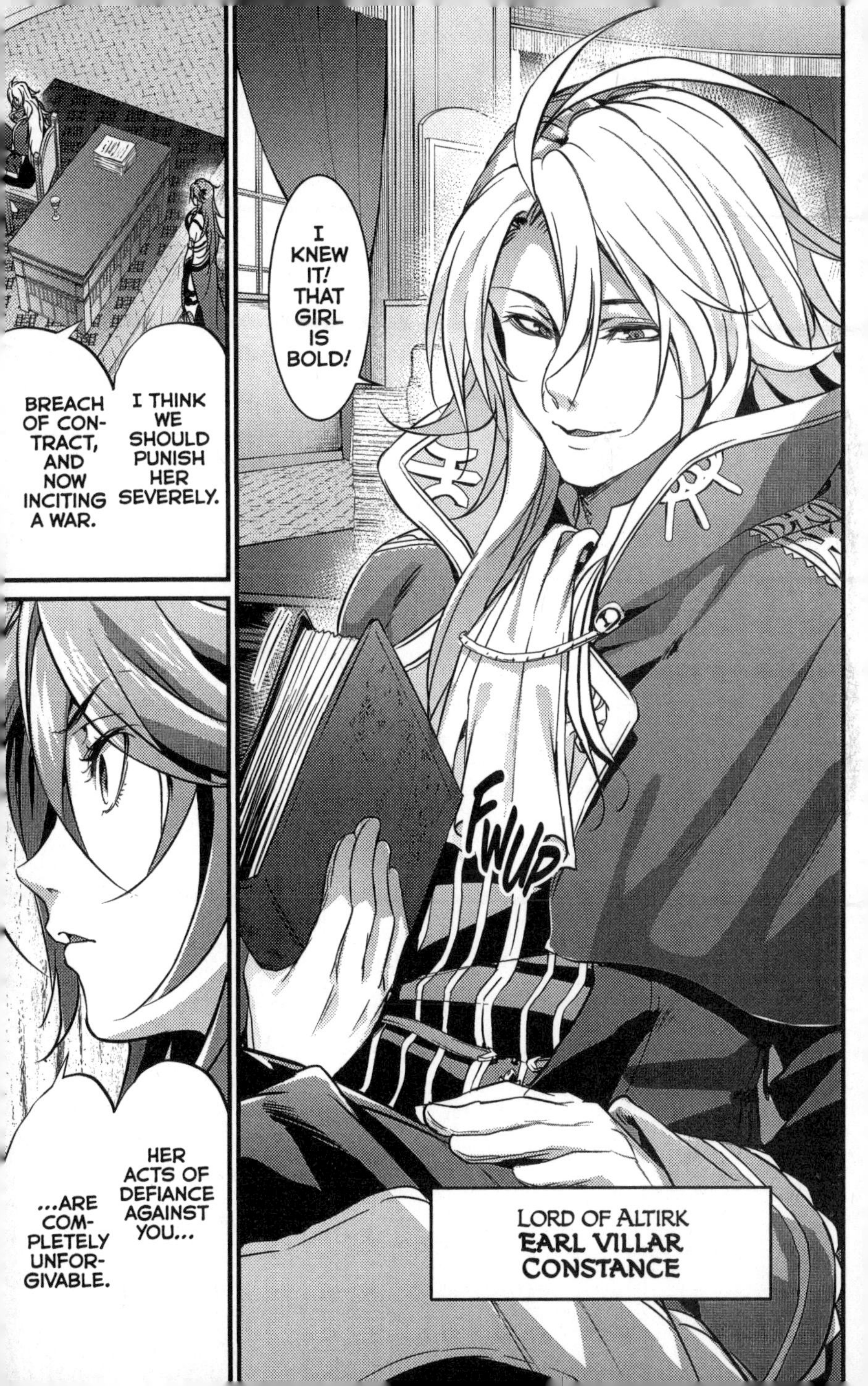
I KNEW IT! THAT GIRL IS BOLD!
FWUP
LORD OF ALTIRK
EARL VILLAR CONSTANCE
I THINK WE SHOULD PUNISH HER SEVERELY.
BREACH OF CON-TRACT, AND NOW INCITING A WAR.
HER ACTS OF DEFIANCE AGAINST YOU...
...ARE COM-PLETELY UNFOR-GIVABLE.

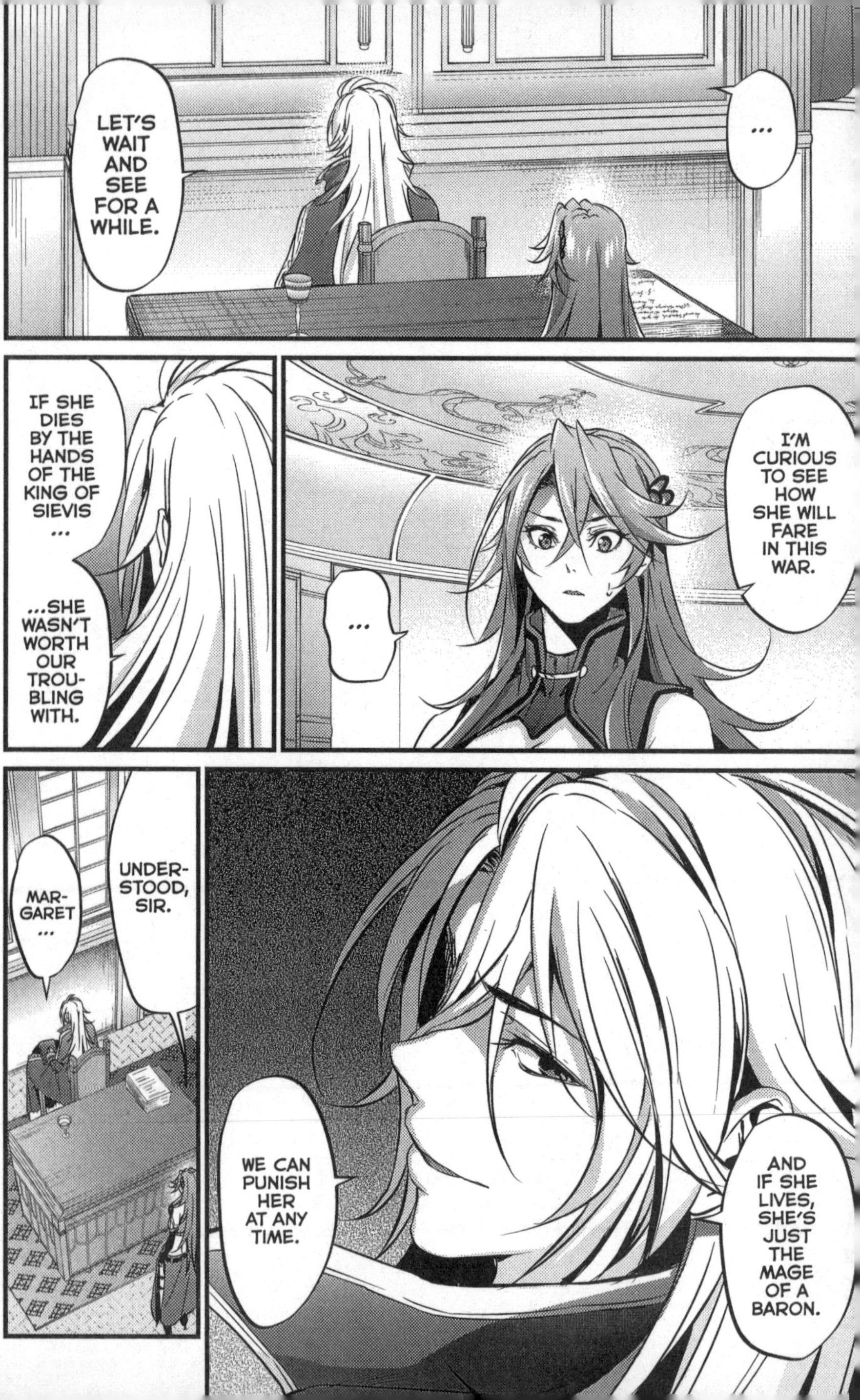
...
LET'S WAIT AND SEE FOR A WHILE.
I'M CURIOUS TO SEE HOW SHE WILL FARE IN THIS WAR.
...
IF SHE DIES BY THE HANDS OF THE KING OF SIEVIS...
...SHE WASN'T WORTH OUR TROUBLING WITH.
AND IF SHE LIVES, SHE'S JUST THE MAGE OF A BARON.
WE CAN PUNISH HER AT ANY TIME.
UNDERSTOOD, SIR.
MARGARET...

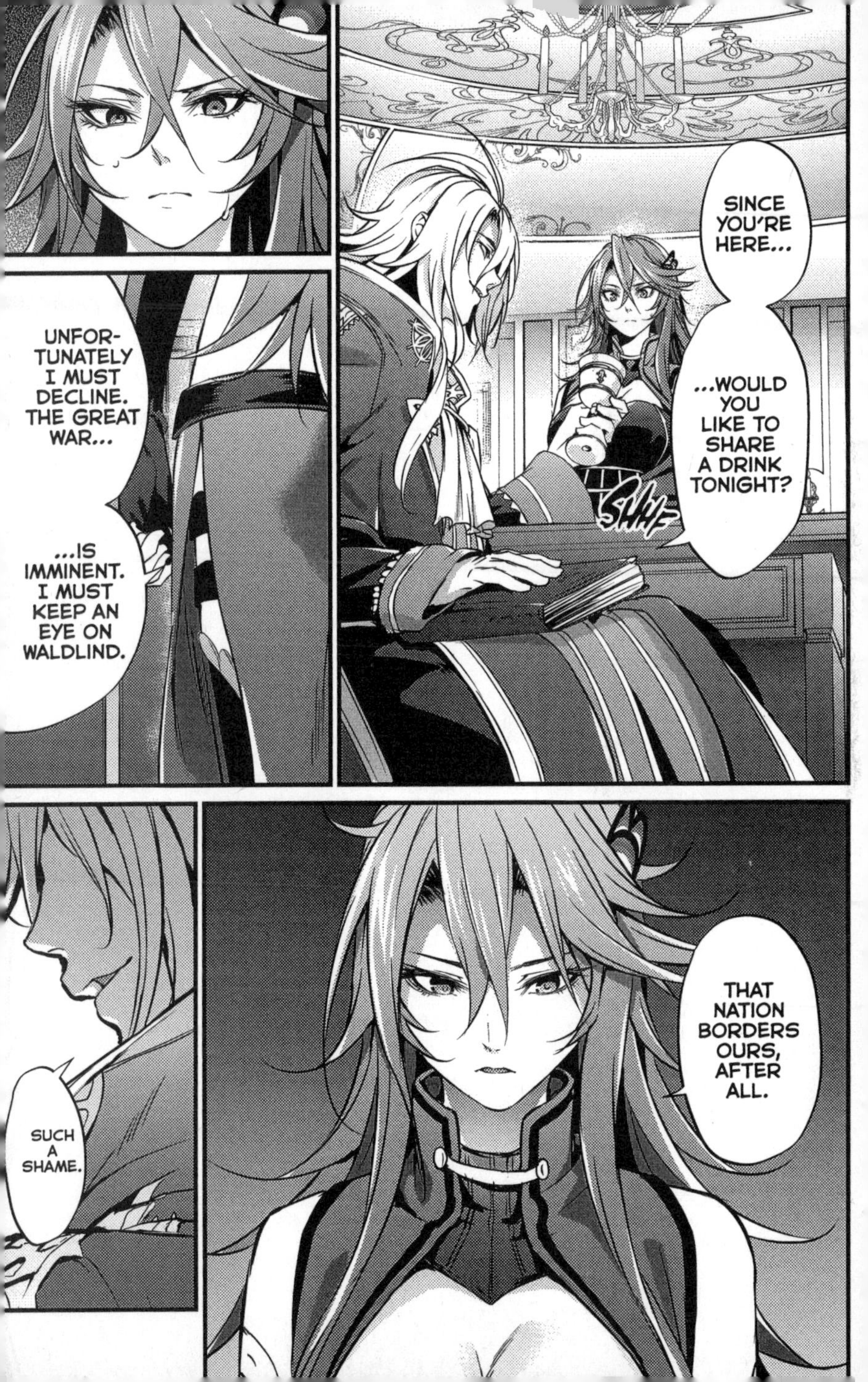

SINCE YOU'RE HERE...
...WOULD YOU LIKE TO SHARE A DRINK TONIGHT?
SHHF
UNFOR-TUNATELY I MUST DECLINE. THE GREAT WAR...
...IS IMMINENT. I MUST KEEP AN EYE ON WALDLIND.
THAT NATION BORDERS OURS, AFTER ALL.
SUCH A SHAME.

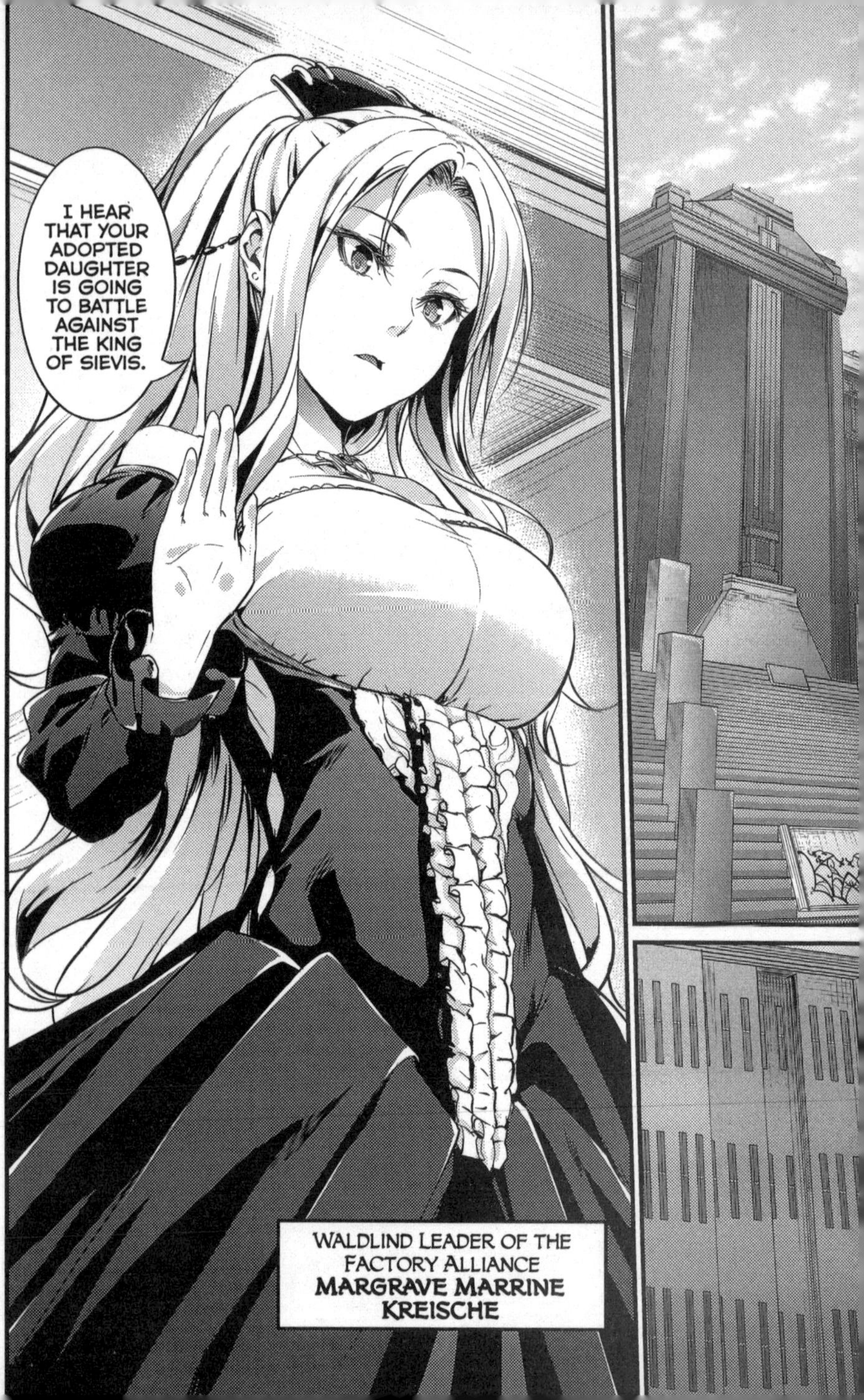
I HEAR THAT YOUR ADOPTED DAUGHTER IS GOING TO BATTLE AGAINST THE KING OF SIEVIS.
WALDLIND LEADER OF THE FACTORY ALLIANCE
MARGRAVE MARRINE KREISCHE

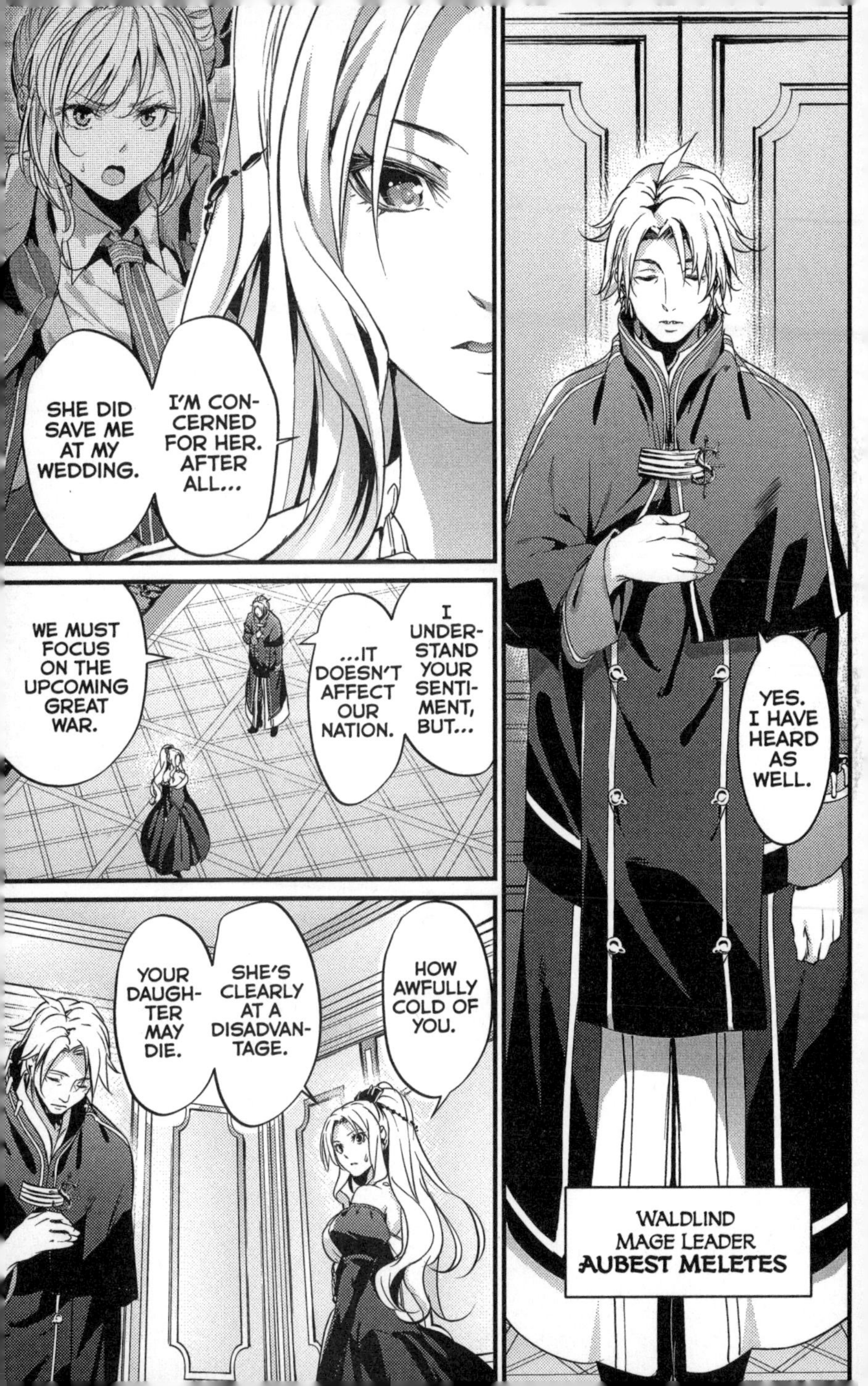
YES. I HAVE HEARD AS WELL.
WALDLIND MAGE LEADER AUBEST MELETES
I'M CONCERNED FOR HER. AFTER ALL...
SHE DID SAVE ME AT MY WEDDING.
I UNDERSTAND YOUR SENTIMENT, BUT...
...IT DOESN'T AFFECT OUR NATION.
WE MUST FOCUS ON THE UPCOMING GREAT WAR.
HOW AWFULLY COLD OF YOU.
SHE'S CLEARLY AT A DISADVANTAGE.
YOUR DAUGHTER MAY DIE.

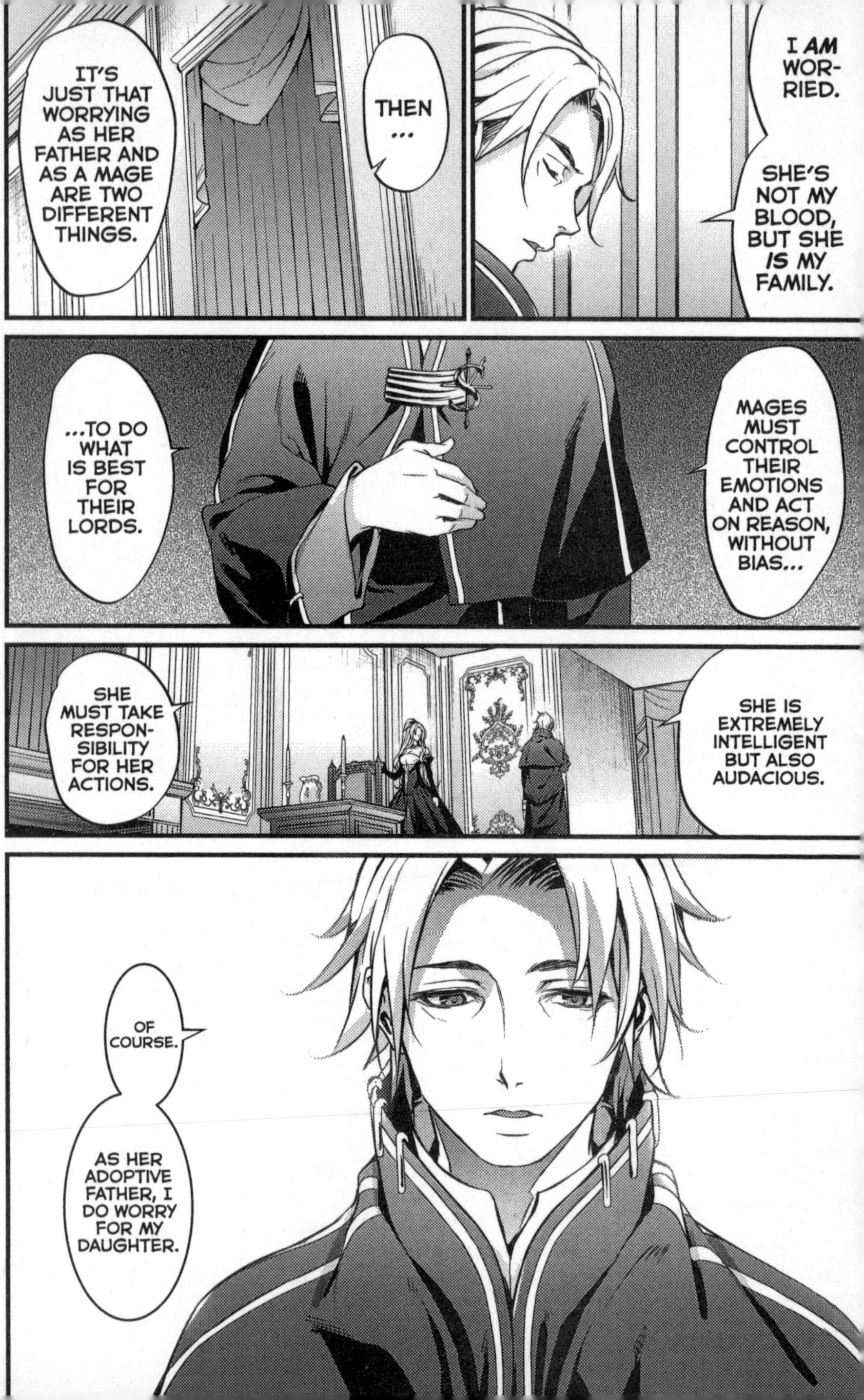
I *AM* WORRIED.
SHE'S NOT MY BLOOD, BUT SHE *IS* MY FAMILY.
THEN…
IT'S JUST THAT WORRYING AS HER FATHER AND AS A MAGE ARE TWO DIFFERENT THINGS.
MAGES MUST CONTROL THEIR EMOTIONS AND ACT ON REASON, WITHOUT BIAS…
…TO DO WHAT IS BEST FOR THEIR LORDS.
SHE IS EXTREMELY INTELLIGENT BUT ALSO AUDACIOUS.
SHE MUST TAKE RESPONSIBILITY FOR HER ACTIONS.
OF COURSE.
AS HER ADOPTIVE FATHER, I DO WORRY FOR MY DAUGHTER.

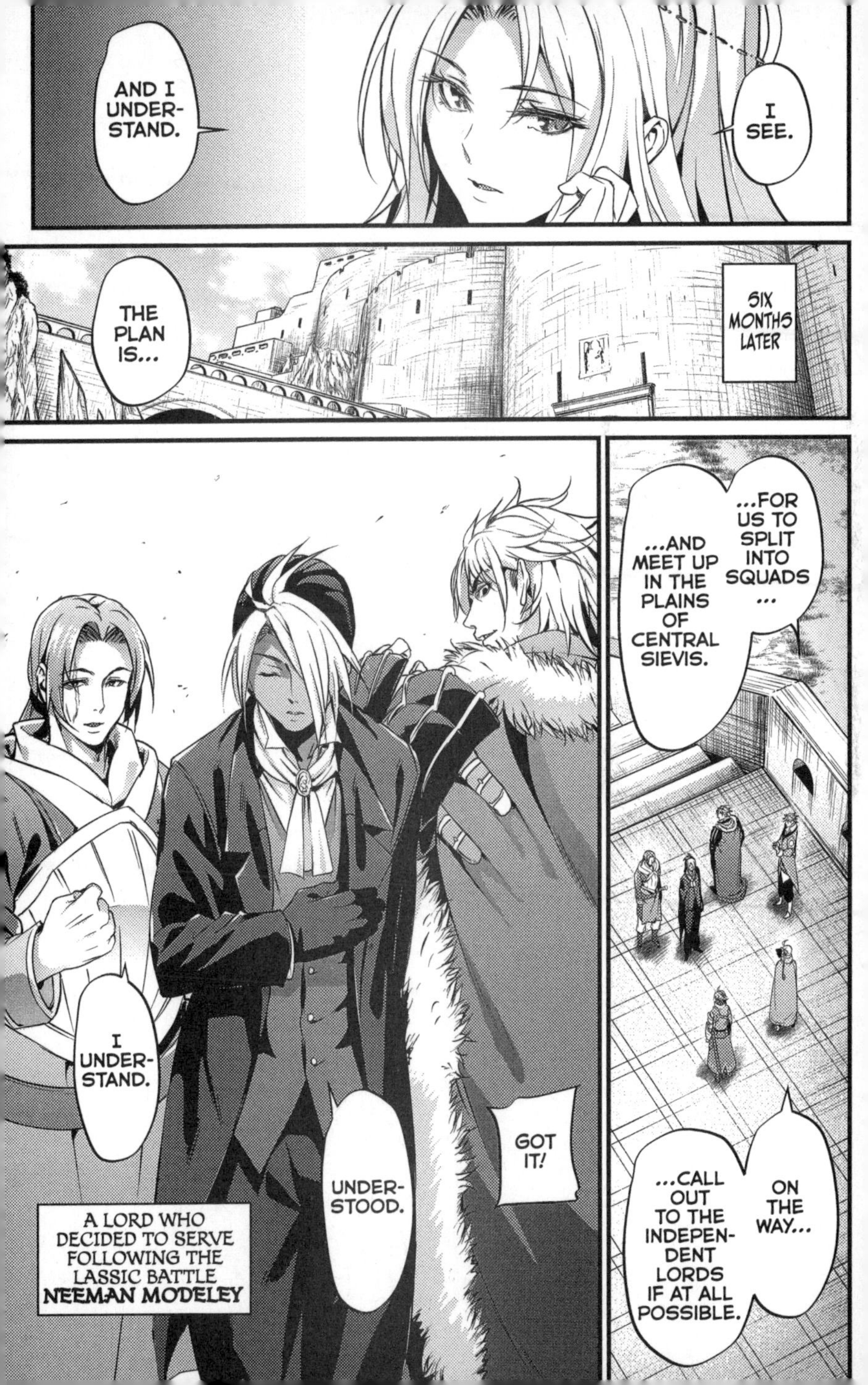
I SEE.
AND I UNDERSTAND.
SIX MONTHS LATER
THE PLAN IS...
...FOR US TO SPLIT INTO SQUADS...
...AND MEET UP IN THE PLAINS OF CENTRAL SIEVIS.
ON THE WAY...
...CALL OUT TO THE INDEPENDENT LORDS IF AT ALL POSSIBLE.
GOT IT!
UNDERSTOOD.
I UNDERSTAND.
A LORD WHO DECIDED TO SERVE FOLLOWING THE LASSIC BATTLE
NEEMAN MODELEY

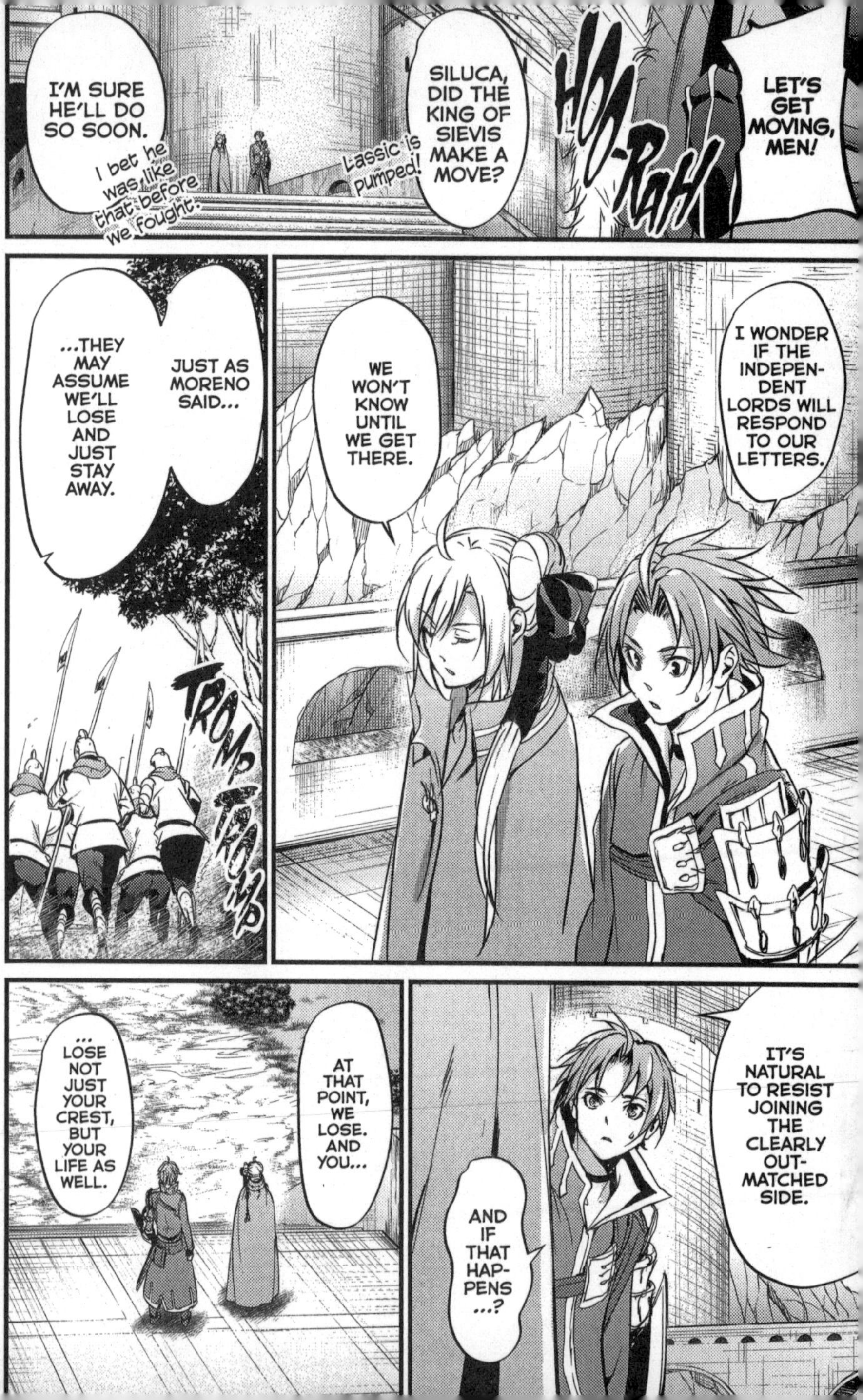
LET'S GET MOVING, MEN!
HOO-RAH
SILUCA, DID THE KING OF SIEVIS MAKE A MOVE?
Lassic is pumped!
I'M SURE HE'LL DO SO SOON.
I bet he was like that before we fought.
I WONDER IF THE INDEPENDENT LORDS WILL RESPOND TO OUR LETTERS.
WE WON'T KNOW UNTIL WE GET THERE.
JUST AS MORENO SAID...
...THEY MAY ASSUME WE'LL LOSE AND JUST STAY AWAY.
TROMP TROMP TROMP
IT'S NATURAL TO RESIST JOINING THE CLEARLY OUTMATCHED SIDE.
AND IF THAT HAPPENS...?
AT THAT POINT, WE LOSE. AND YOU...
...LOSE NOT JUST YOUR CREST, BUT YOUR LIFE AS WELL.

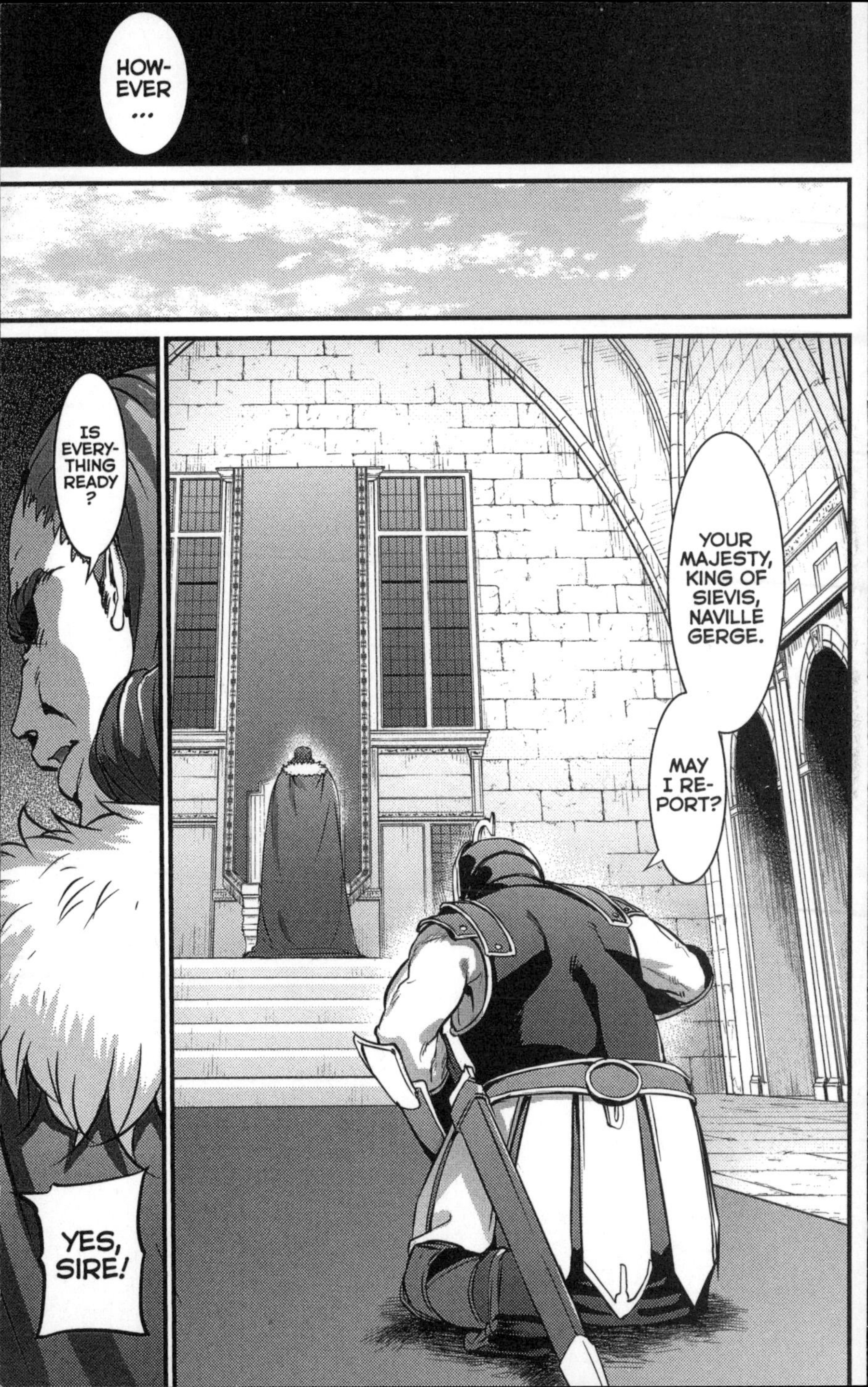
HOW-EVER...
YOUR MAJESTY, KING OF SIEVIS, NAVILLE GERGE.
MAY I RE-PORT?
IS EVERY-THING READY?
YES, SIRE!

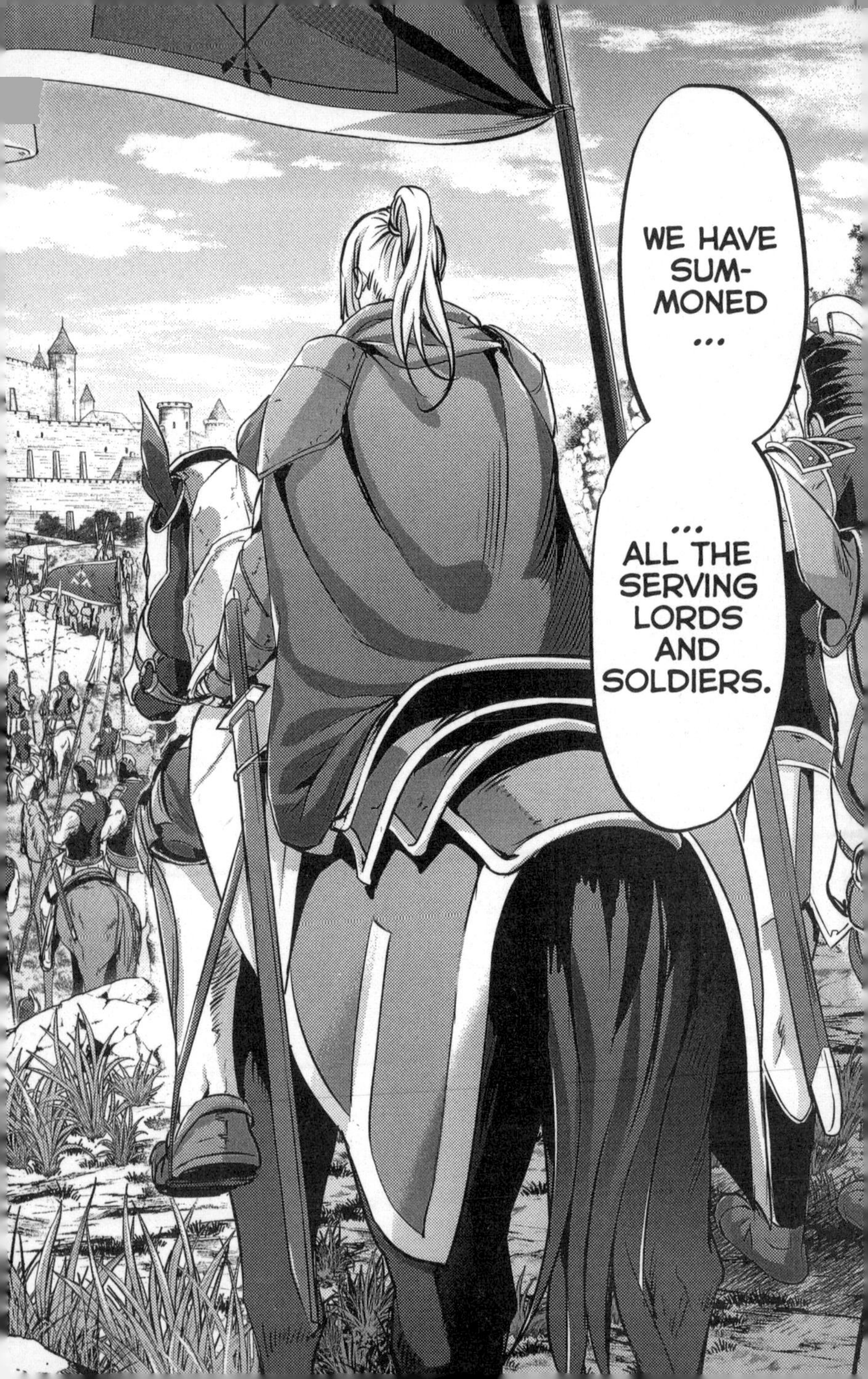
WE HAVE SUM-MONED ...
... ALL THE SERVING LORDS AND SOLDIERS.

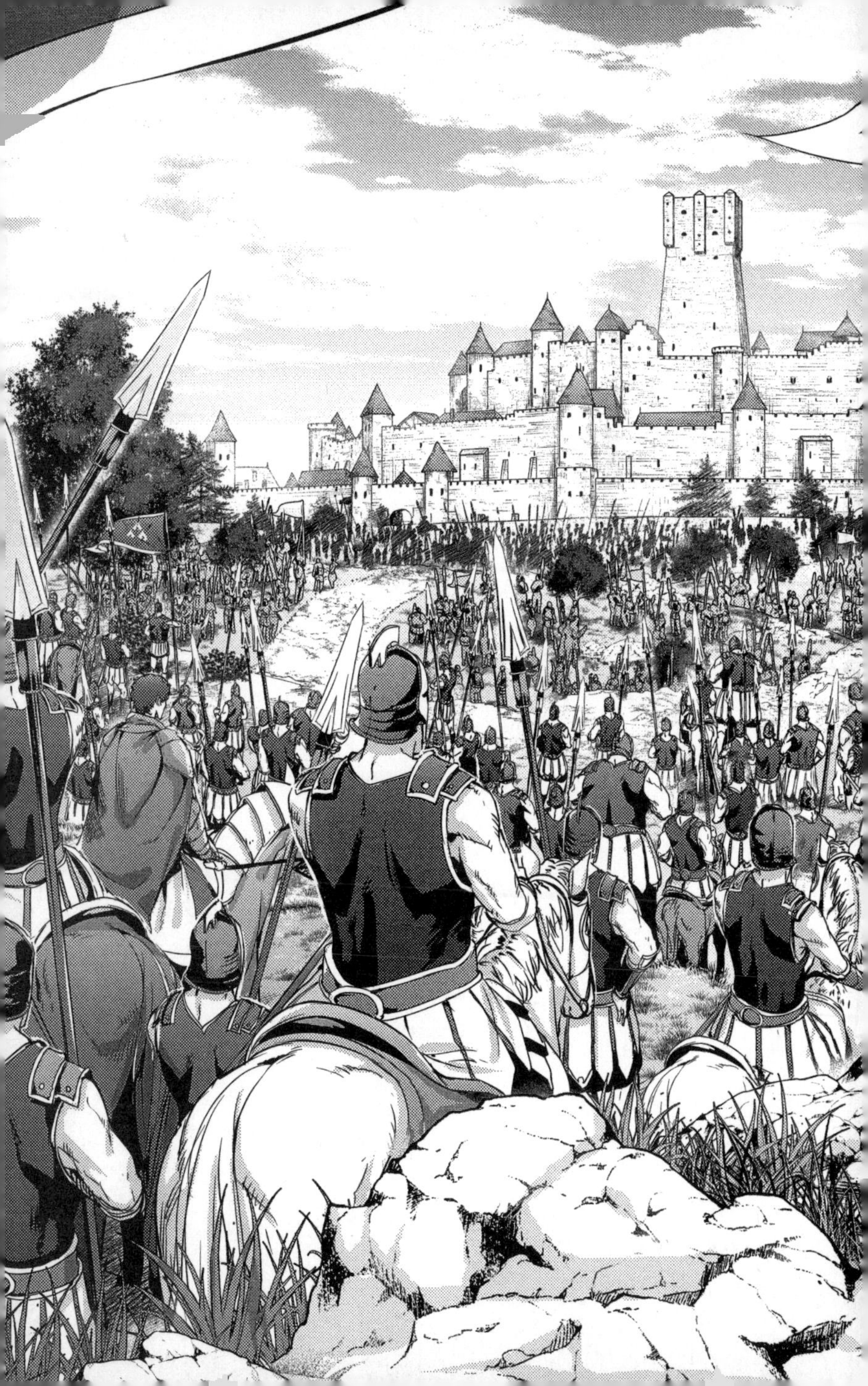

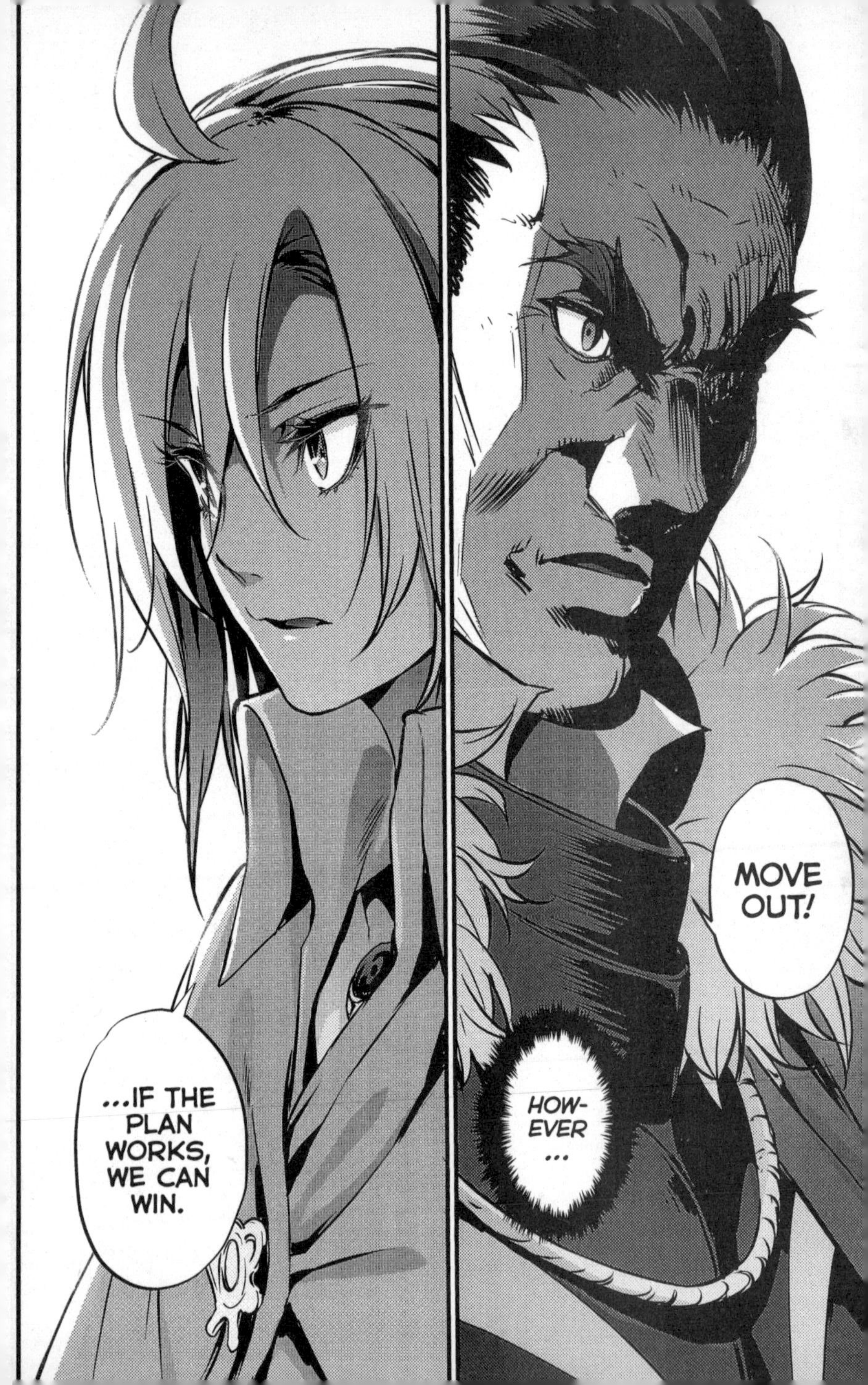
MOVE OUT!
HOW-EVER ...
...IF THE PLAN WORKS, WE CAN WIN.

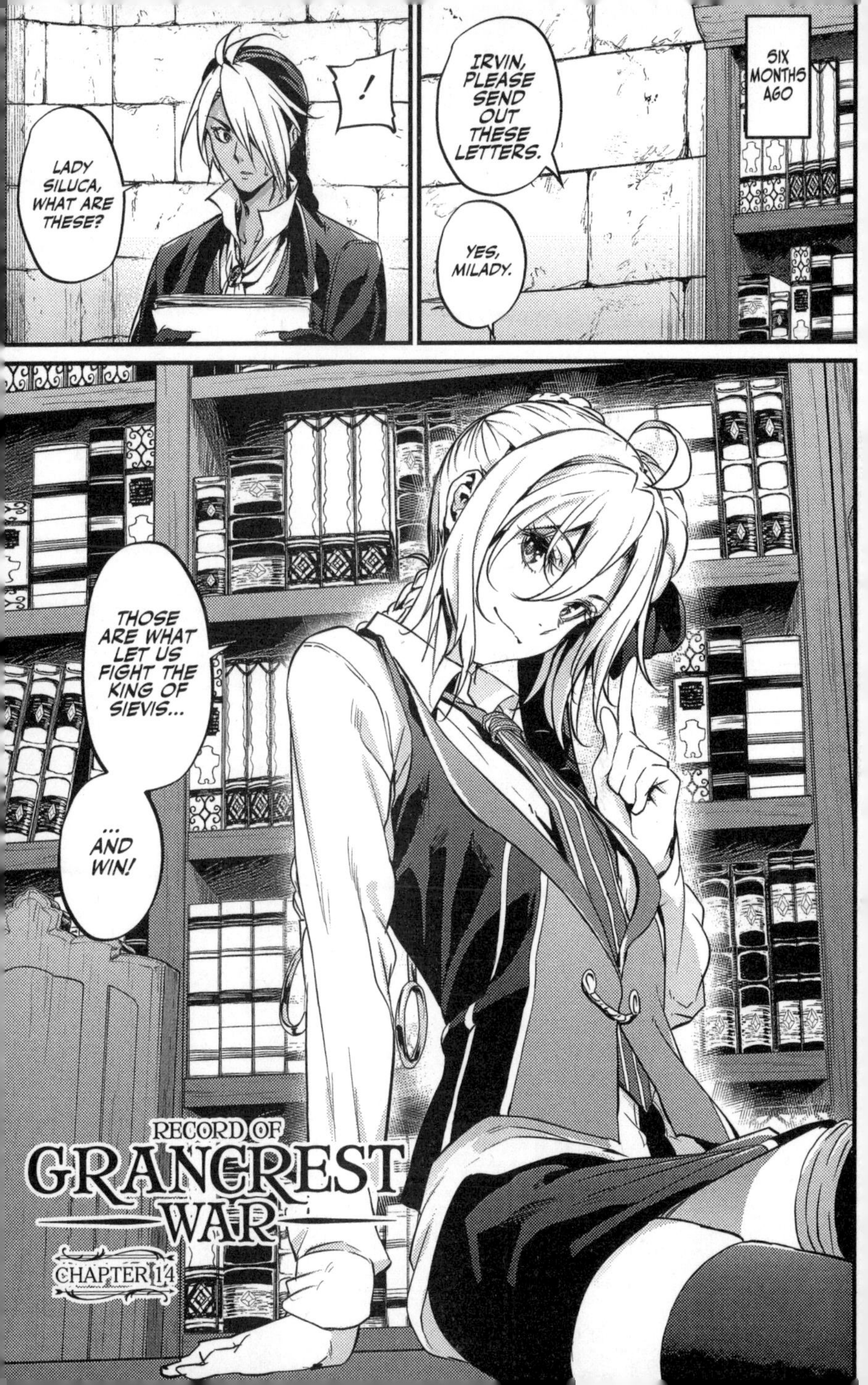
SIX MONTHS AGO
IRVIN, PLEASE SEND OUT THESE LETTERS.
YES, MILADY.
!
LADY SILUCA, WHAT ARE THESE?
THOSE ARE WHAT LET US FIGHT THE KING OF SIEVIS...
... AND WIN!
RECORD OF GRANCREST WAR
CHAPTER 14

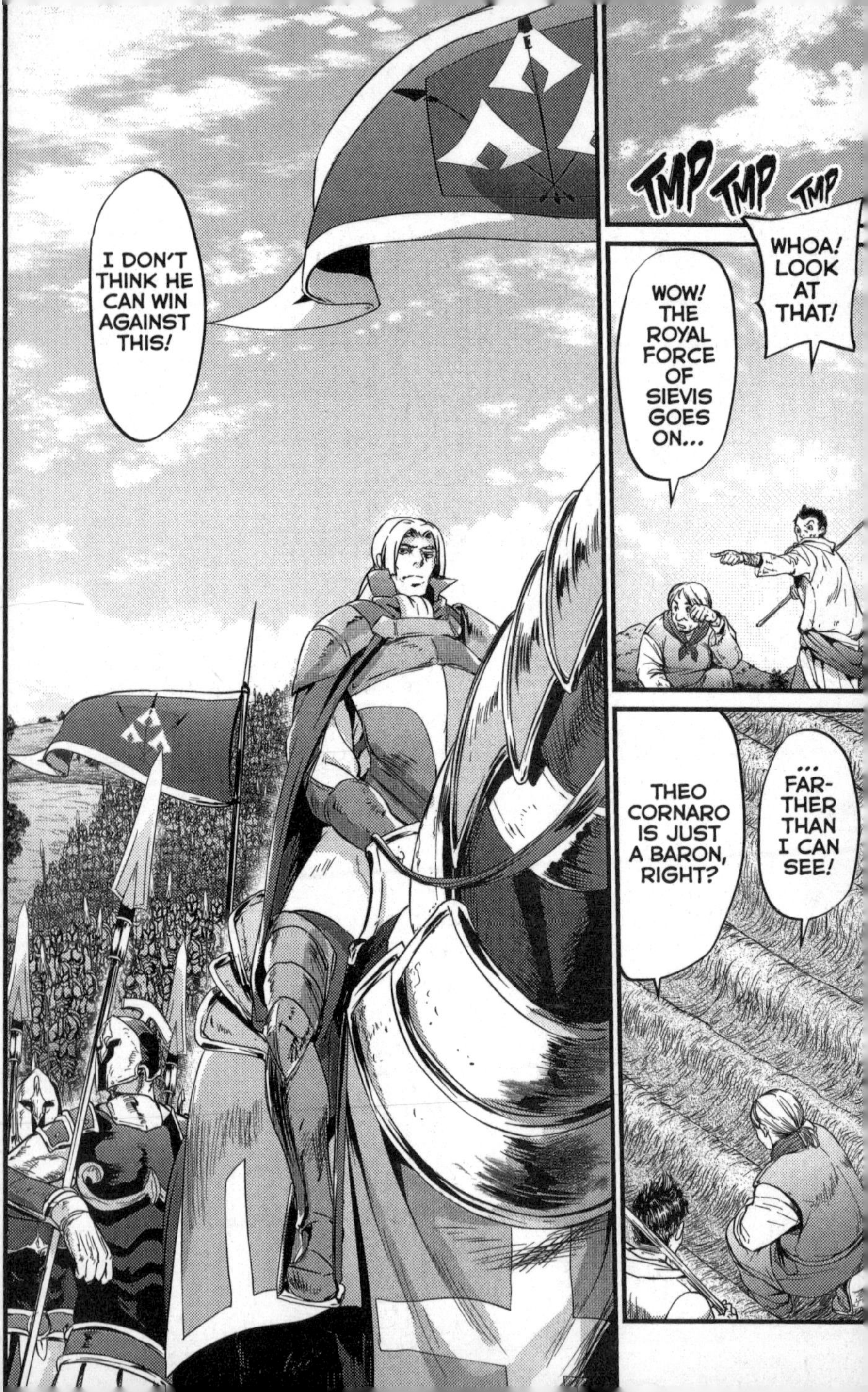
TMP TMP TMP
WHOA! LOOK AT THAT!
WOW! THE ROYAL FORCE OF SIEVIS GOES ON...
...FAR-THER THAN I CAN SEE!
THEO CORNARO IS JUST A BARON, RIGHT?
I DON'T THINK HE CAN WIN AGAINST THIS!

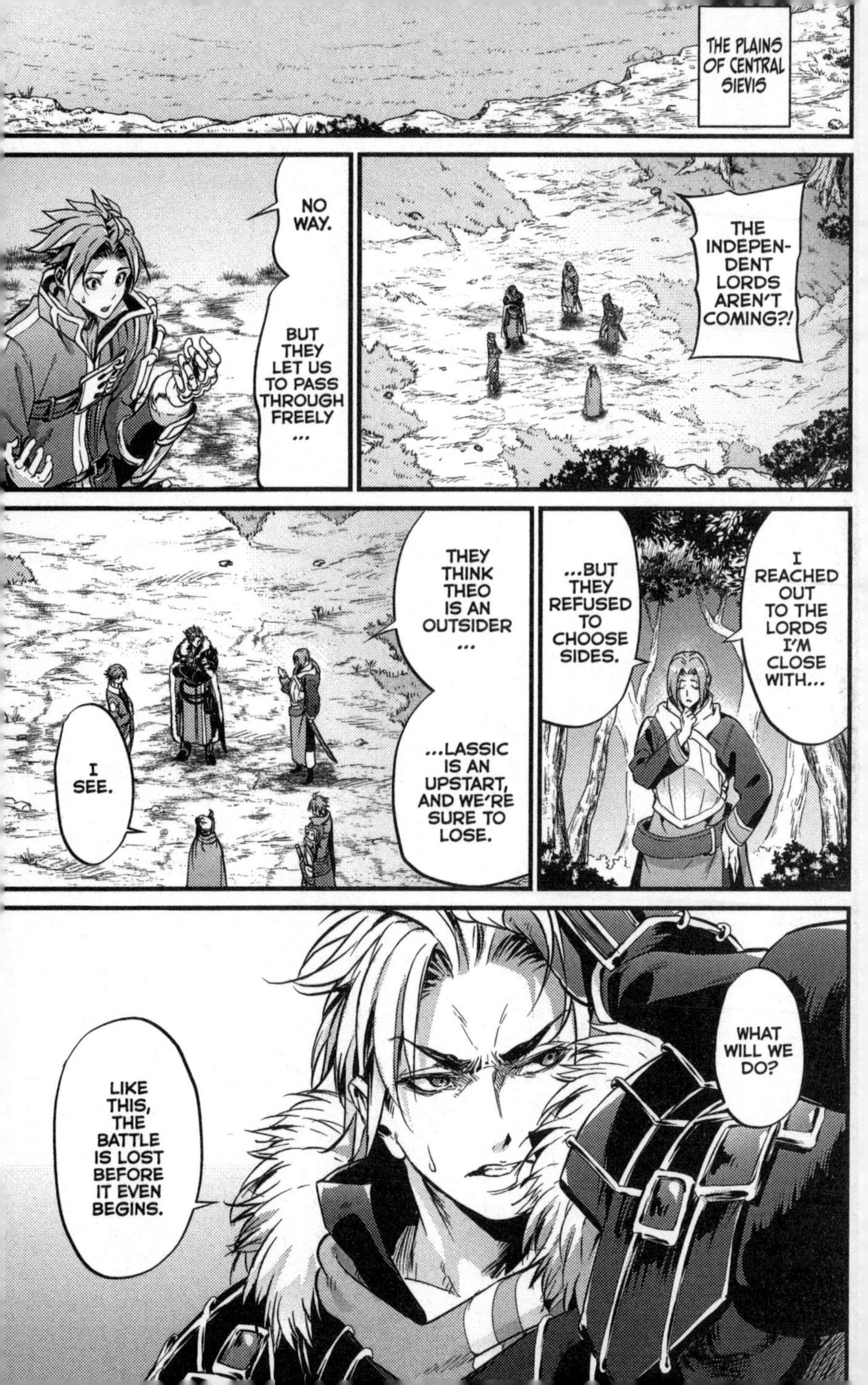
THE PLAINS OF CENTRAL SIEVIS
THE INDEPENDENT LORDS AREN'T COMING?!
NO WAY.
BUT THEY LET US TO PASS THROUGH FREELY ...
I REACHED OUT TO THE LORDS I'M CLOSE WITH...
...BUT THEY REFUSED TO CHOOSE SIDES.
THEY THINK THEO IS AN OUTSIDER ...
...LASSIC IS AN UPSTART, AND WE'RE SURE TO LOSE.
I SEE.
WHAT WILL WE DO?
LIKE THIS, THE BATTLE IS LOST BEFORE IT EVEN BEGINS.

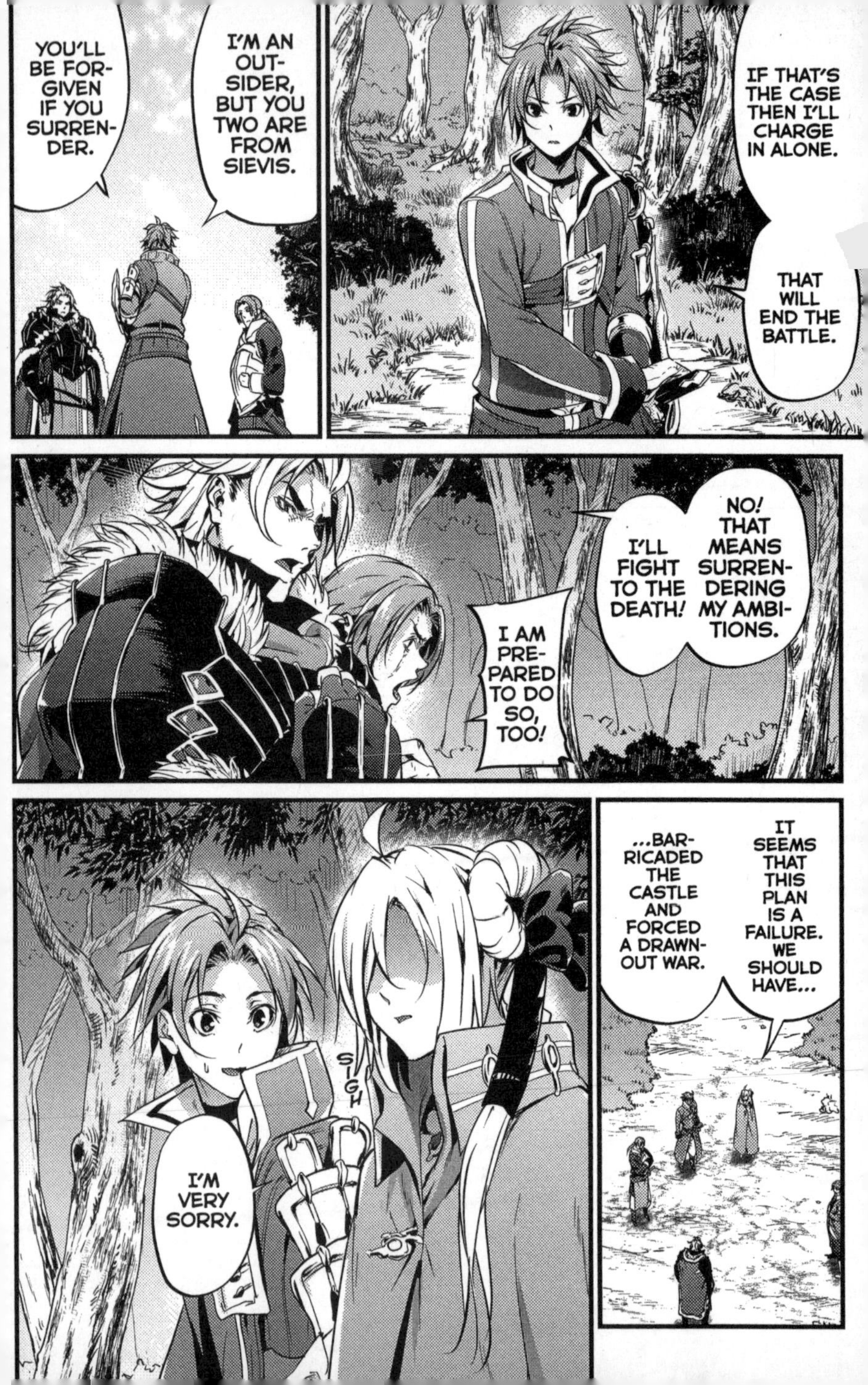
IF THAT'S THE CASE THEN I'LL CHARGE IN ALONE.
THAT WILL END THE BATTLE.
I'M AN OUTSIDER, BUT YOU TWO ARE FROM SIEVIS.
YOU'LL BE FORGIVEN IF YOU SURRENDER.
NO! THAT MEANS SURRENDERING MY AMBITIONS.
I'LL FIGHT TO THE DEATH!
I AM PREPARED TO DO SO, TOO!
IT SEEMS THAT THIS PLAN IS A FAILURE. WE SHOULD HAVE...
...BARRICADED THE CASTLE AND FORCED A DRAWN-OUT WAR.
SIGH
I'M VERY SORRY.

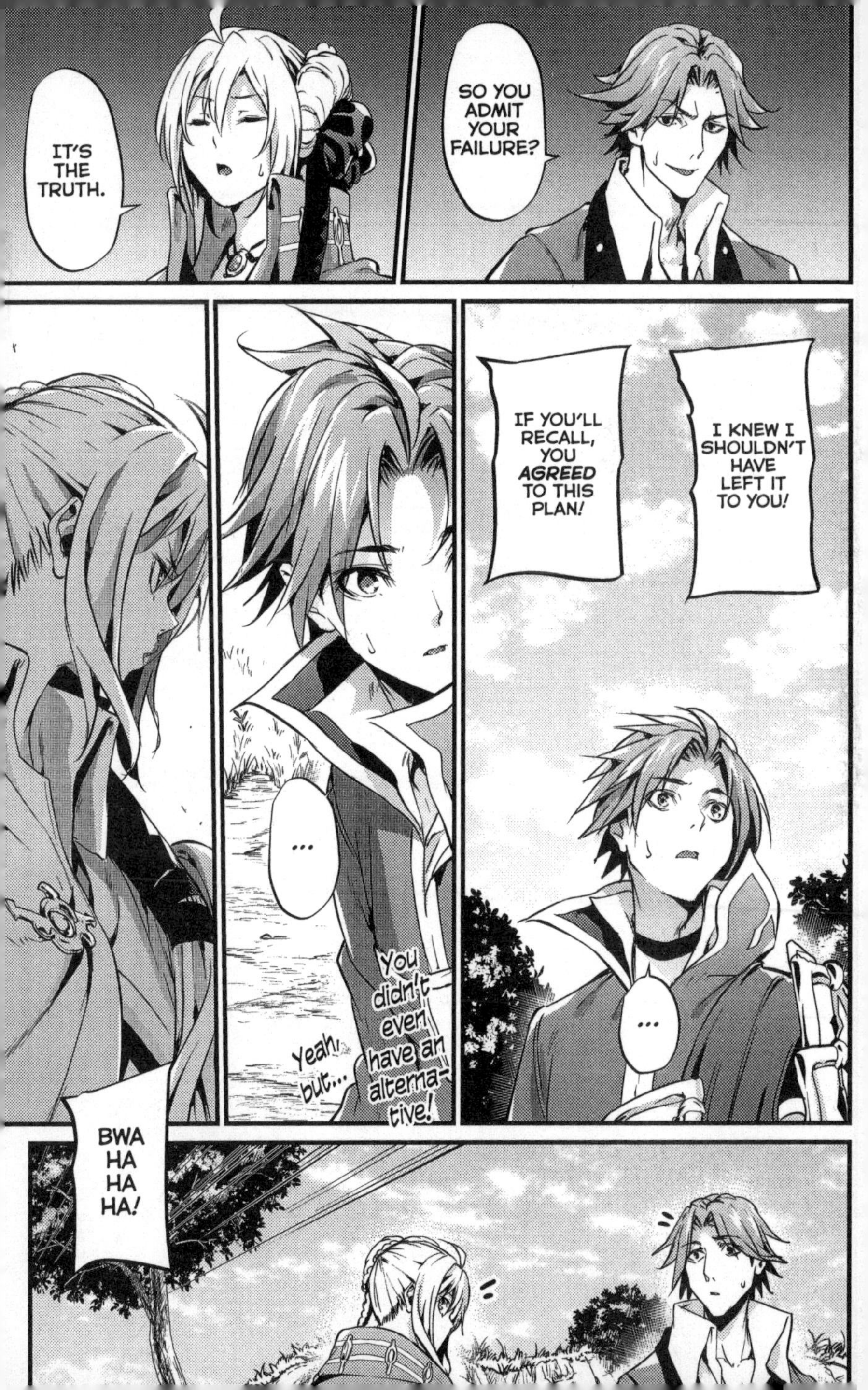
SO YOU ADMIT YOUR FAILURE?
IT'S THE TRUTH.
I KNEW I SHOULDN'T HAVE LEFT IT TO YOU!
IF YOU'LL RECALL, YOU AGREED TO THIS PLAN!
...
You didn't even have an alterna-tive!
Yeah, but...
...
BWA HA HA HA!

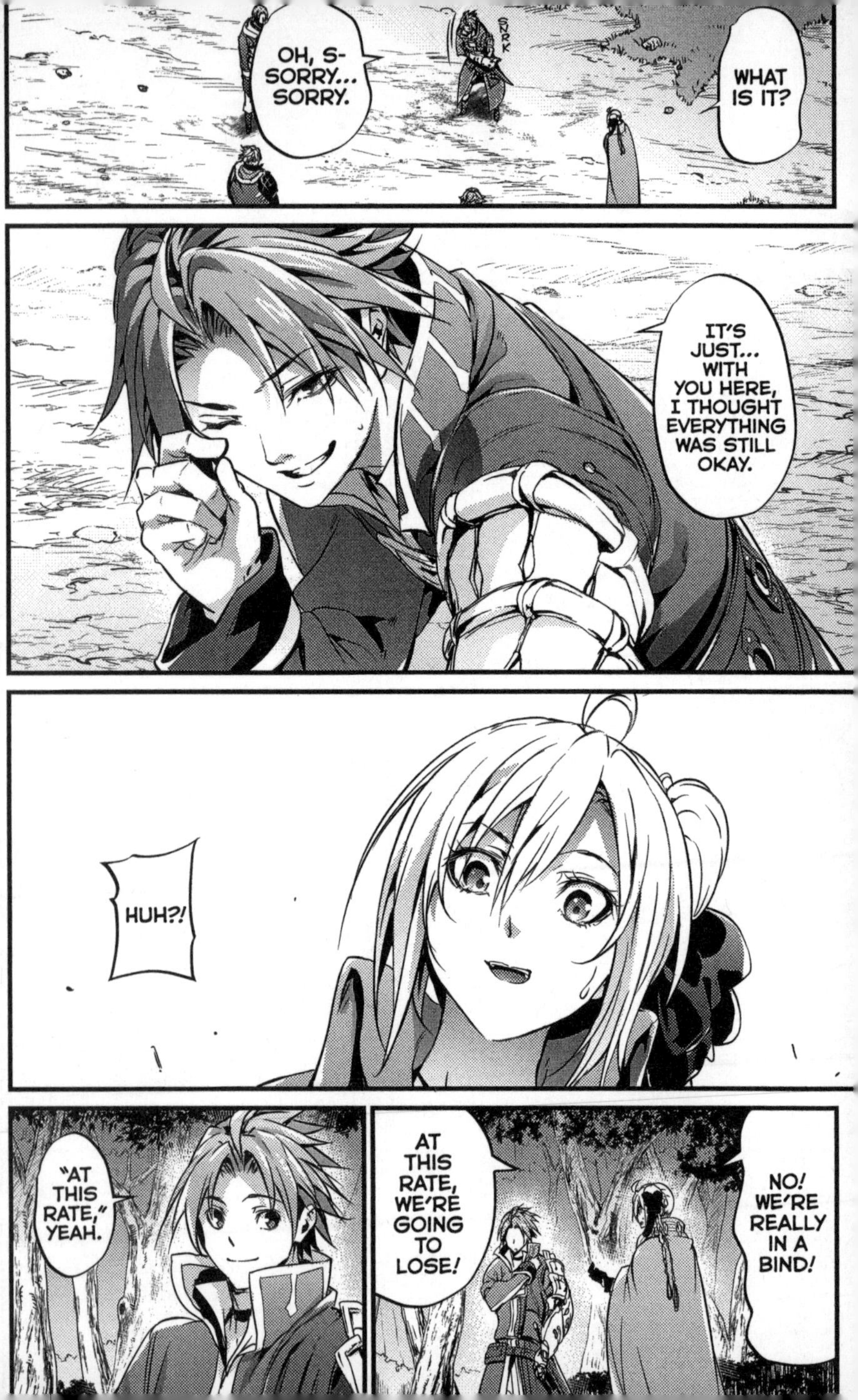
WHAT IS IT?
SNRK
OH, S-SORRY... SORRY.
IT'S JUST... WITH YOU HERE, I THOUGHT EVERYTHING WAS STILL OKAY.
HUH?!
NO! WE'RE REALLY IN A BIND!
AT THIS RATE, WE'RE GOING TO LOSE!
"AT THIS RATE," YEAH.

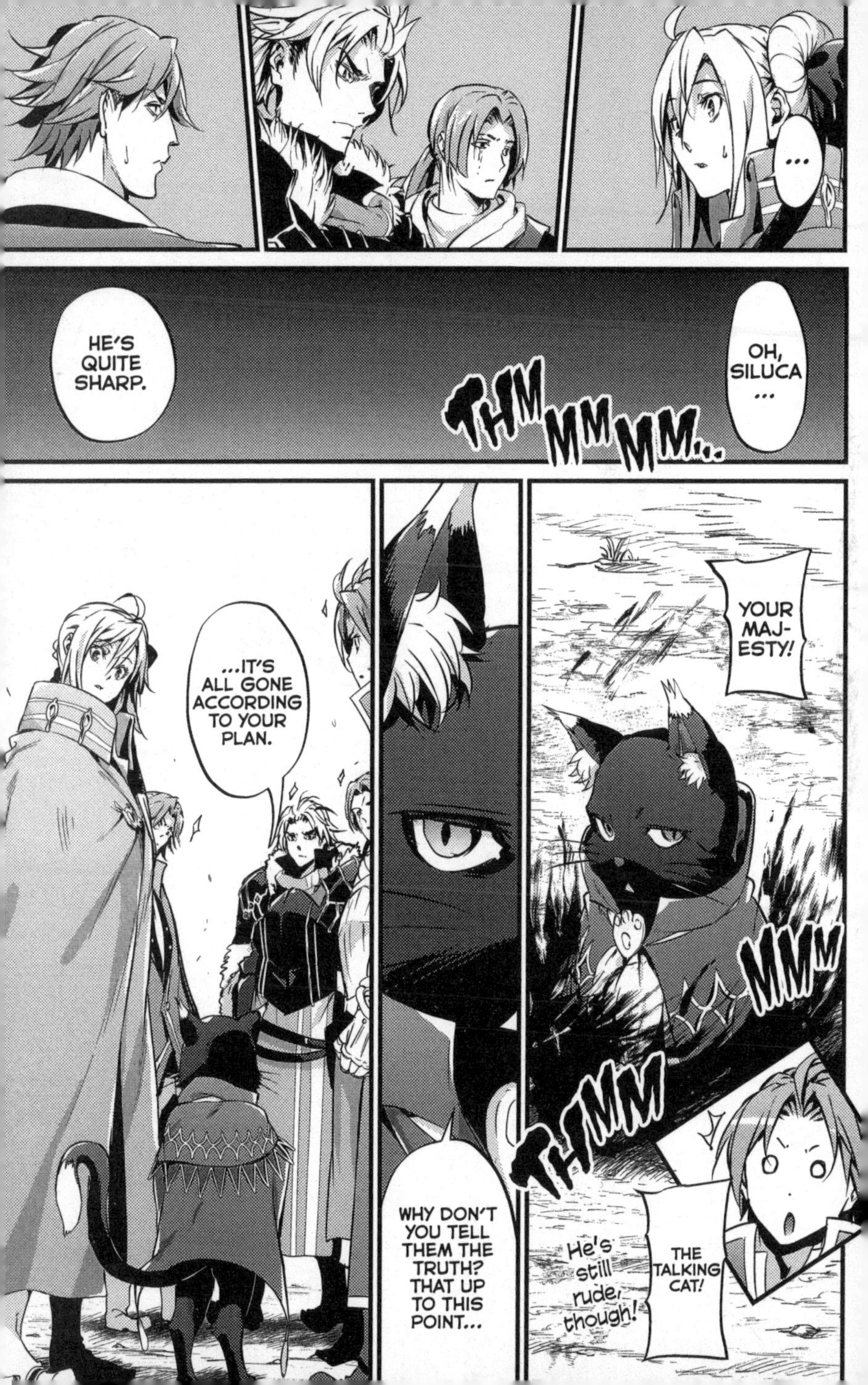
...
OH, SILUCA ...
THMMMMMM..
HE'S QUITE SHARP.
YOUR MAJ-ESTY!
MMM
THMM
THE TALKING CAT!
He's still rude, though!
WHY DON'T YOU TELL THEM THE TRUTH? THAT UP TO THIS POINT...
...IT'S ALL GONE ACCORDING TO YOUR PLAN.

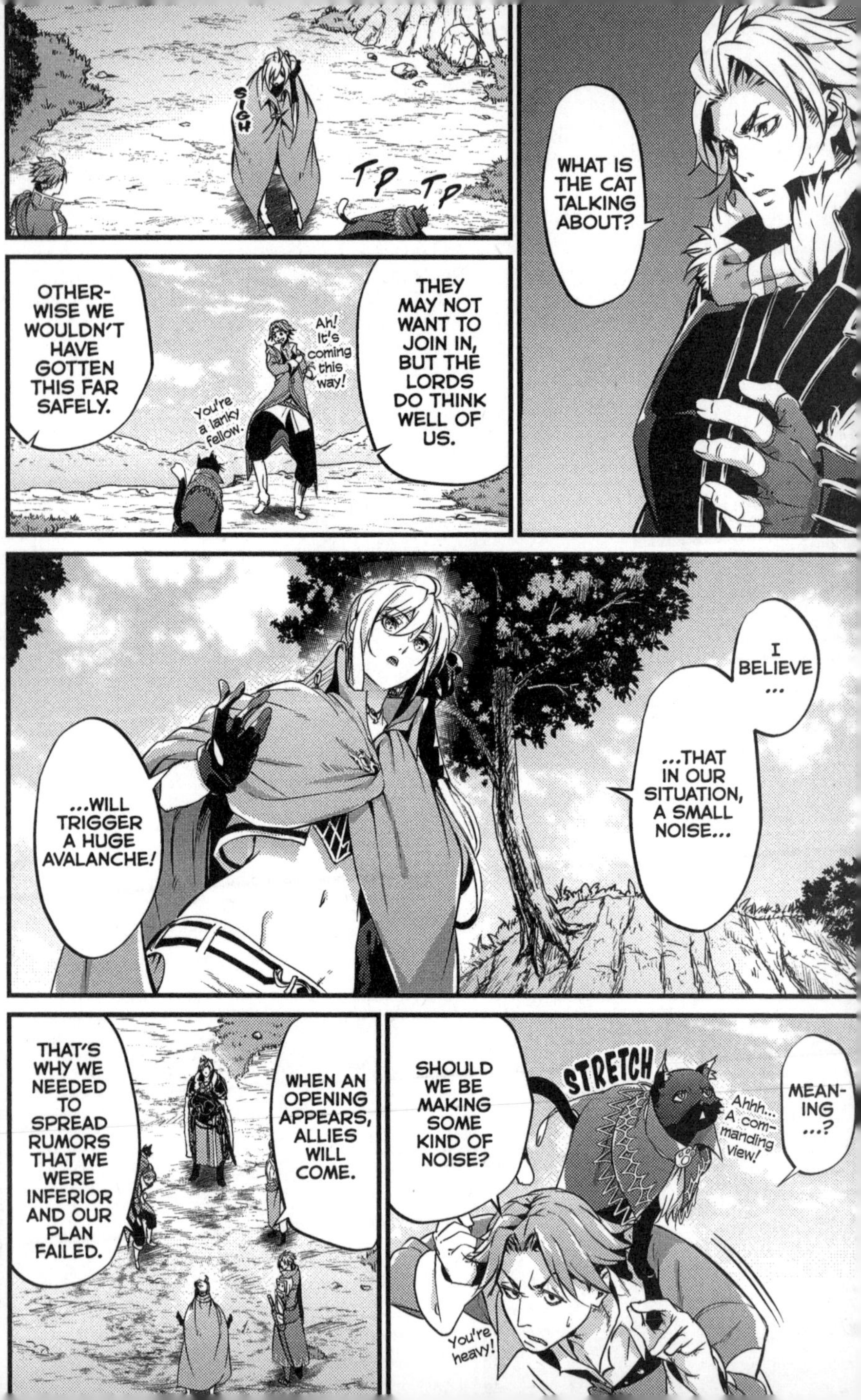
WHAT IS THE CAT TALKING ABOUT?
SIGH
TP TP TP
THEY MAY NOT WANT TO JOIN IN, BUT THE LORDS DO THINK WELL OF US.
OTHERWISE WE WOULDN'T HAVE GOTTEN THIS FAR SAFELY.
Ah! It's coming this way!
You're a lanky fellow.
I BELIEVE...
...THAT IN OUR SITUATION, A SMALL NOISE...
...WILL TRIGGER A HUGE AVALANCHE!
MEANING...?
Ahhh... A commanding view!
STRETCH
SHOULD WE BE MAKING SOME KIND OF NOISE?
You're heavy!
WHEN AN OPENING APPEARS, ALLIES WILL COME.
THAT'S WHY WE NEEDED TO SPREAD RUMORS THAT WE WERE INFERIOR AND OUR PLAN FAILED.

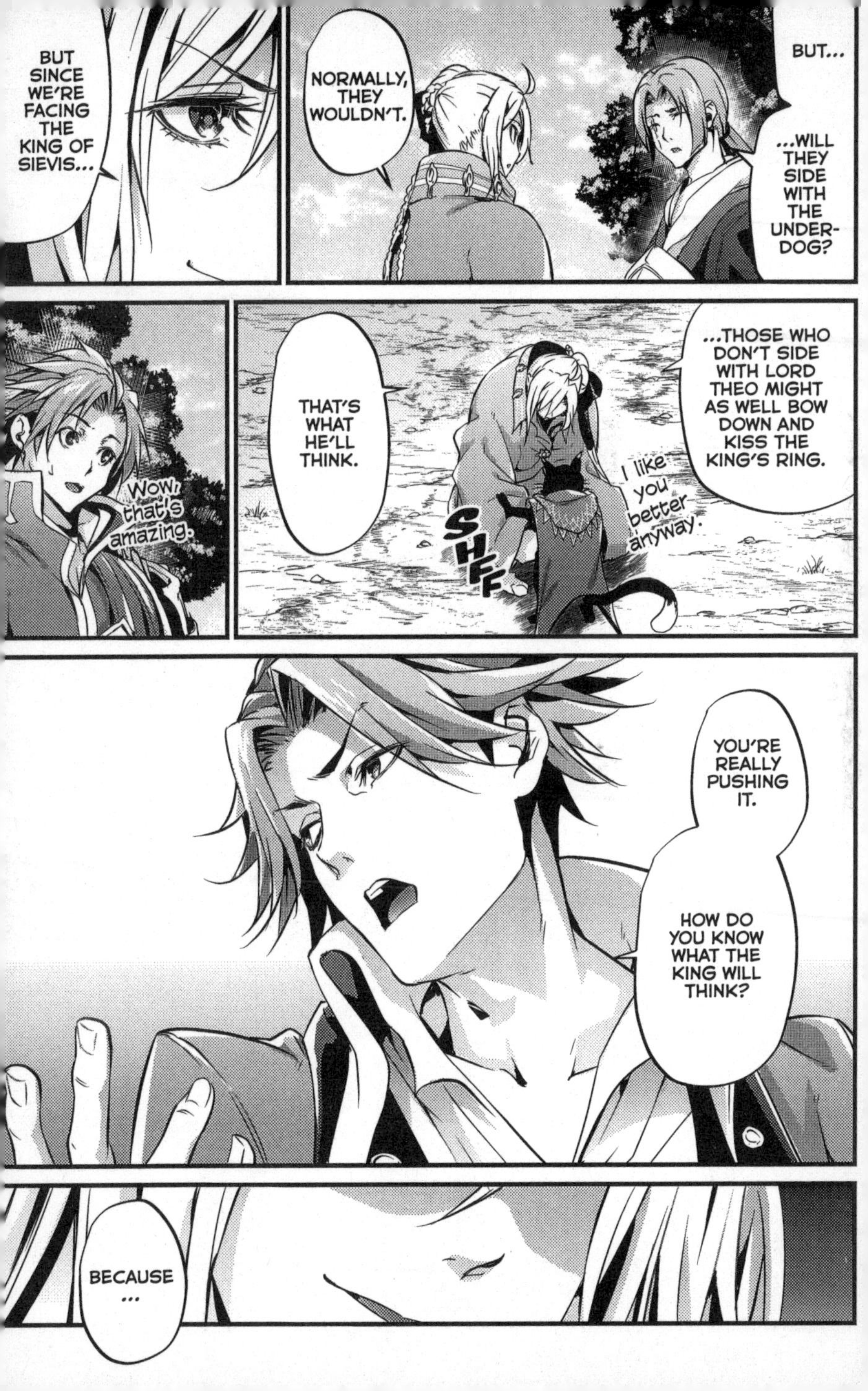
BUT...
...WILL THEY SIDE WITH THE UNDER-DOG?
NORMALLY, THEY WOULDN'T.
BUT SINCE WE'RE FACING THE KING OF SIEVIS...
...THOSE WHO DON'T SIDE WITH LORD THEO MIGHT AS WELL BOW DOWN AND KISS THE KING'S RING.
I like you better anyway.
SHFF
THAT'S WHAT HE'LL THINK.
Wow, that's amazing.
YOU'RE REALLY PUSHING IT.
HOW DO YOU KNOW WHAT THE KING WILL THINK?
BECAUSE...

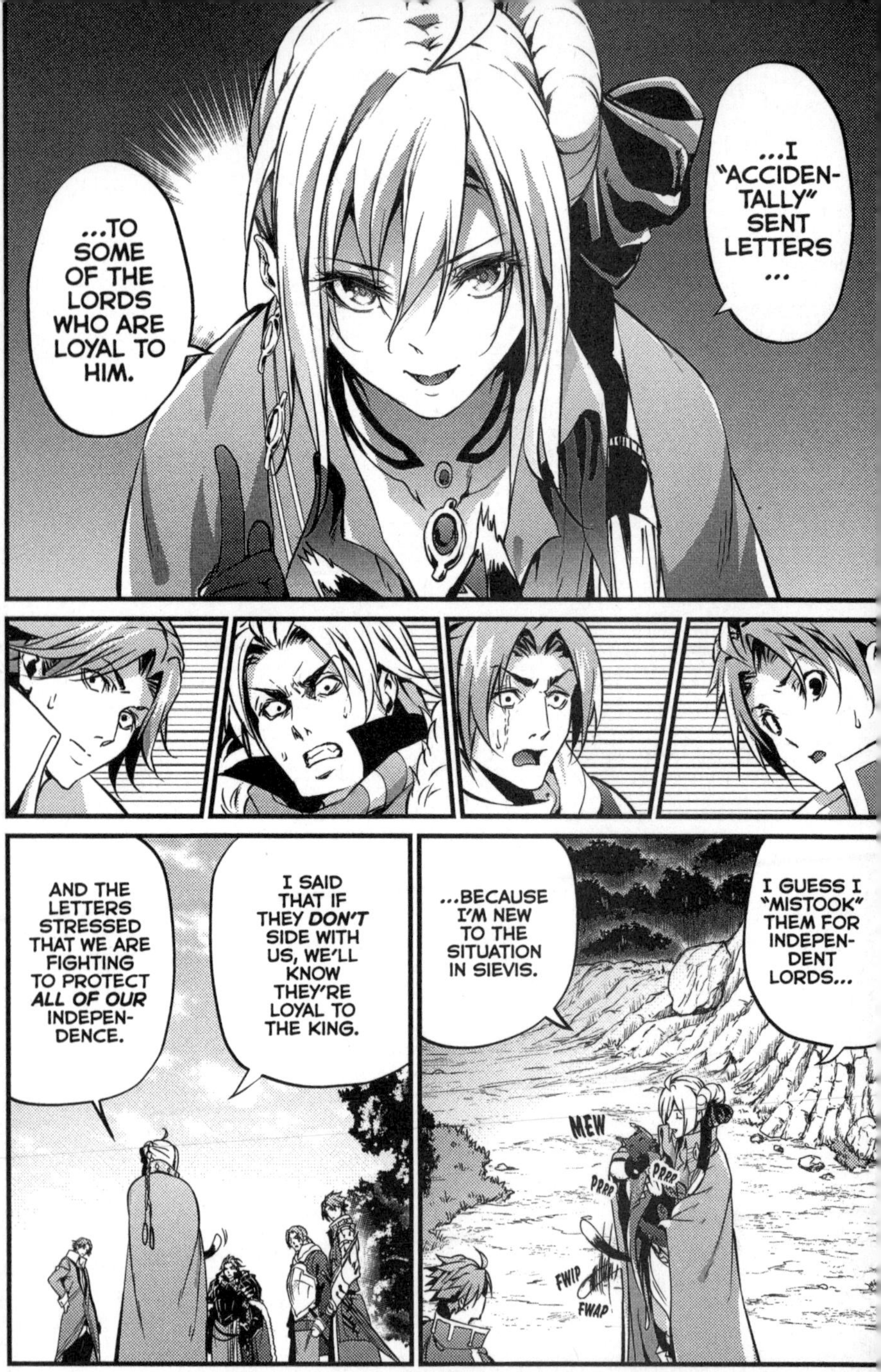
...I "ACCIDEN-TALLY" SENT LETTERS ...
...TO SOME OF THE LORDS WHO ARE LOYAL TO HIM.
I GUESS I "MISTOOK" THEM FOR INDEPEN-DENT LORDS...
...BECAUSE I'M NEW TO THE SITUATION IN SIEVIS.
MEW
PRRP
PRRP
FWIP
FWAP
I SAID THAT IF THEY *DON'T* SIDE WITH US, WE'LL KNOW THEY'RE LOYAL TO THE KING.
AND THE LETTERS STRESSED THAT WE ARE FIGHTING TO PROTECT *ALL OF OUR* INDEPEN-DENCE.

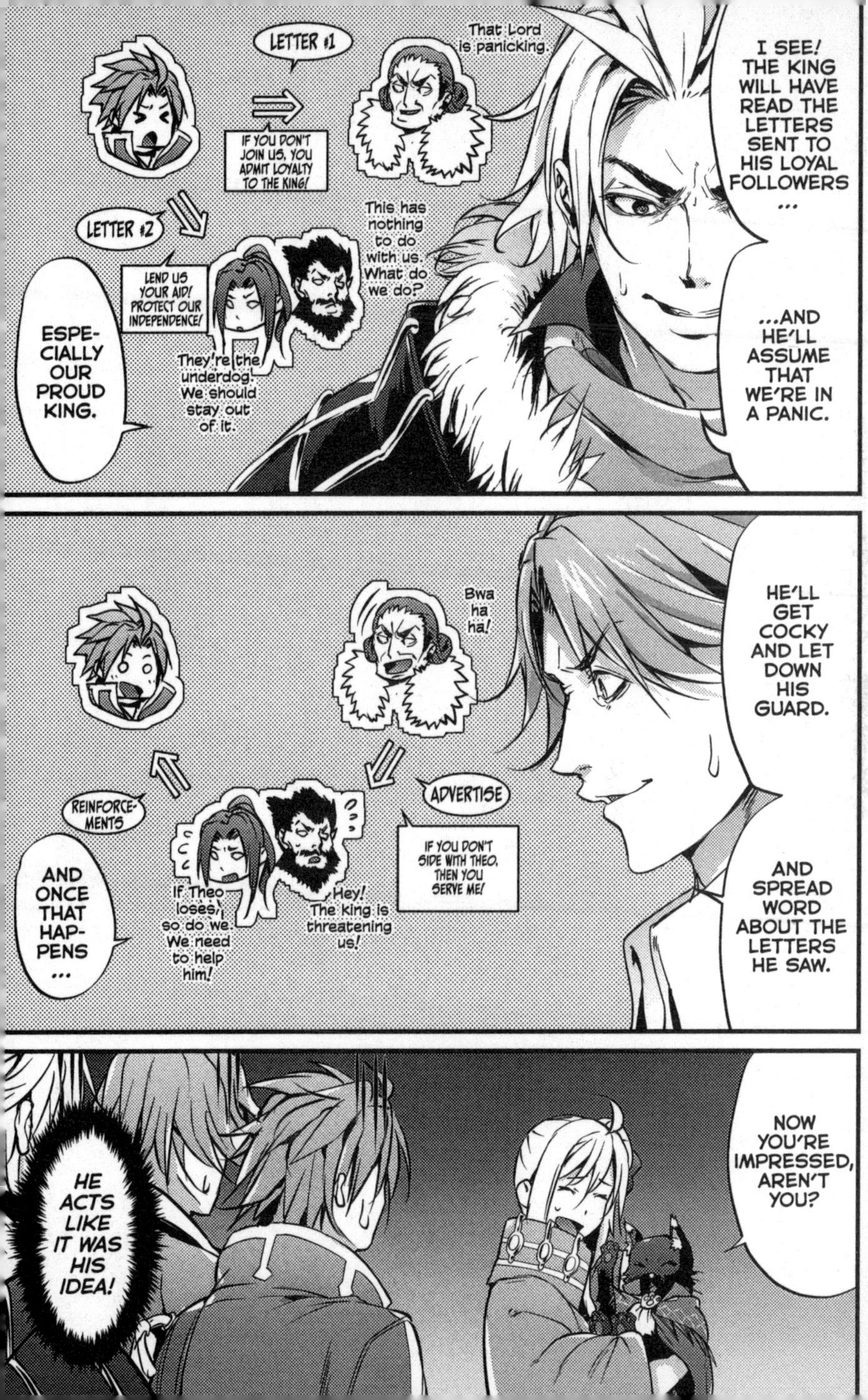
I SEE! THE KING WILL HAVE READ THE LETTERS SENT TO HIS LOYAL FOLLOWERS ...
...AND HE'LL ASSUME THAT WE'RE IN A PANIC.
That Lord is panicking.
LETTER #1
IF YOU DON'T JOIN US, YOU ADMIT LOYALTY TO THE KING!
This has nothing to do with us. What do we do?
LETTER #2
LEND US YOUR AID! PROTECT OUR INDEPENDENCE!
They're the underdog. We should stay out of it.
ESPECIALLY OUR PROUD KING.
HE'LL GET COCKY AND LET DOWN HIS GUARD.
AND SPREAD WORD ABOUT THE LETTERS HE SAW.
Bwa ha ha!
ADVERTISE
IF YOU DON'T SIDE WITH THEO, THEN YOU SERVE ME!
Hey! The king is threatening us!
If Theo loses, so do we. We need to help him!
REINFORCEMENTS
AND ONCE THAT HAPPENS ...
NOW YOU'RE IMPRESSED, AREN'T YOU?
HE ACTS LIKE IT WAS HIS IDEA!

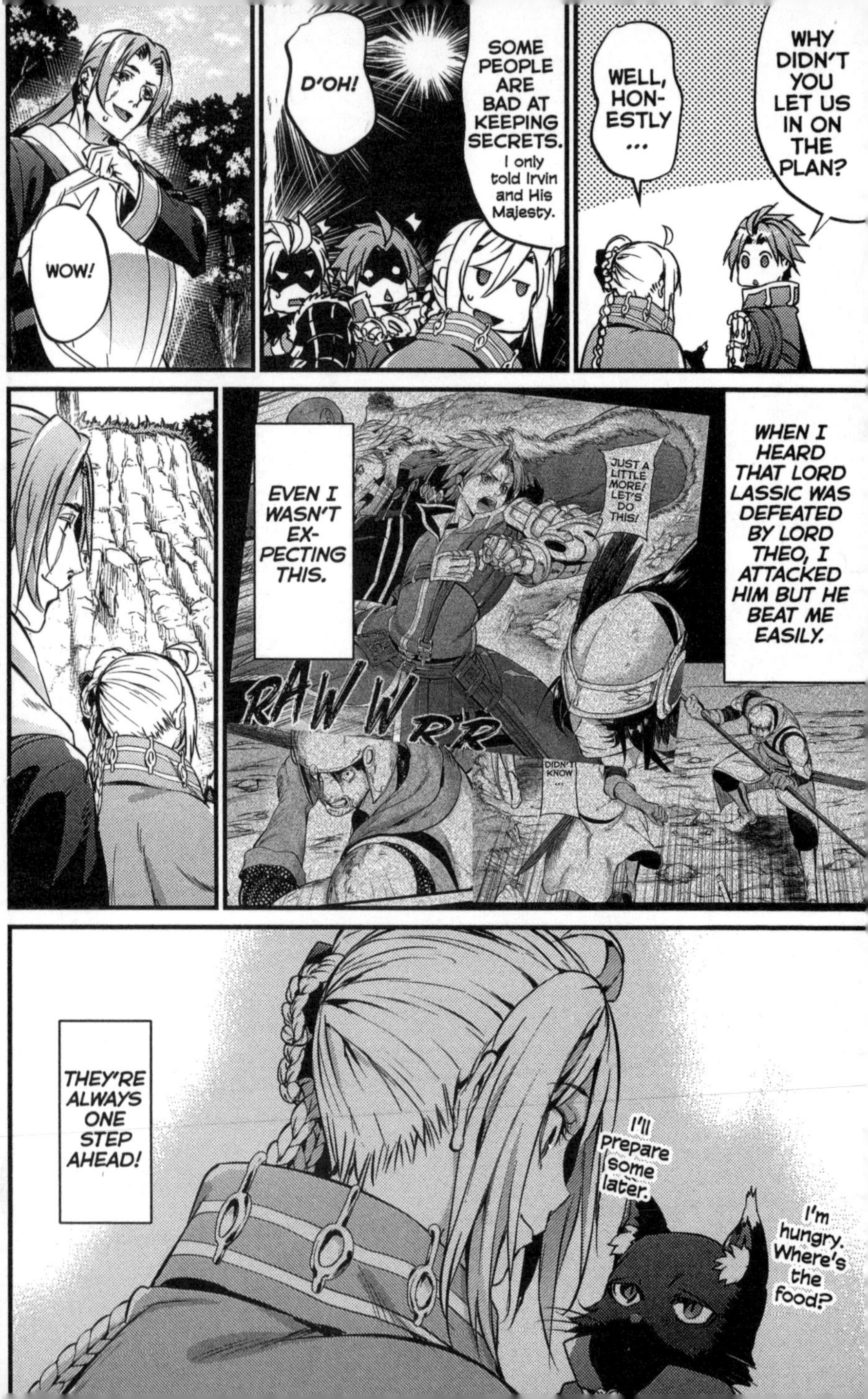
WHY DIDN'T YOU LET US IN ON THE PLAN?
WELL, HON-ESTLY ...
SOME PEOPLE ARE BAD AT KEEPING SECRETS.
I only told Irvin and His Majesty.
D'OH!
WOW!
WHEN I HEARD THAT LORD LASSIC WAS DEFEATED BY LORD THEO, I ATTACKED HIM BUT HE BEAT ME EASILY.
JUST A LITTLE MORE! LET'S DO THIS!
EVEN I WASN'T EX-PECTING THIS.
RAWWRR
DIDN'T KNOW ...
I'm hungry. Where's the food?
I'll prepare some later.
THEY'RE ALWAYS ONE STEP AHEAD!

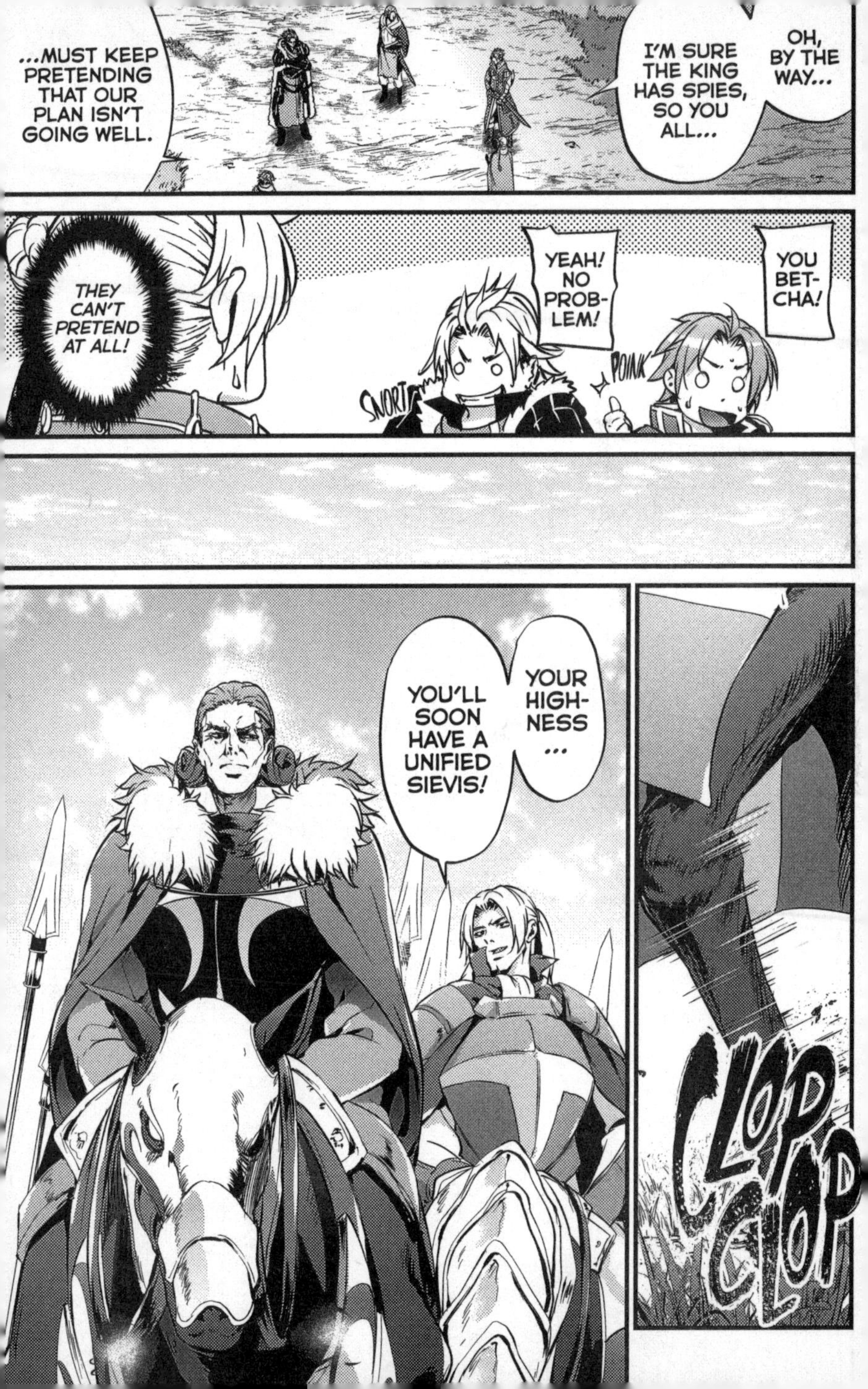
OH, BY THE WAY...
I'M SURE THE KING HAS SPIES, SO YOU ALL...
...MUST KEEP PRETENDING THAT OUR PLAN ISN'T GOING WELL.
YOU BET-CHA!
POINK
YEAH! NO PROB-LEM!
SNORT
THEY CAN'T PRETEND AT ALL!
CLOP CLOP
YOUR HIGH-NESS...
YOU'LL SOON HAVE A UNIFIED SIEVIS!

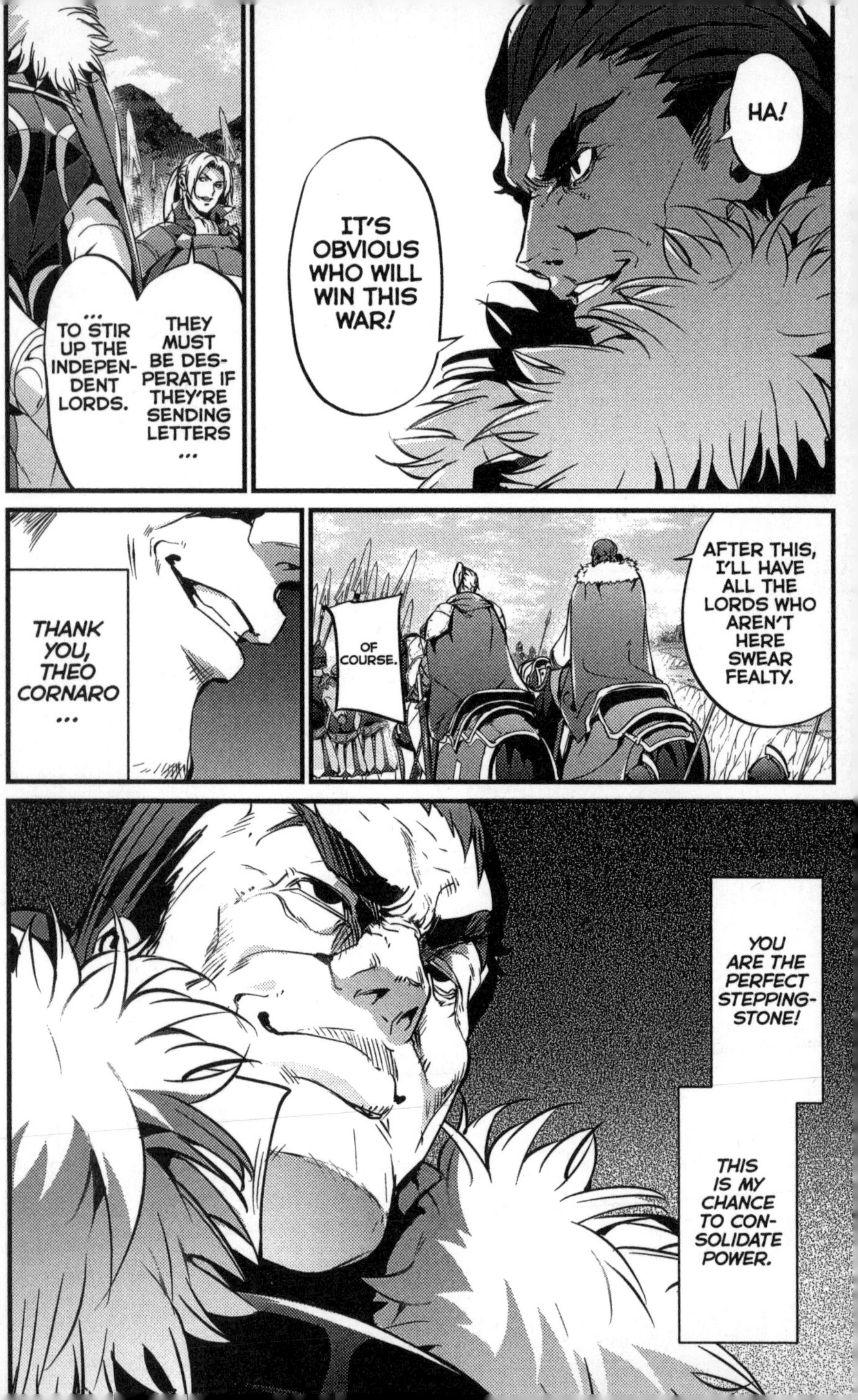
HA!
IT'S OBVIOUS WHO WILL WIN THIS WAR!
THEY MUST BE DES-PERATE IF THEY'RE SENDING LETTERS...
...TO STIR UP THE INDEPEN-DENT LORDS.
AFTER THIS, I'LL HAVE ALL THE LORDS WHO AREN'T HERE SWEAR FEALTY.
OF COURSE.
THANK YOU, THEO CORNARO...
YOU ARE THE PERFECT STEPPING-STONE!
THIS IS MY CHANCE TO CON-SOLIDATE POWER.

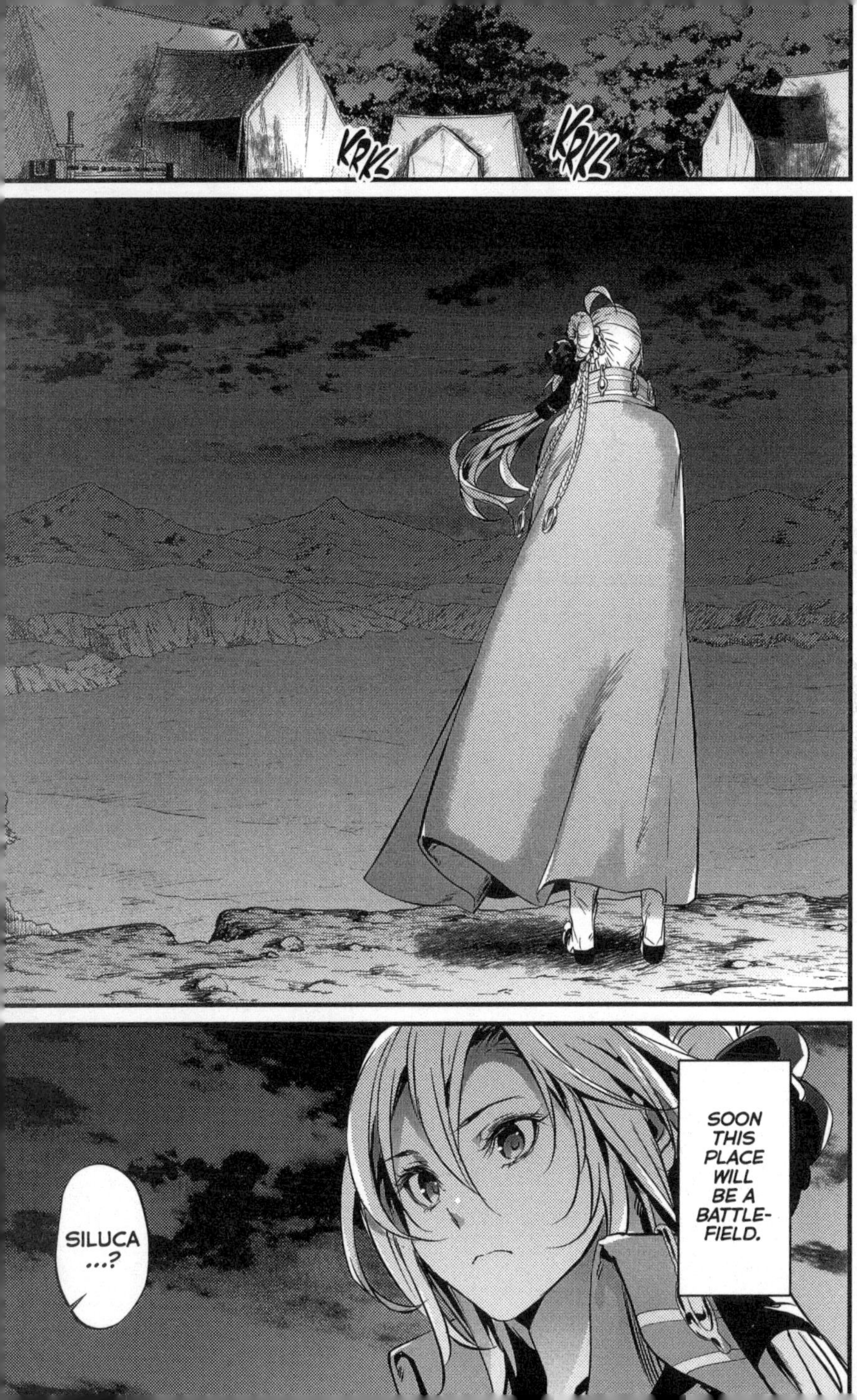
KRKL
KRKL
SOON THIS PLACE WILL BE A BATTLE-FIELD.
SILUCA ...?

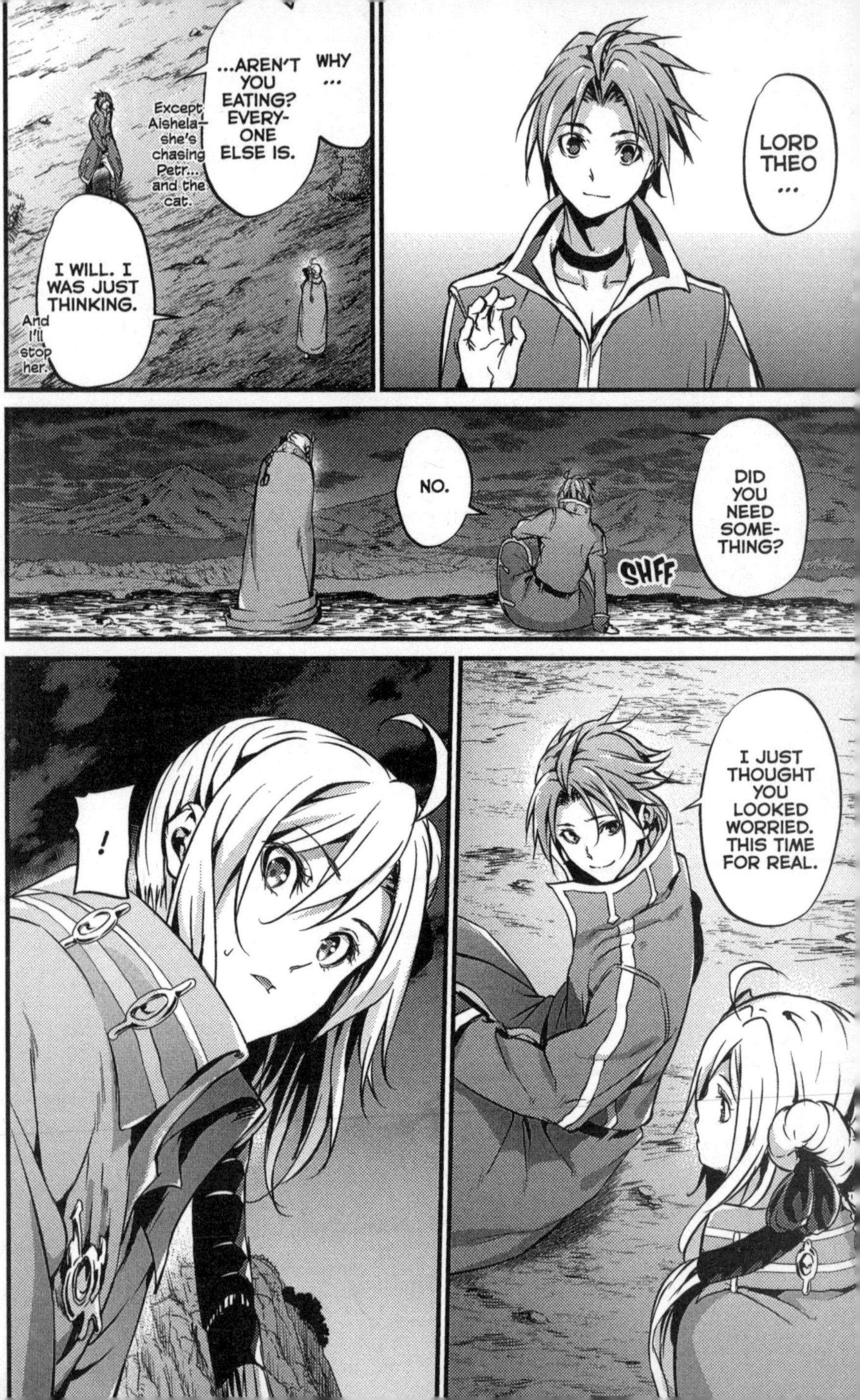
LORD THEO ...
WHY ...
...AREN'T YOU EATING? EVERY-ONE ELSE IS.
Except Aishela— she's chasing Petr... and the cat.
I WILL. I WAS JUST THINKING.
And I'll stop her.
DID YOU NEED SOME-THING?
SHFF
NO.
I JUST THOUGHT YOU LOOKED WORRIED. THIS TIME FOR REAL.
!

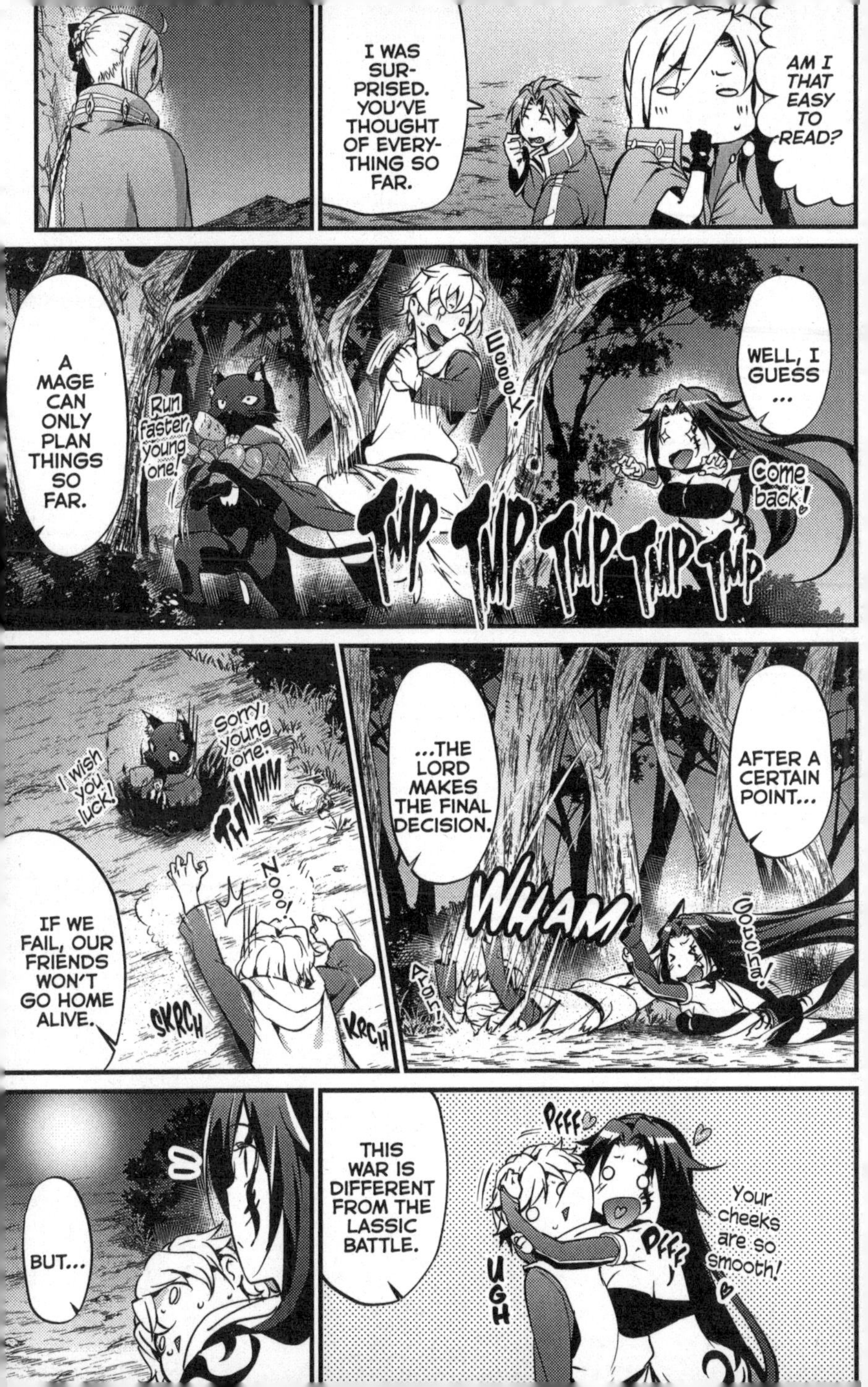
AM I THAT EASY TO READ?
I WAS SURPRISED. YOU'VE THOUGHT OF EVERYTHING SO FAR.
WELL, I GUESS ...
Come back!
TMP TMP TMP TMP TMP
Eeeek!
Run faster, young one!
A MAGE CAN ONLY PLAN THINGS SO FAR.
AFTER A CERTAIN POINT...
...THE LORD MAKES THE FINAL DECISION.
WHAM
Gotcha!
Argh!
Sorry, young one.
I wish you luck!
THMMM
Nooo!
IF WE FAIL, OUR FRIENDS WON'T GO HOME ALIVE.
SKRCH
KRCH
THIS WAR IS DIFFERENT FROM THE LASSIC BATTLE.
PFFF
Your cheeks are so smooth!
PFFF
UGH
BUT...

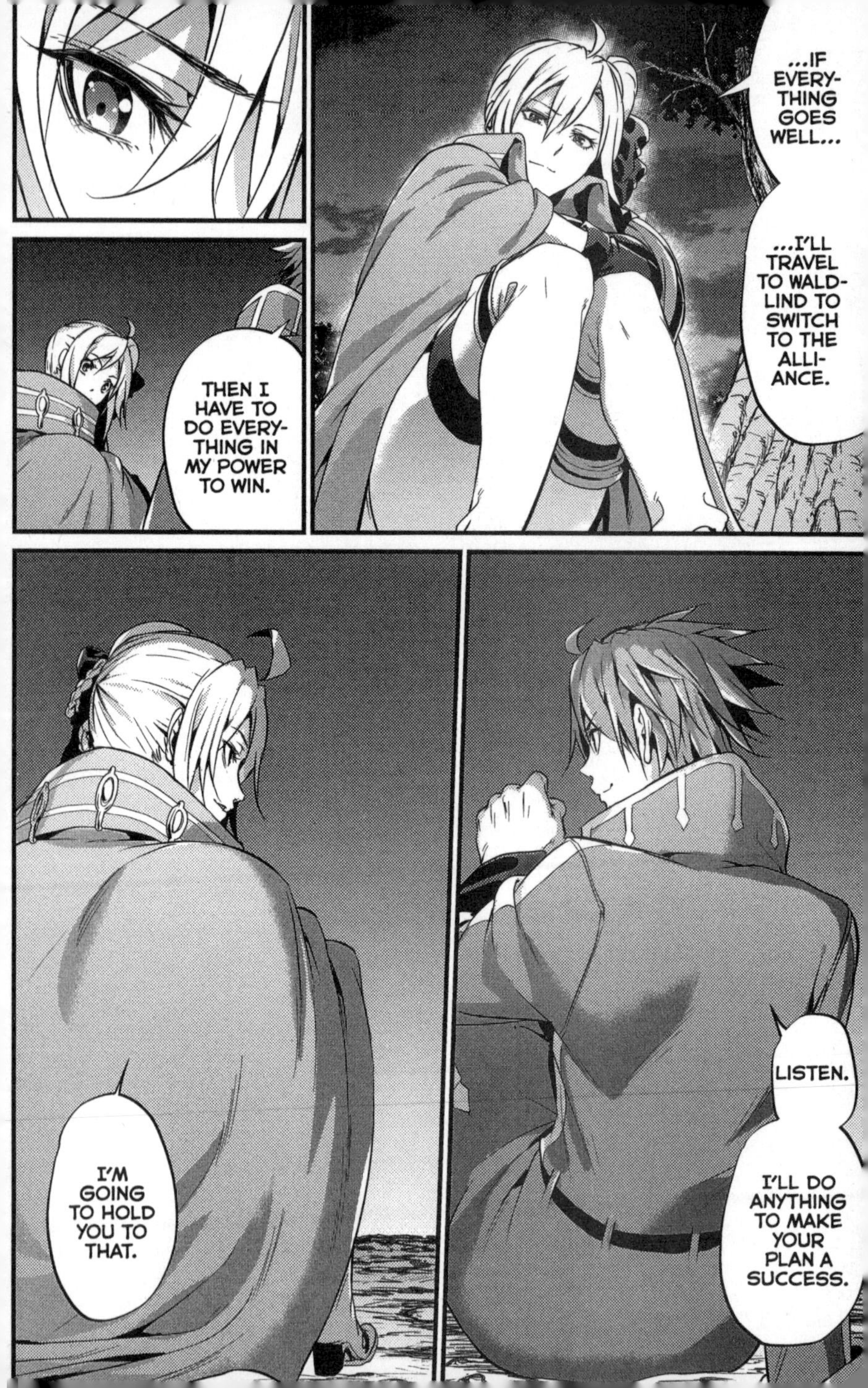
...IF EVERY-THING GOES WELL...
...I'LL TRAVEL TO WALD-LIND TO SWITCH TO THE ALLI-ANCE.
THEN I HAVE TO DO EVERY-THING IN MY POWER TO WIN.
LISTEN.
I'LL DO ANYTHING TO MAKE YOUR PLAN A SUCCESS.
I'M GOING TO HOLD YOU TO THAT.

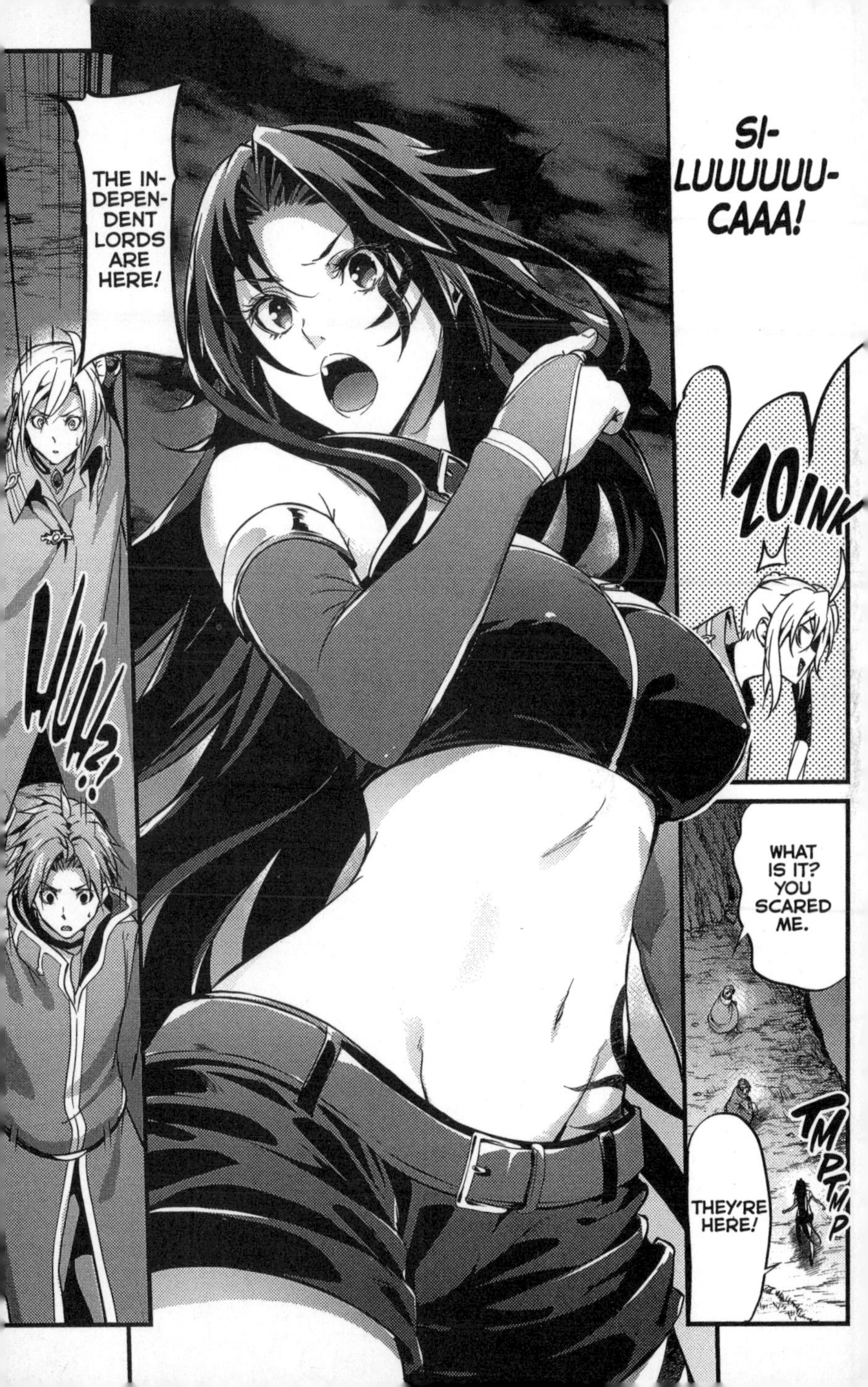
SI-LUUUUUU-CAAA!
ZOINK
WHAT IS IT? YOU SCARED ME.
THEY'RE HERE!
TMPTMP
THE IN-DEPEN-DENT LORDS ARE HERE!
HUH?!

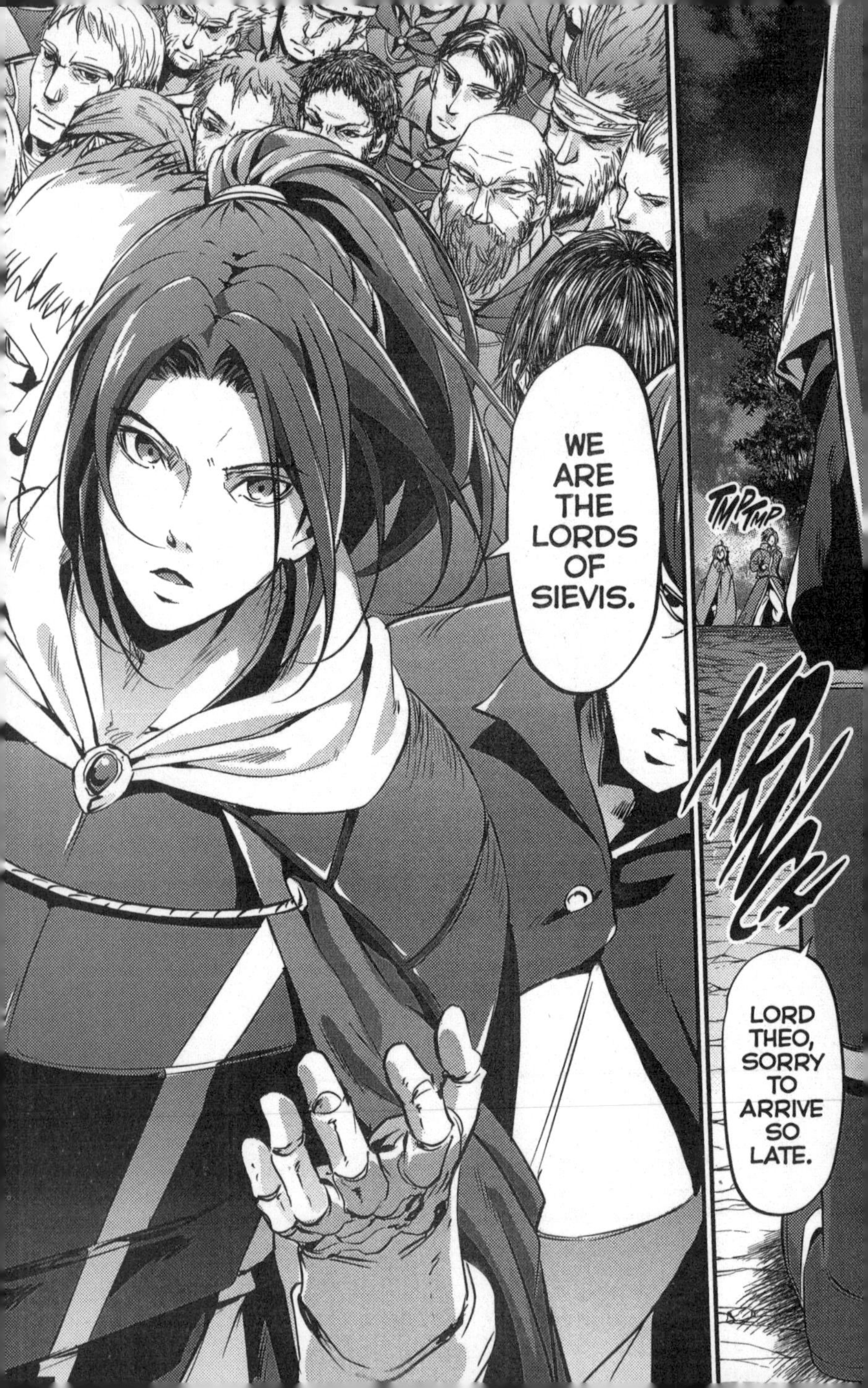
TMP TMP
LORD THEO, SORRY TO ARRIVE SO LATE.
WE ARE THE LORDS OF SIEVIS.

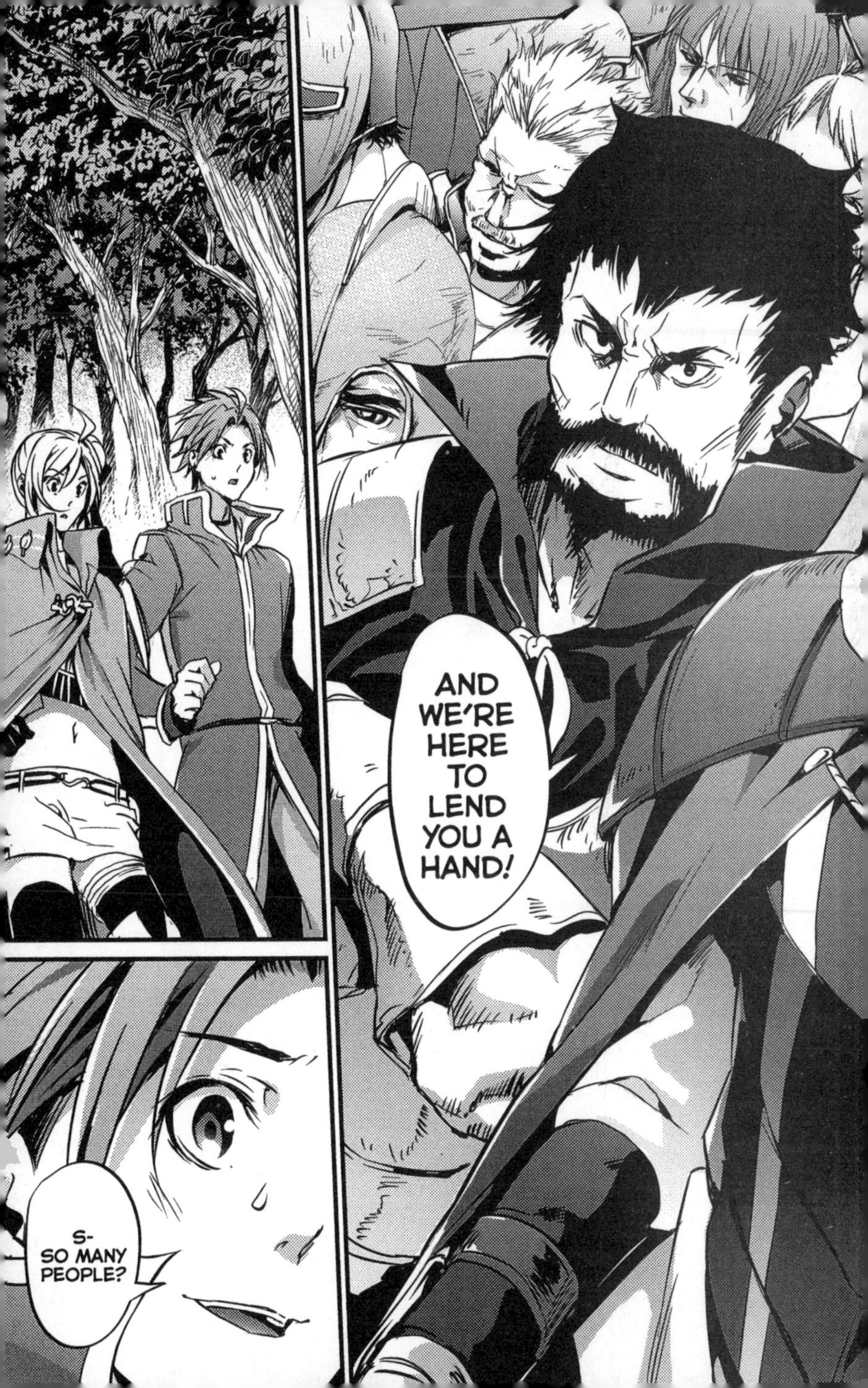
AND WE'RE HERE TO LEND YOU A HAND!
S- SO MANY PEOPLE?

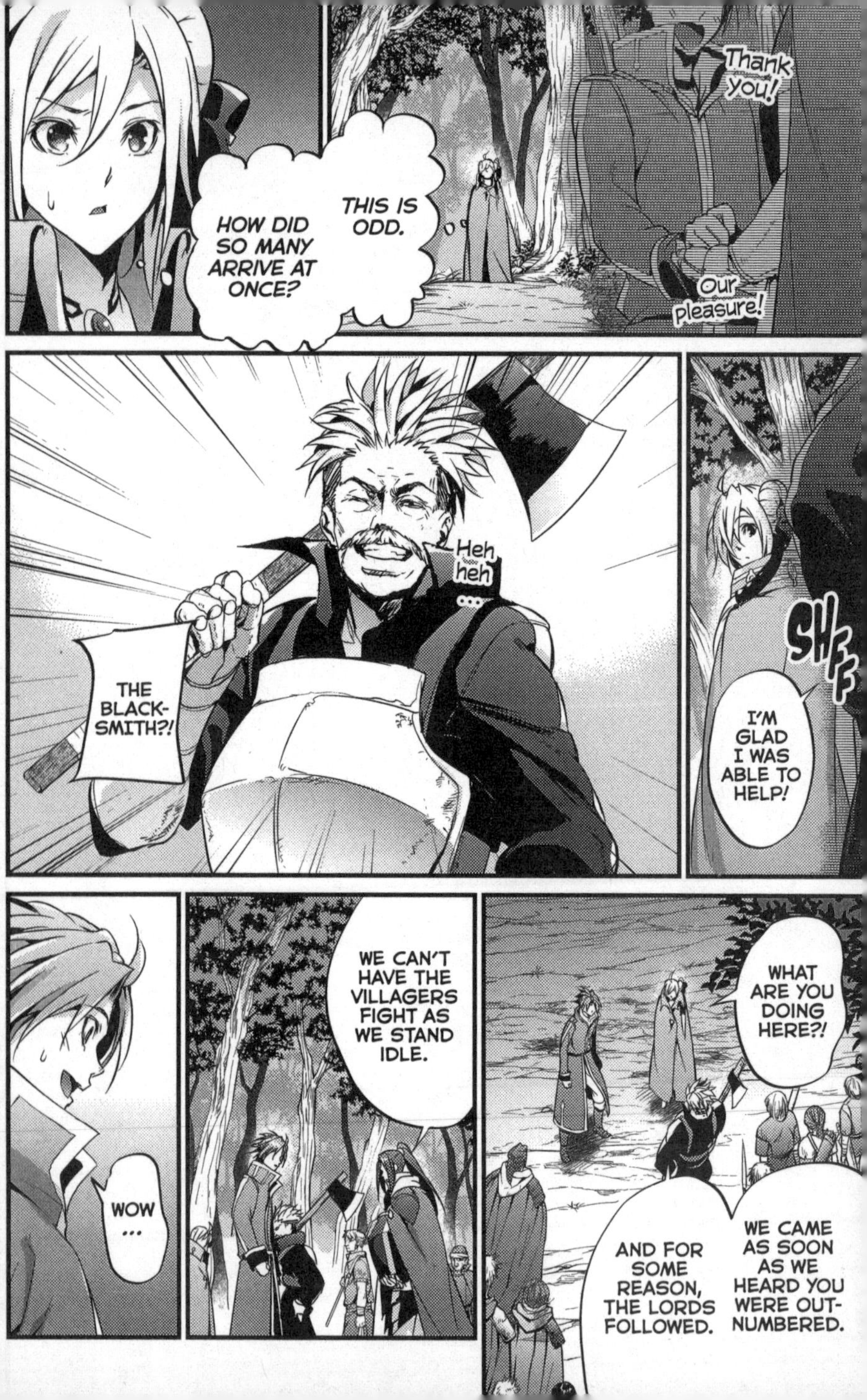
Thank you!
Our pleasure!
THIS IS ODD.
HOW DID SO MANY ARRIVE AT ONCE?
SHFF
I'M GLAD I WAS ABLE TO HELP!
Heh heh ...
THE BLACK-SMITH?!
WHAT ARE YOU DOING HERE?!
WE CAME AS SOON AS WE HEARD YOU WERE OUT-NUMBERED.
AND FOR SOME REASON, THE LORDS FOLLOWED.
WE CAN'T HAVE THE VILLAGERS FIGHT AS WE STAND IDLE.
WOW ...

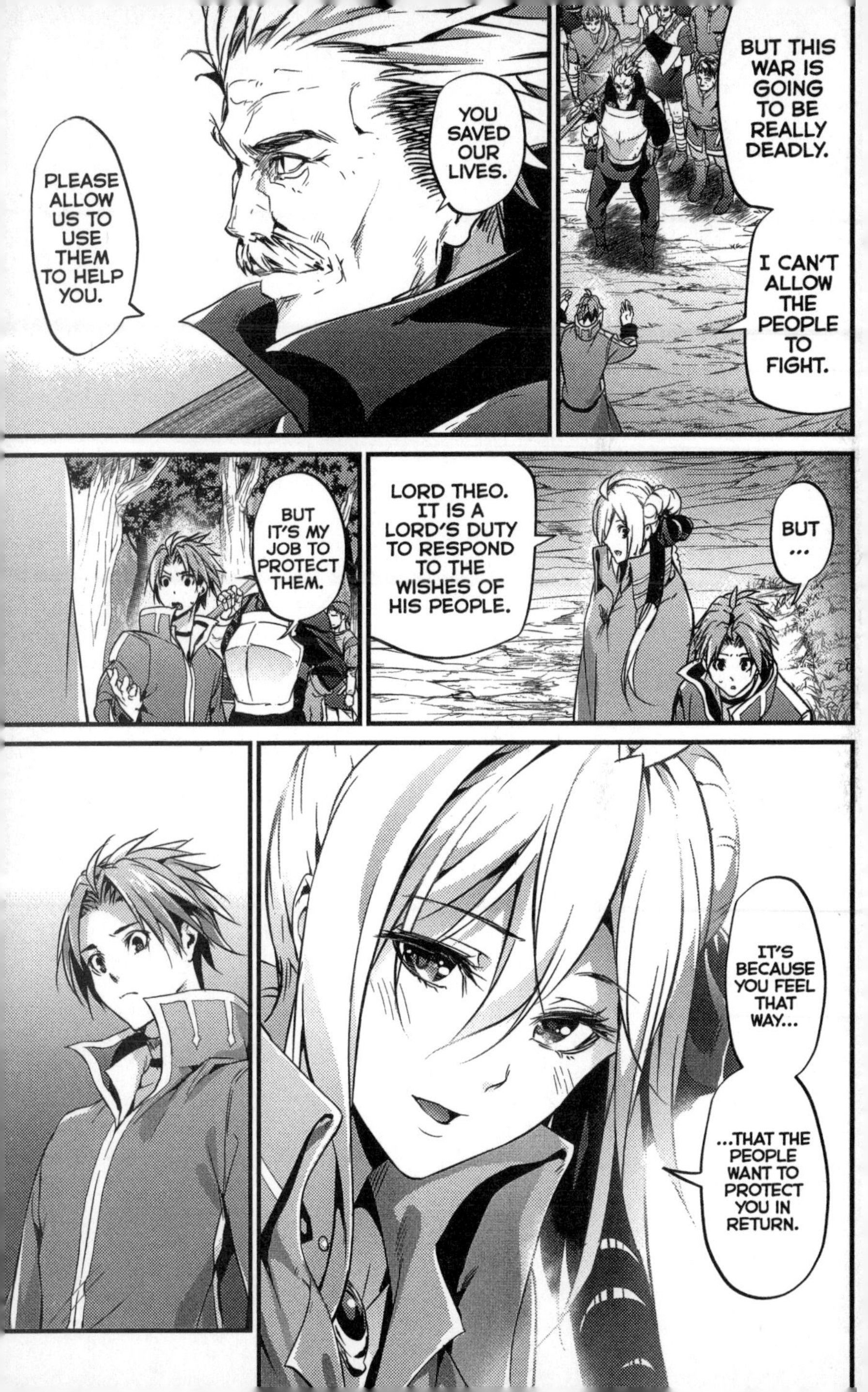
BUT THIS WAR IS GOING TO BE REALLY DEADLY.
I CAN'T ALLOW THE PEOPLE TO FIGHT.
YOU SAVED OUR LIVES.
PLEASE ALLOW US TO USE THEM TO HELP YOU.
BUT ...
LORD THEO. IT IS A LORD'S DUTY TO RESPOND TO THE WISHES OF HIS PEOPLE.
BUT IT'S MY JOB TO PROTECT THEM.
IT'S BECAUSE YOU FEEL THAT WAY...
...THAT THE PEOPLE WANT TO PROTECT YOU IN RETURN.

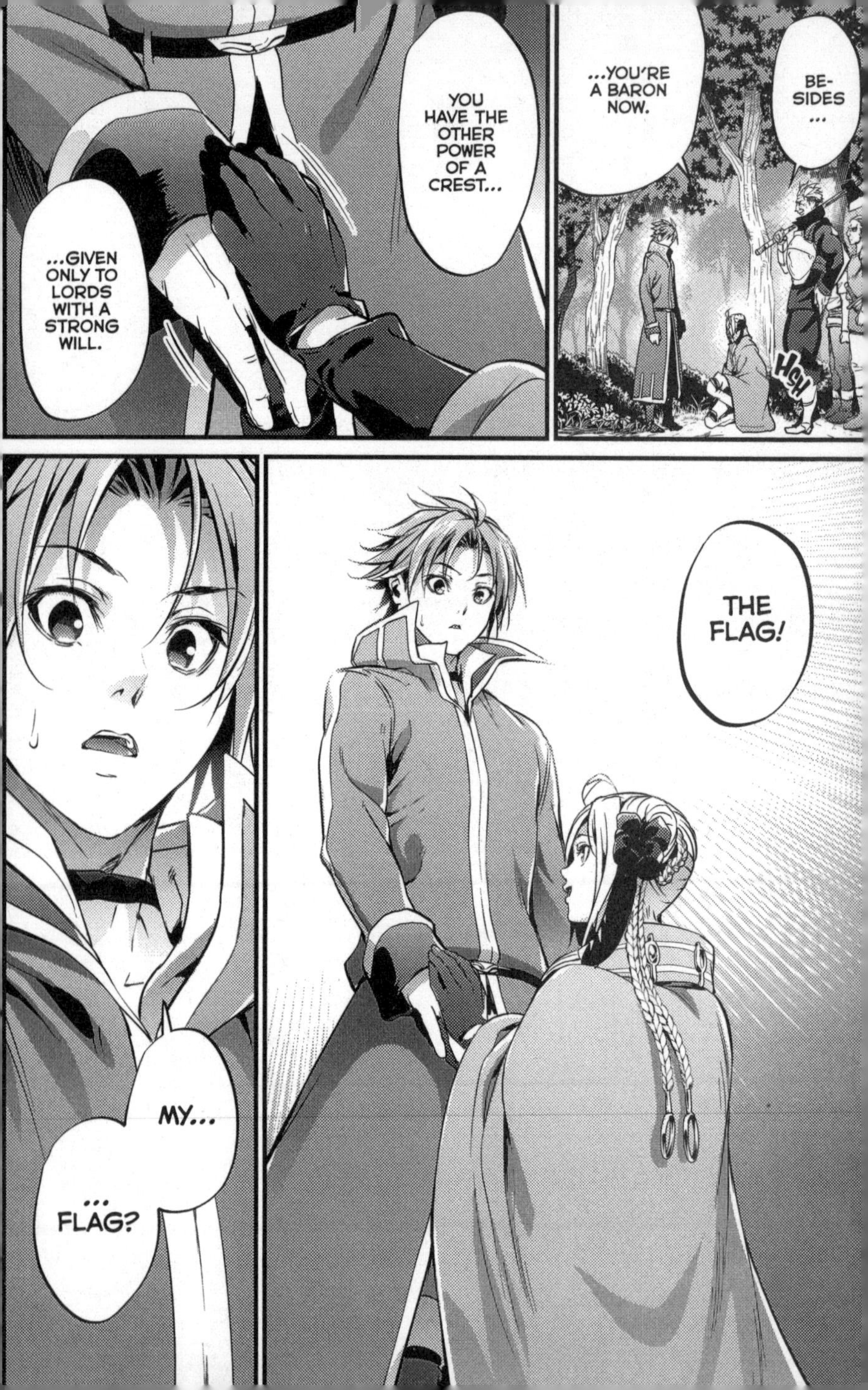
BE-
SIDES
...
...YOU'RE
A BARON
NOW.
HSH
YOU
HAVE THE
OTHER
POWER
OF A
CREST...
...GIVEN
ONLY TO
LORDS
WITH A
STRONG
WILL.
THE
FLAG!
MY...
...
FLAG?

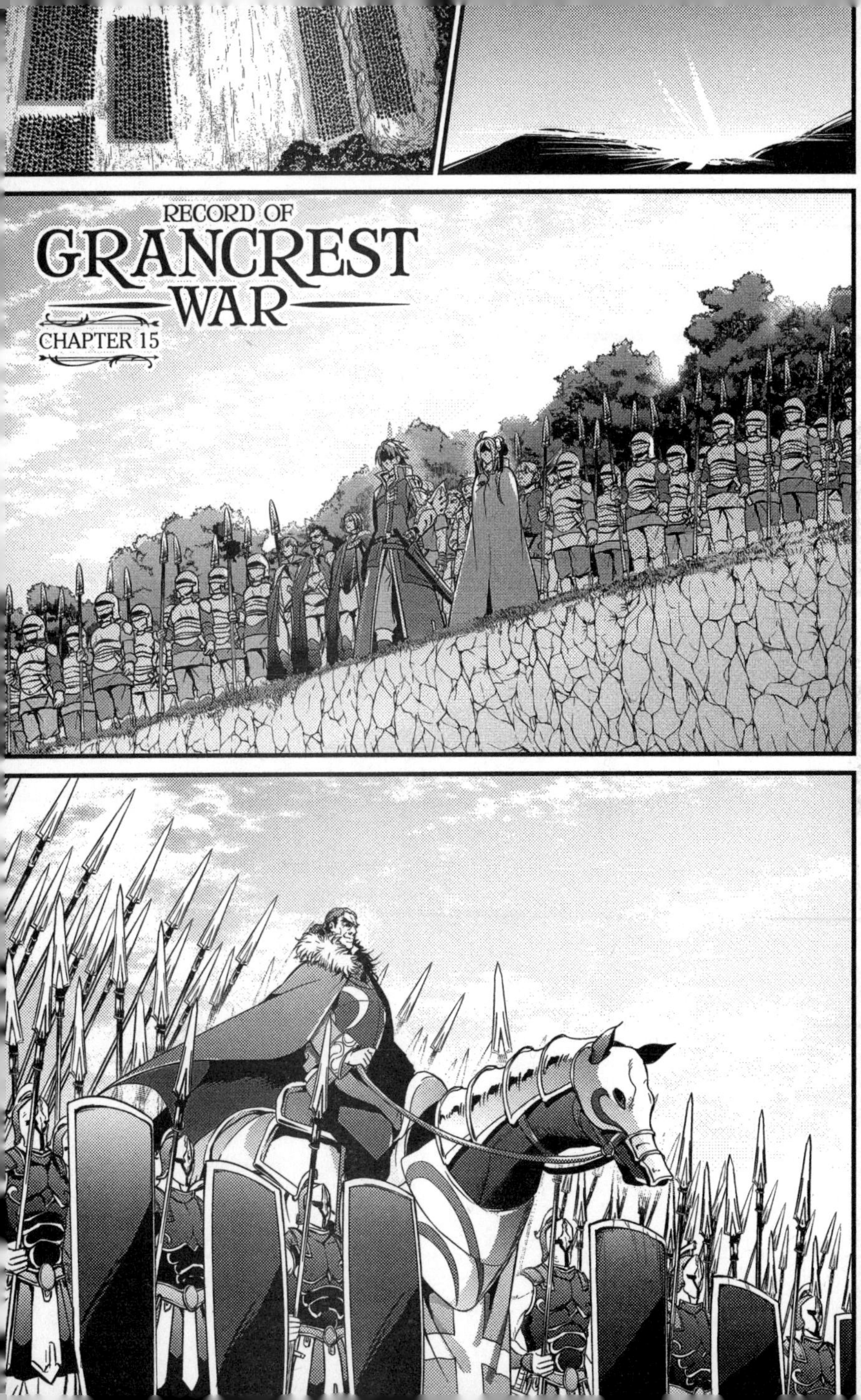
RECORD OF
GRANCREST
WAR
CHAPTER 15

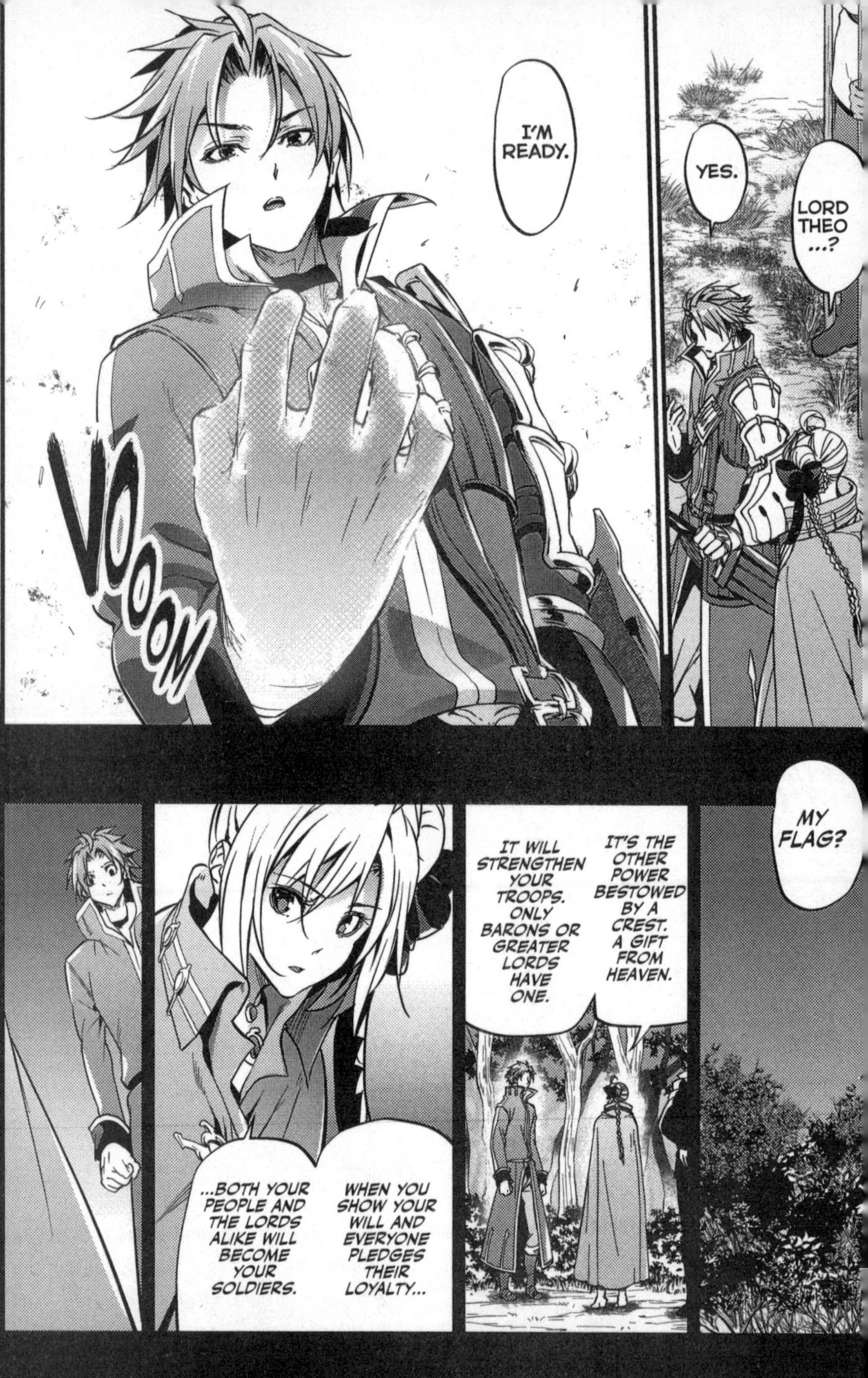
LORD THEO ...?
YES.
I'M READY.
VOOOM
MY FLAG?
IT'S THE OTHER POWER BESTOWED BY A CREST. A GIFT FROM HEAVEN.
IT WILL STRENGTHEN YOUR TROOPS. ONLY BARONS OR GREATER LORDS HAVE ONE.
WHEN YOU SHOW YOUR WILL AND EVERYONE PLEDGES THEIR LOYALTY...
...BOTH YOUR PEOPLE AND THE LORDS ALIKE WILL BECOME YOUR SOLDIERS.

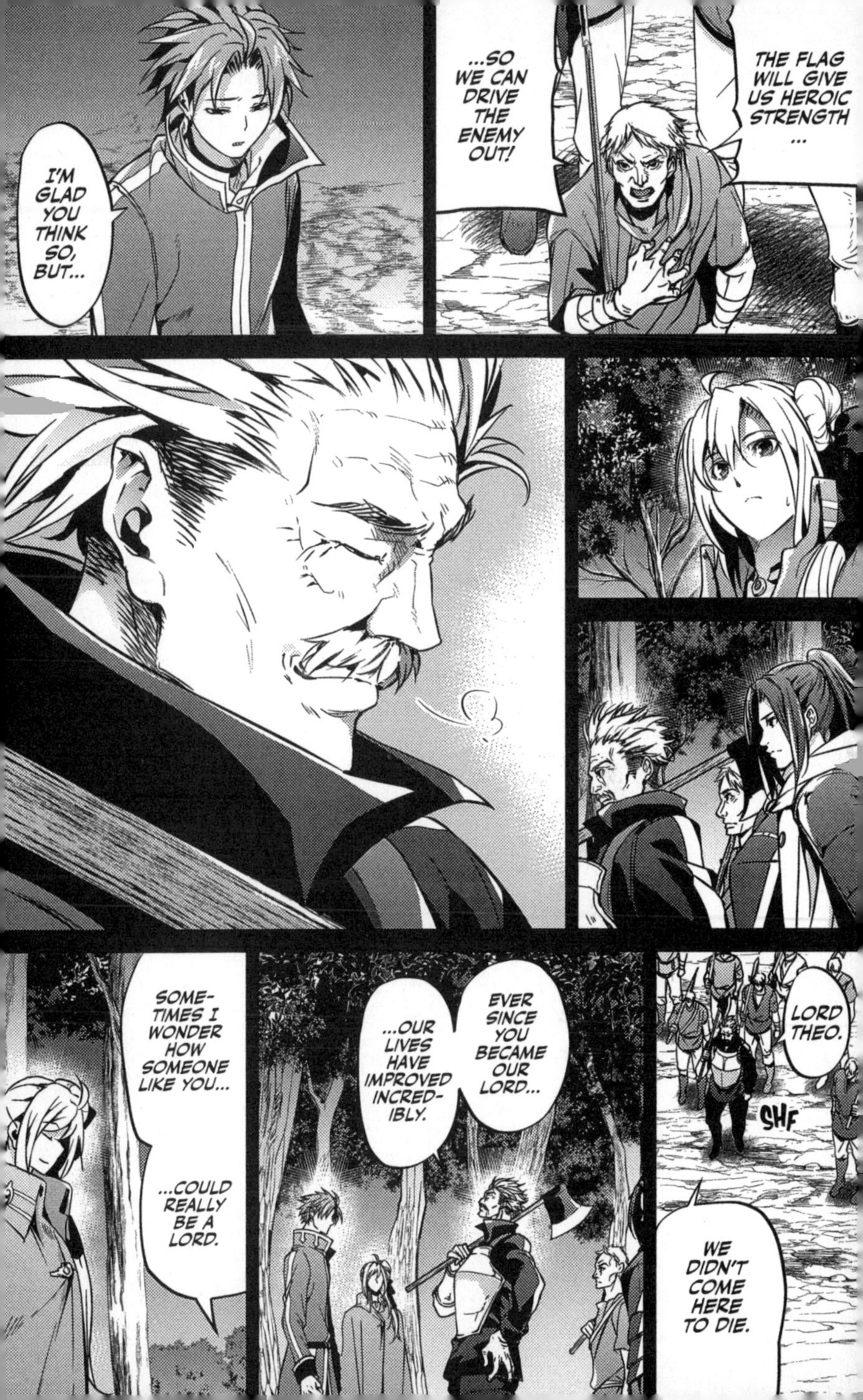
THE FLAG WILL GIVE US HEROIC STRENGTH...
...SO WE CAN DRIVE THE ENEMY OUT!
I'M GLAD YOU THINK SO, BUT...
LORD THEO.
SHF
WE DIDN'T COME HERE TO DIE.
EVER SINCE YOU BECAME OUR LORD...
...OUR LIVES HAVE IMPROVED INCREDIBLY.
SOME-TIMES I WONDER HOW SOMEONE LIKE YOU...
...COULD REALLY BE A LORD.

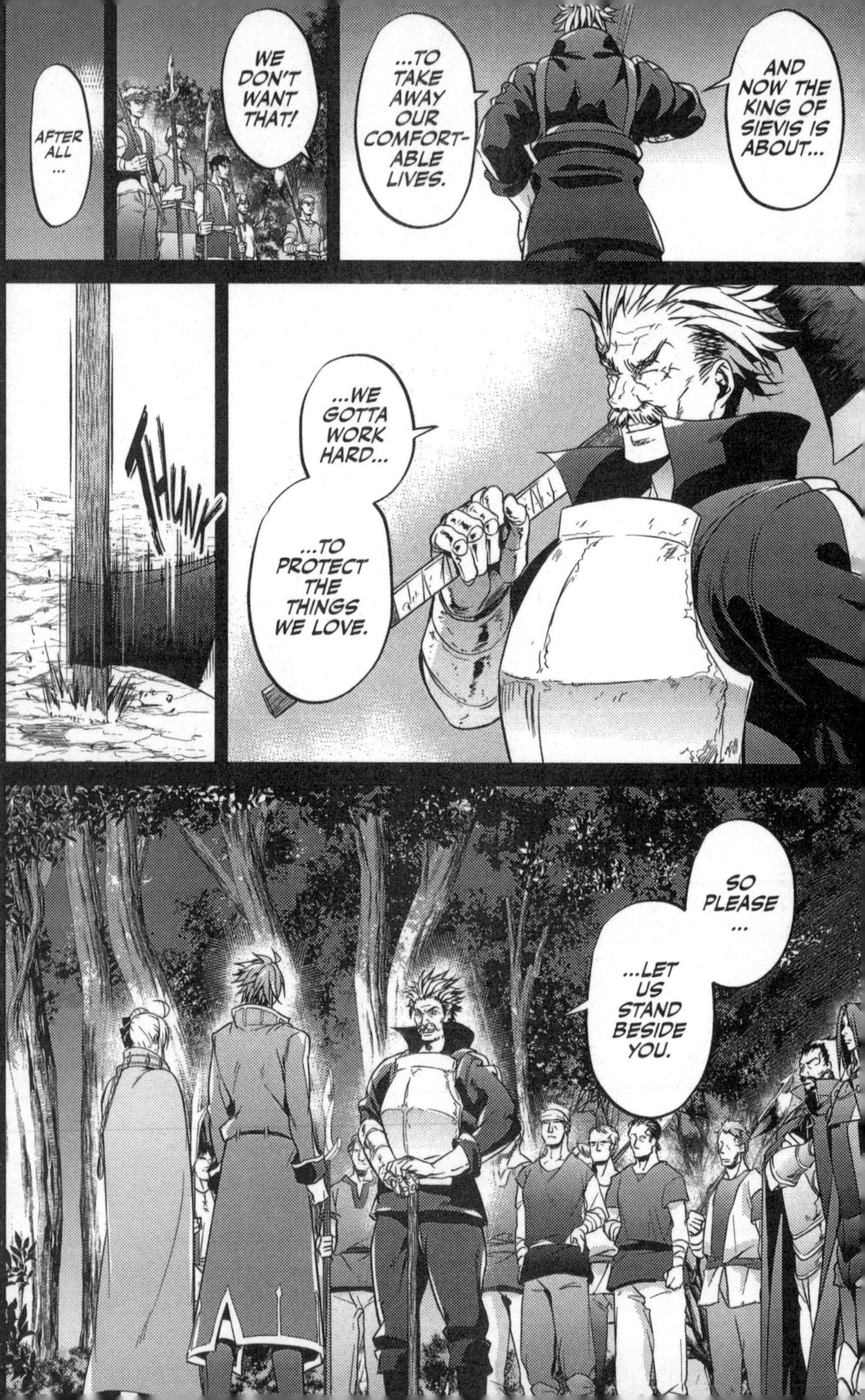
AND NOW THE KING OF SIEVIS IS ABOUT...
...TO TAKE AWAY OUR COMFORTABLE LIVES.
WE DON'T WANT THAT!
AFTER ALL ...
...WE GOTTA WORK HARD...
...TO PROTECT THE THINGS WE LOVE.
THUNK
SO PLEASE ...
...LET US STAND BESIDE YOU.

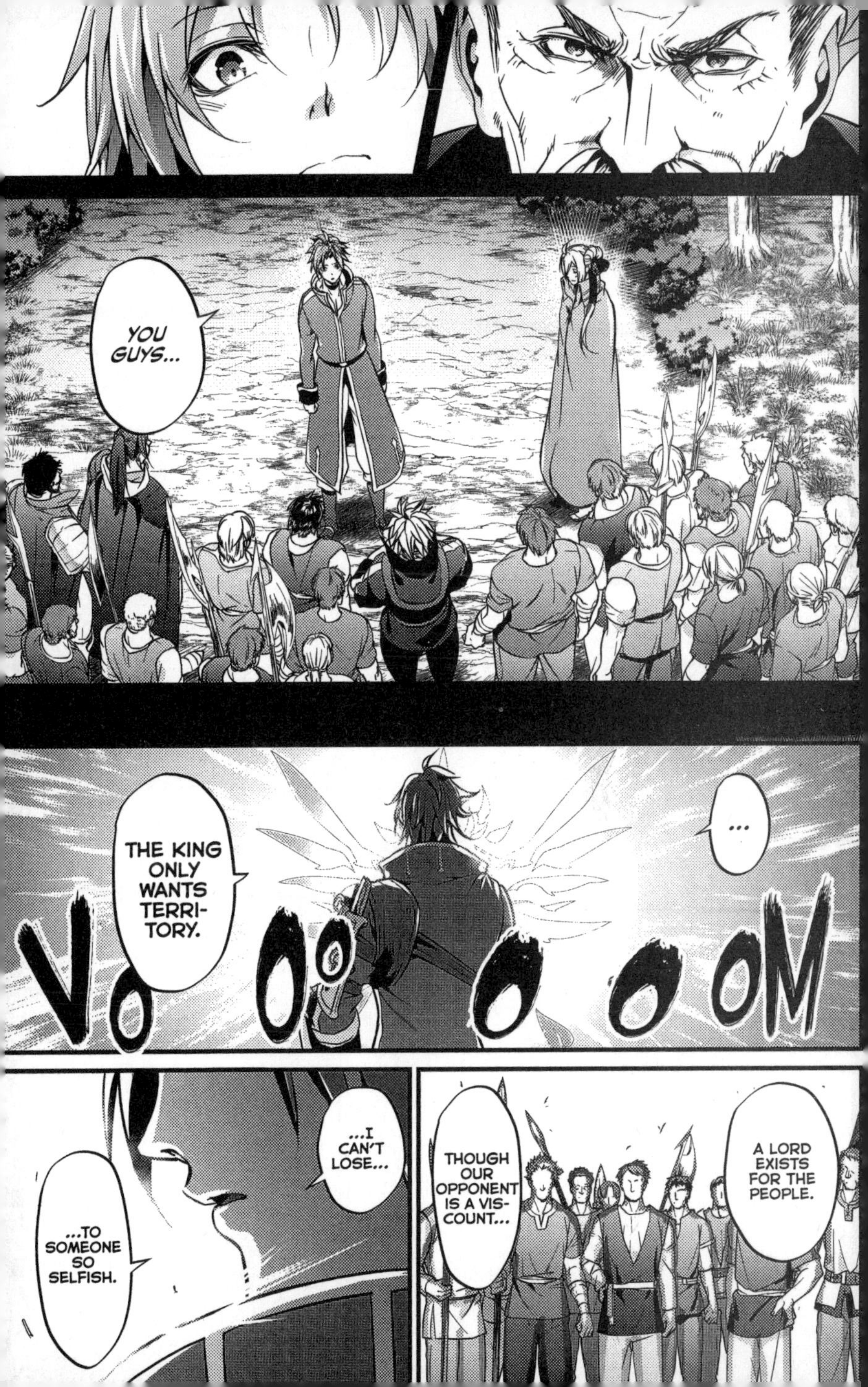
YOU GUYS...
...
THE KING ONLY WANTS TERRI-TORY.
VOOOOOOM
A LORD EXISTS FOR THE PEOPLE.
THOUGH OUR OPPONENT IS A VIS-COUNT...
...I CAN'T LOSE...
...TO SOMEONE SO SELFISH.

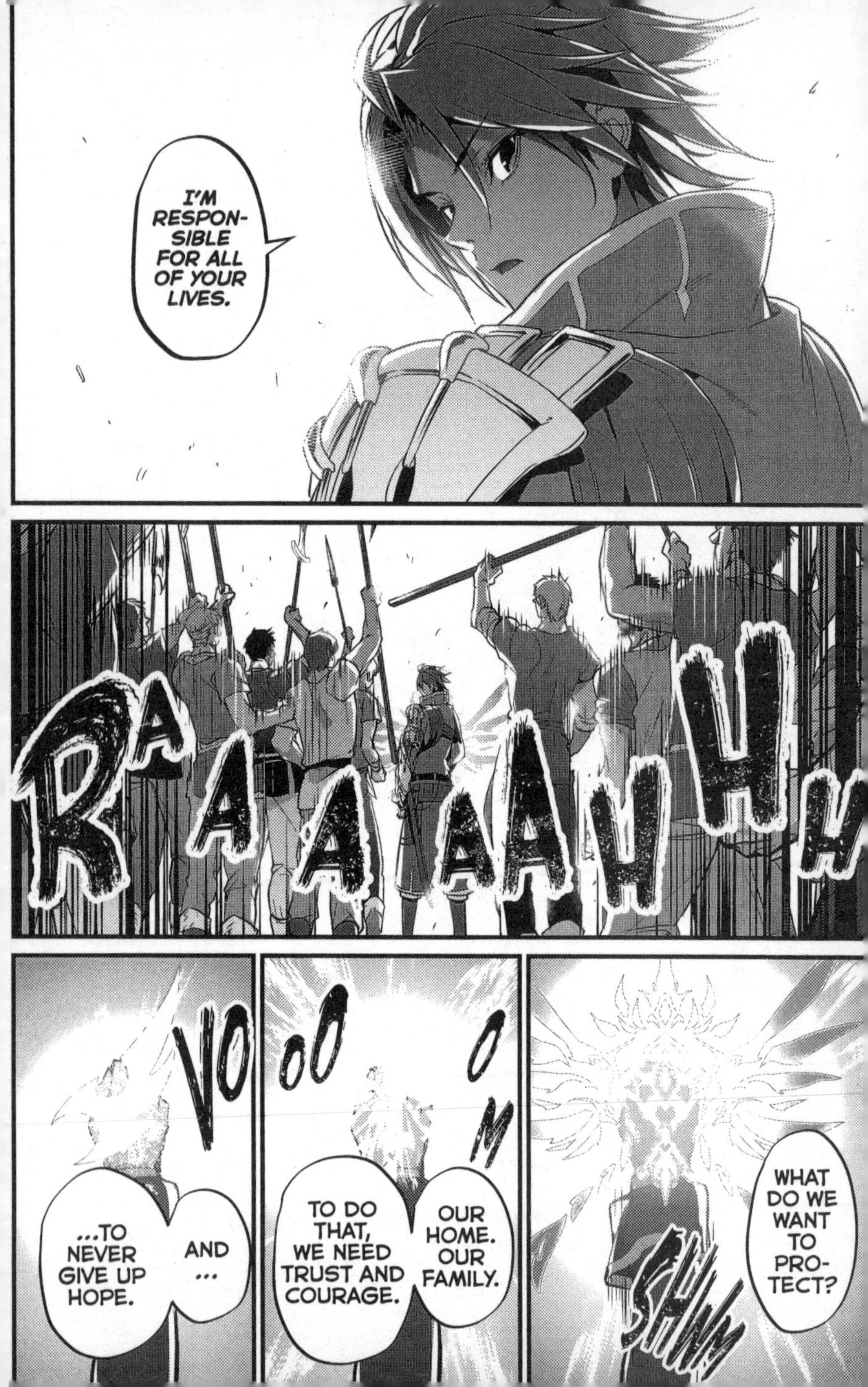
I'M RESPONSIBLE FOR ALL OF YOUR LIVES.
RAAAAHHH
WHAT DO WE WANT TO PROTECT?
SHWM
VOOOOM
OUR HOME. OUR FAMILY.
TO DO THAT, WE NEED TRUST AND COURAGE.
AND...
...TO NEVER GIVE UP HOPE.

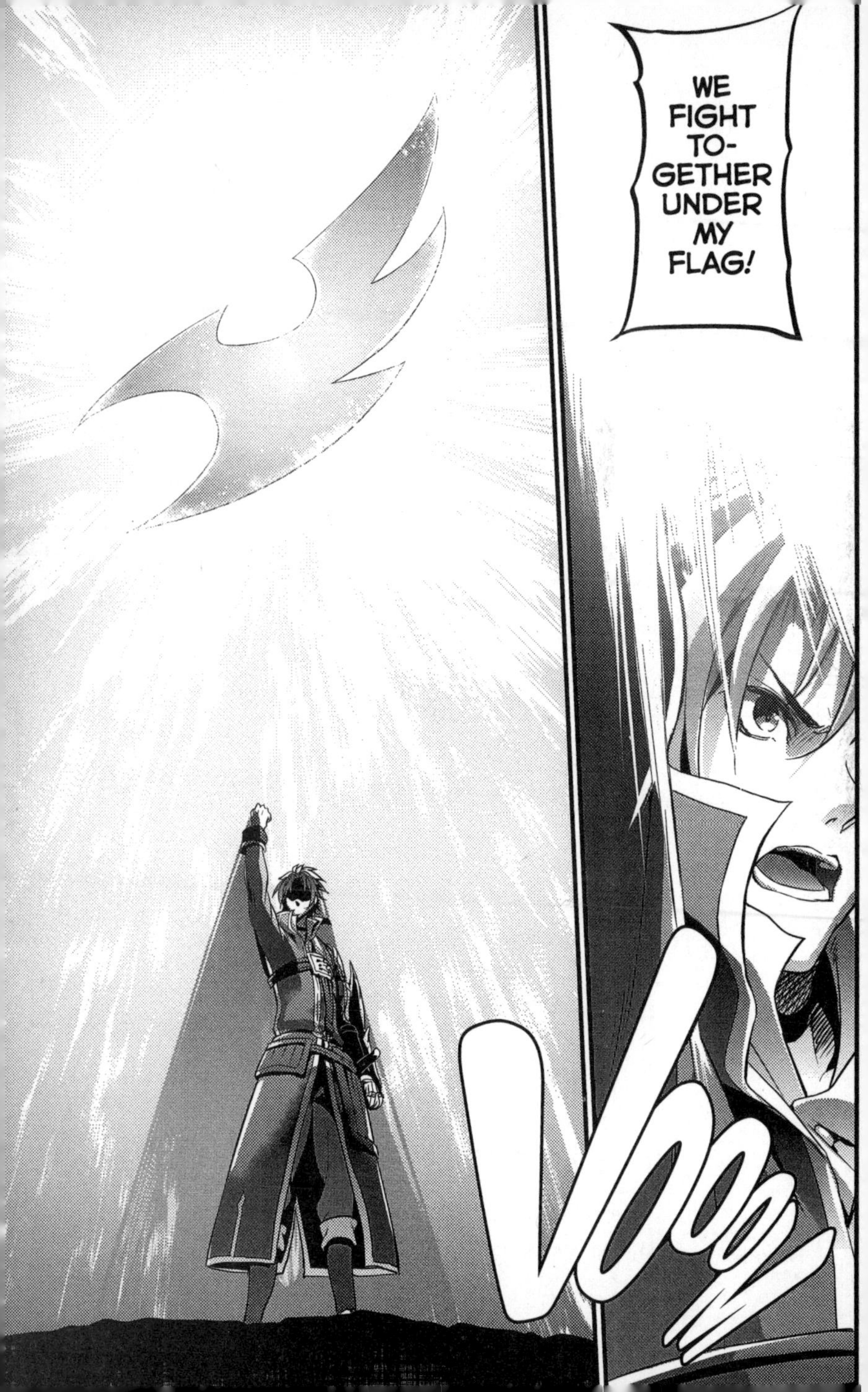
WE FIGHT TO-GETHER UNDER MY FLAG!

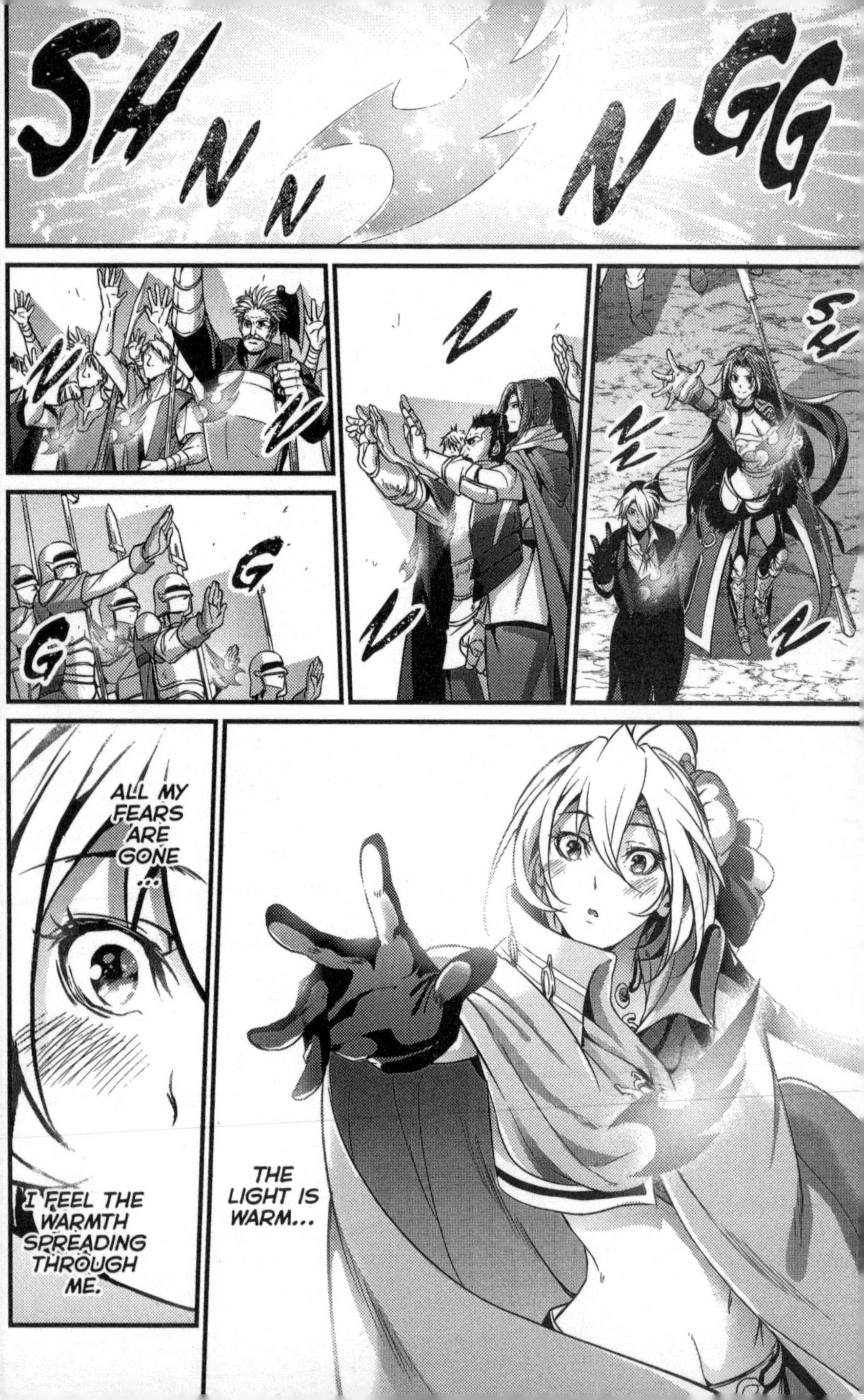
SHNNNNGG
SH
N
N
N
N
N
N
G
G
THE LIGHT IS WARM...
ALL MY FEARS ARE GONE...
I FEEL THE WARMTH SPREADING THROUGH ME.

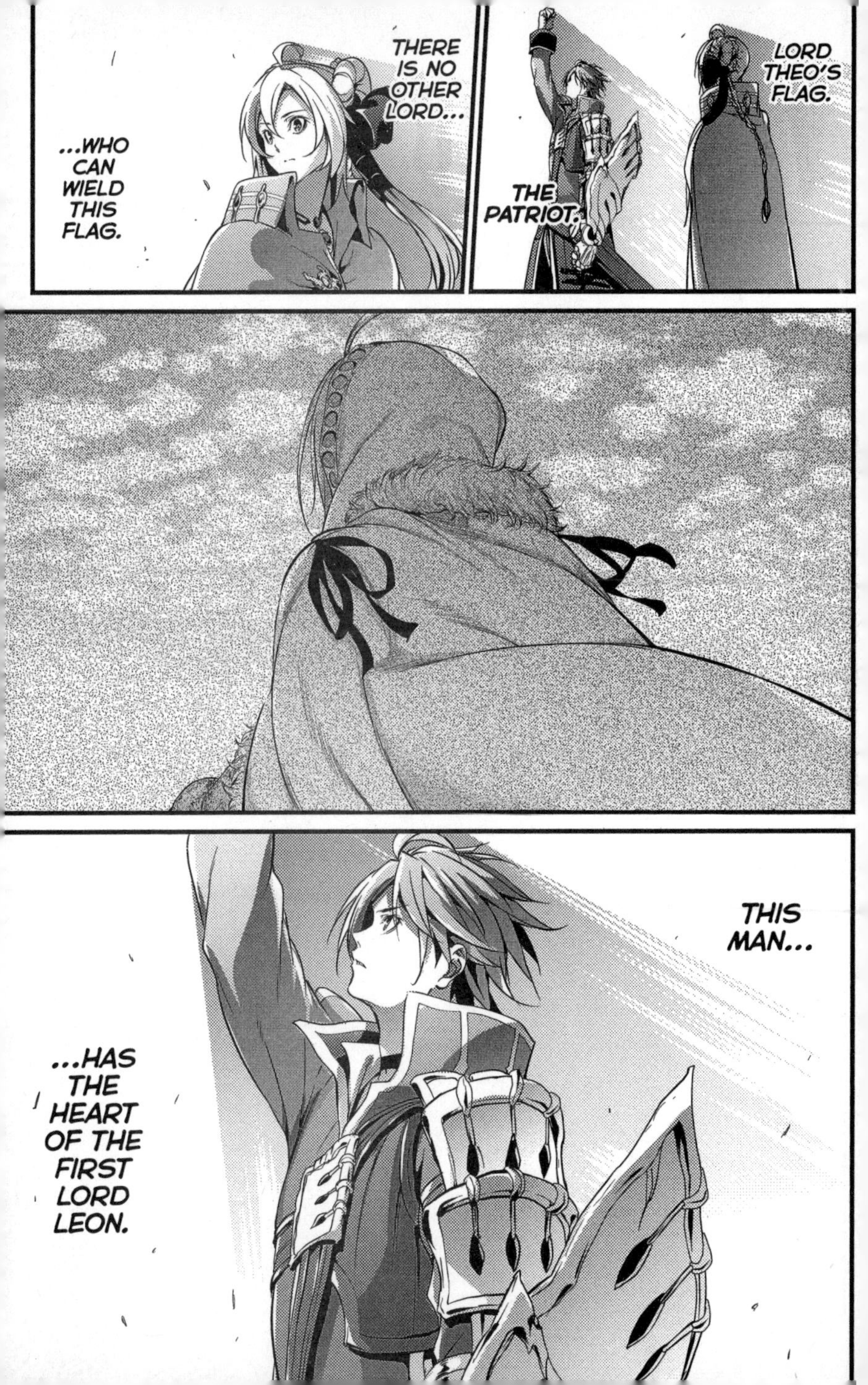
LORD THEO'S FLAG.
THE PATRIOT.
THERE IS NO OTHER LORD...
...WHO CAN WIELD THIS FLAG.
THIS MAN...
...HAS THE HEART OF THE FIRST LORD LEON.

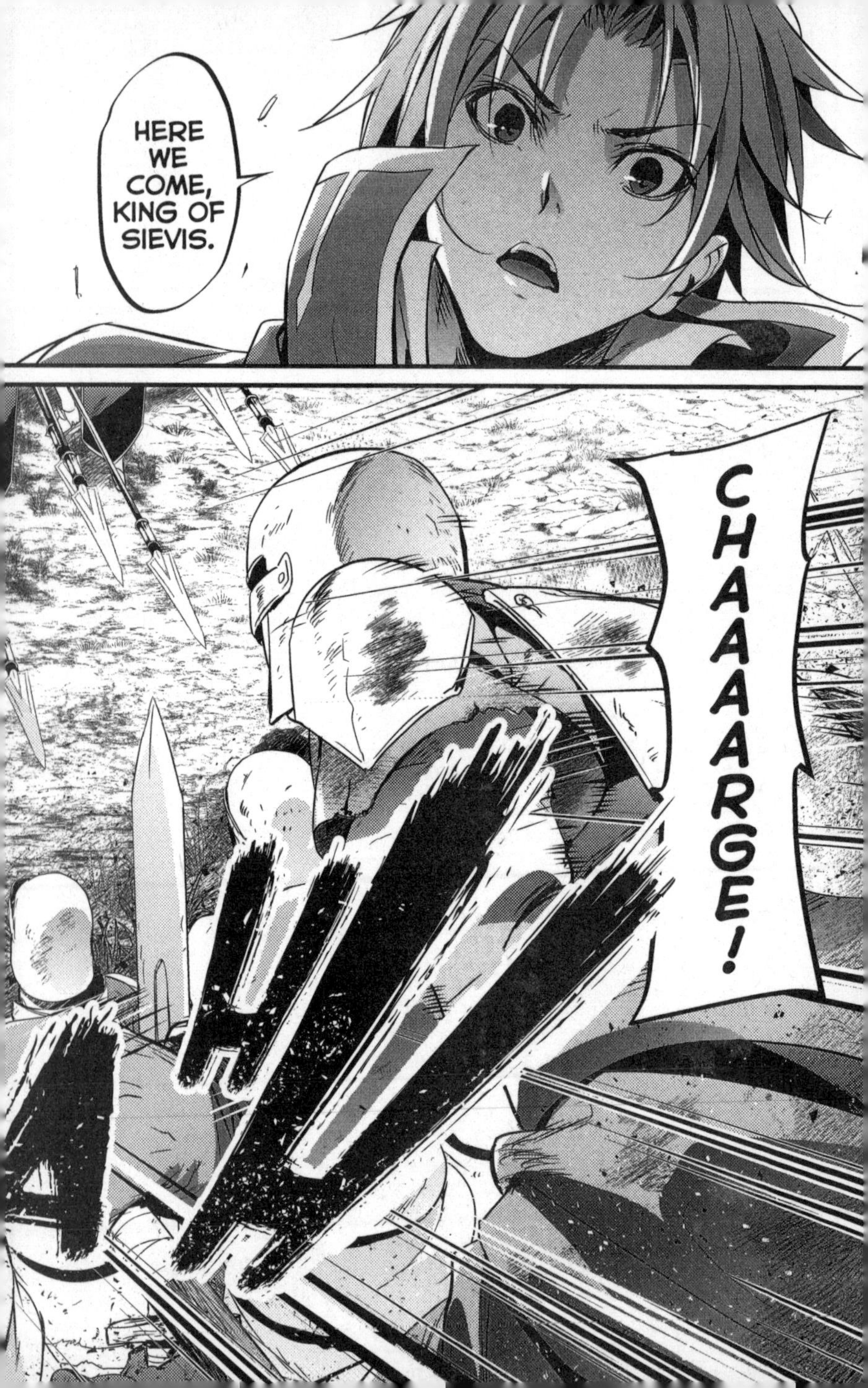
HERE WE COME, KING OF SIEVIS.
CHAAAARGE!

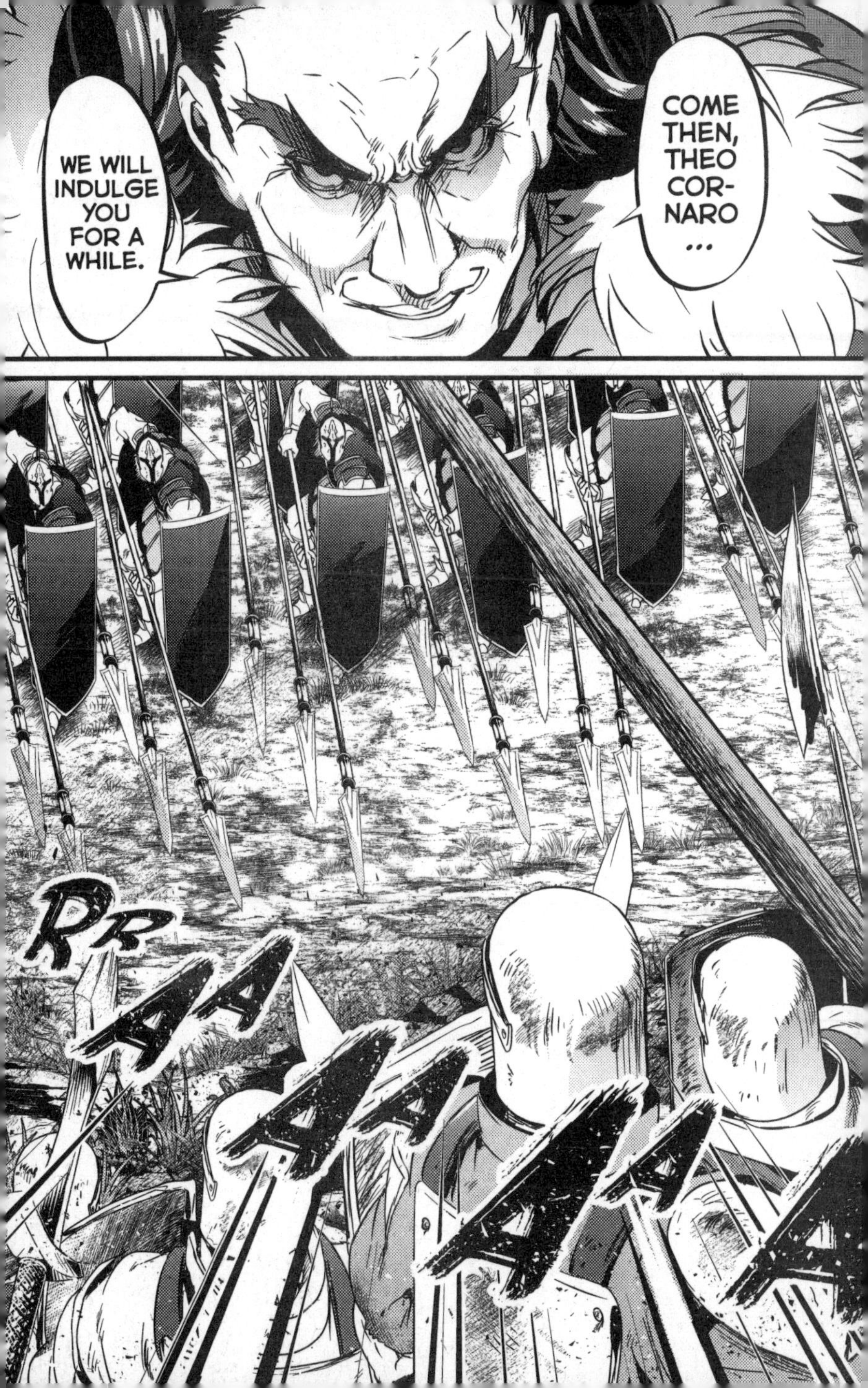
COME THEN, THEO COR-NARO ...
WE WILL INDULGE YOU FOR A WHILE.
RRAAAAAAA

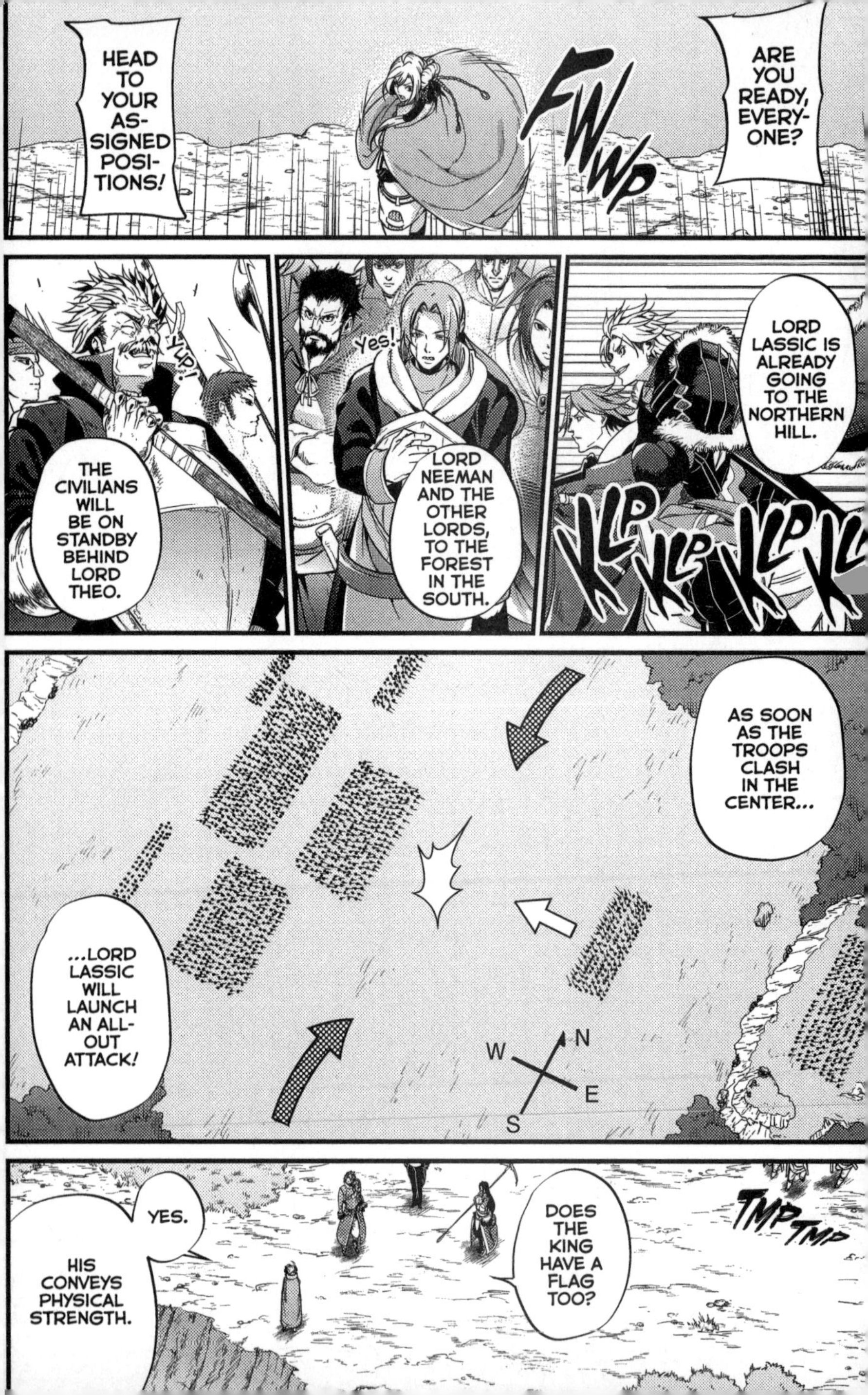
ARE YOU READY, EVERYONE?
FWWP
HEAD TO YOUR AS-SIGNED POSITIONS!
LORD LASSIC IS ALREADY GOING TO THE NORTHERN HILL.
KLP KLP KLP KL
Yes!
LORD NEEMAN AND THE OTHER LORDS, TO THE FOREST IN THE SOUTH.
YUP!
THE CIVILIANS WILL BE ON STANDBY BEHIND LORD THEO.
AS SOON AS THE TROOPS CLASH IN THE CENTER...
...LORD LASSIC WILL LAUNCH AN ALL-OUT ATTACK!
N
W
E
S
TMP TMP
DOES THE KING HAVE A FLAG TOO?
YES.
HIS CONVEYS PHYSICAL STRENGTH.

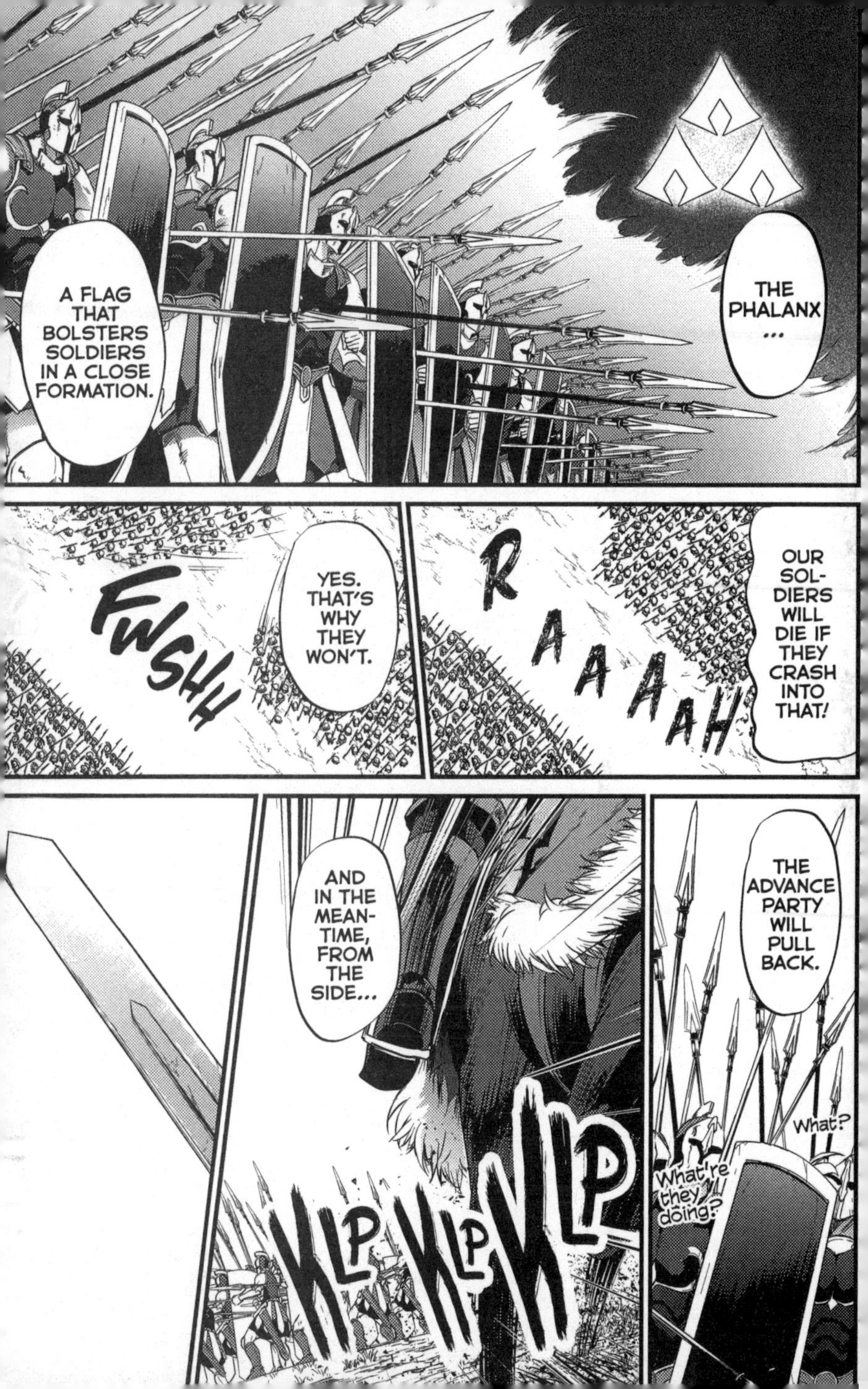
THE PHALANX...
A FLAG THAT BOLSTERS SOLDIERS IN A CLOSE FORMATION.
OUR SOLDIERS WILL DIE IF THEY CRASH INTO THAT!
RAAAAH
YES. THAT'S WHY THEY WON'T.
FWSHH
THE ADVANCE PARTY WILL PULL BACK.
What?
What're they doing?
AND IN THE MEANTIME, FROM THE SIDE...
KLP KLP KLP

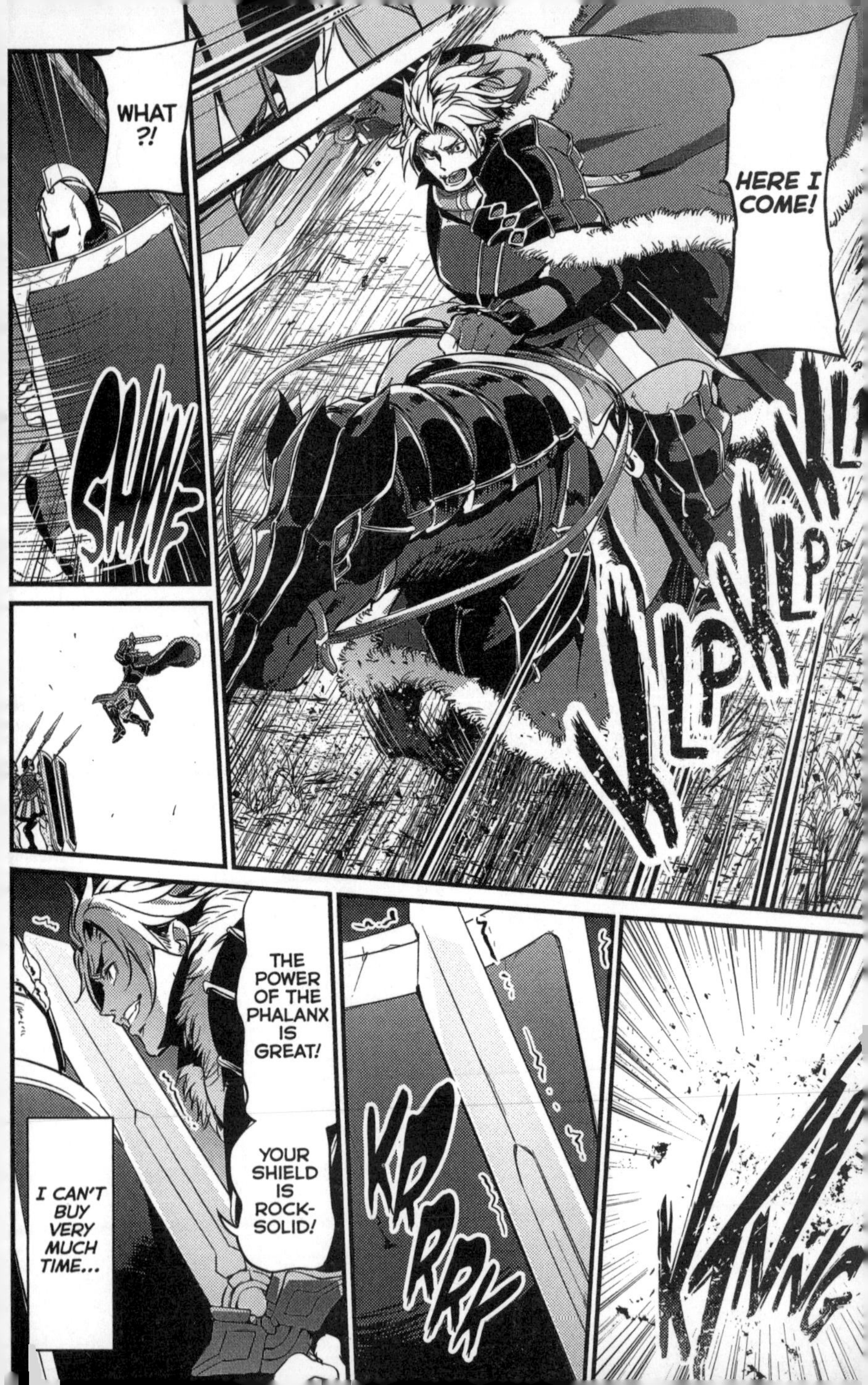
HERE I COME!
WHAT ?!
THE POWER OF THE PHALANX IS GREAT!
YOUR SHIELD IS ROCK-SOLID!
I CAN'T BUY VERY MUCH TIME...

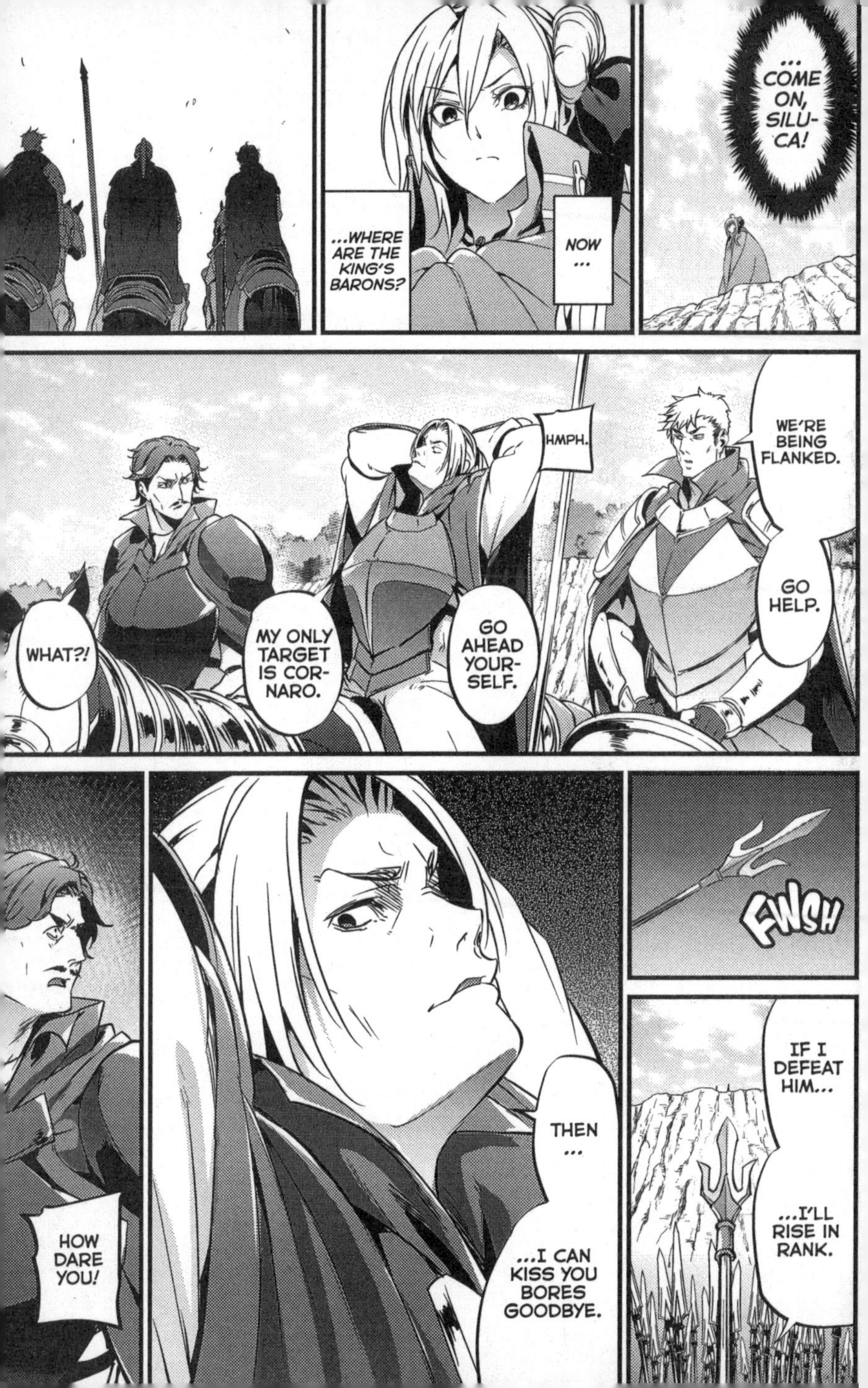
...COME ON, SILU-CA!
NOW...
...WHERE ARE THE KING'S BARONS?
WE'RE BEING FLANKED.
GO HELP.
HMPH.
GO AHEAD YOUR-SELF.
MY ONLY TARGET IS COR-NARO.
WHAT?!
FWSH
IF I DEFEAT HIM...
...I'LL RISE IN RANK.
THEN...
...I CAN KISS YOU BORES GOODBYE.
HOW DARE YOU!

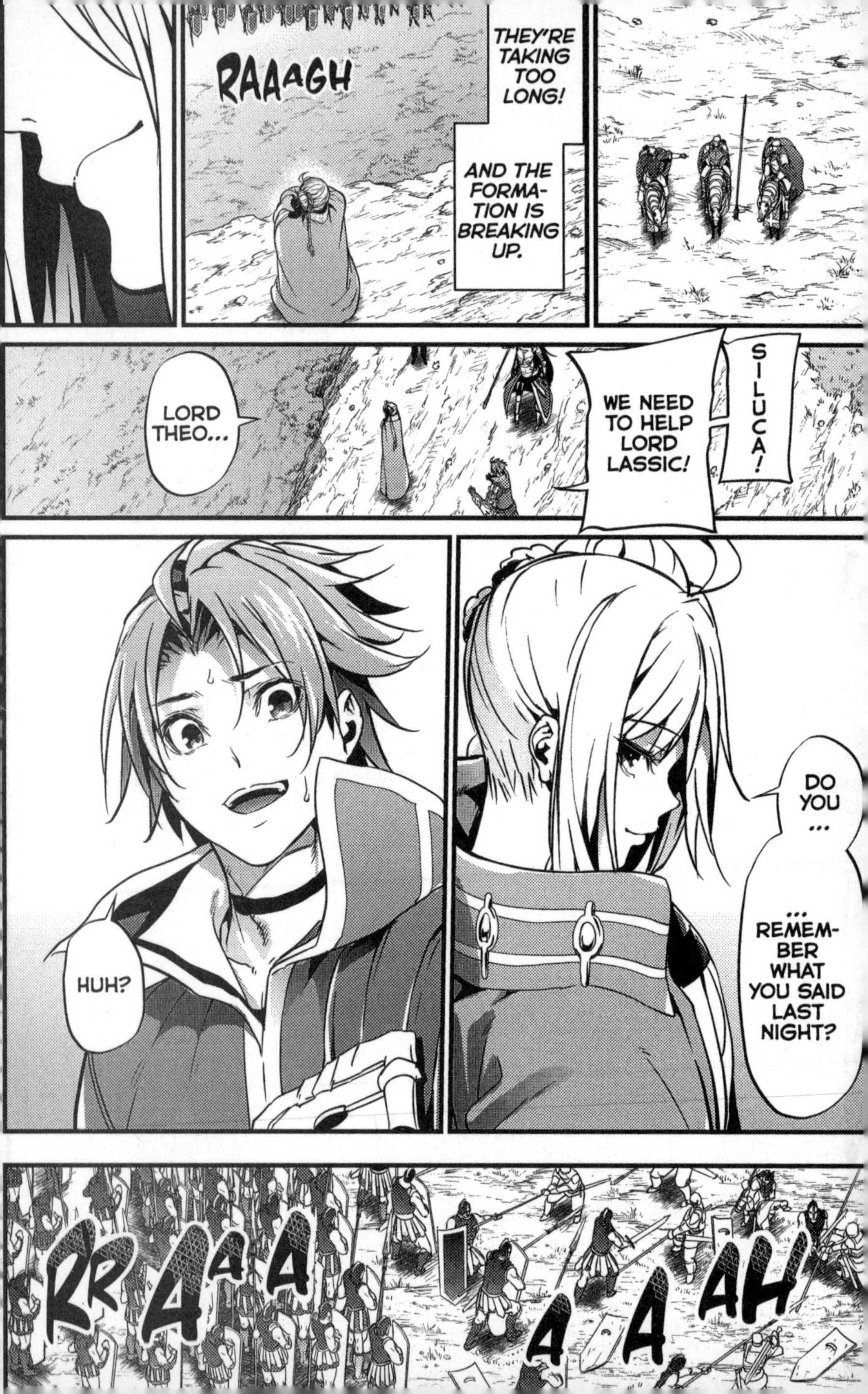
THEY'RE TAKING TOO LONG!
RAAAGH
AND THE FORMATION IS BREAKING UP.
SILUCA!
WE NEED TO HELP LORD LASSIC!
LORD THEO...
DO YOU...
...REMEMBER WHAT YOU SAID LAST NIGHT?
HUH?
KRAAAAAAH

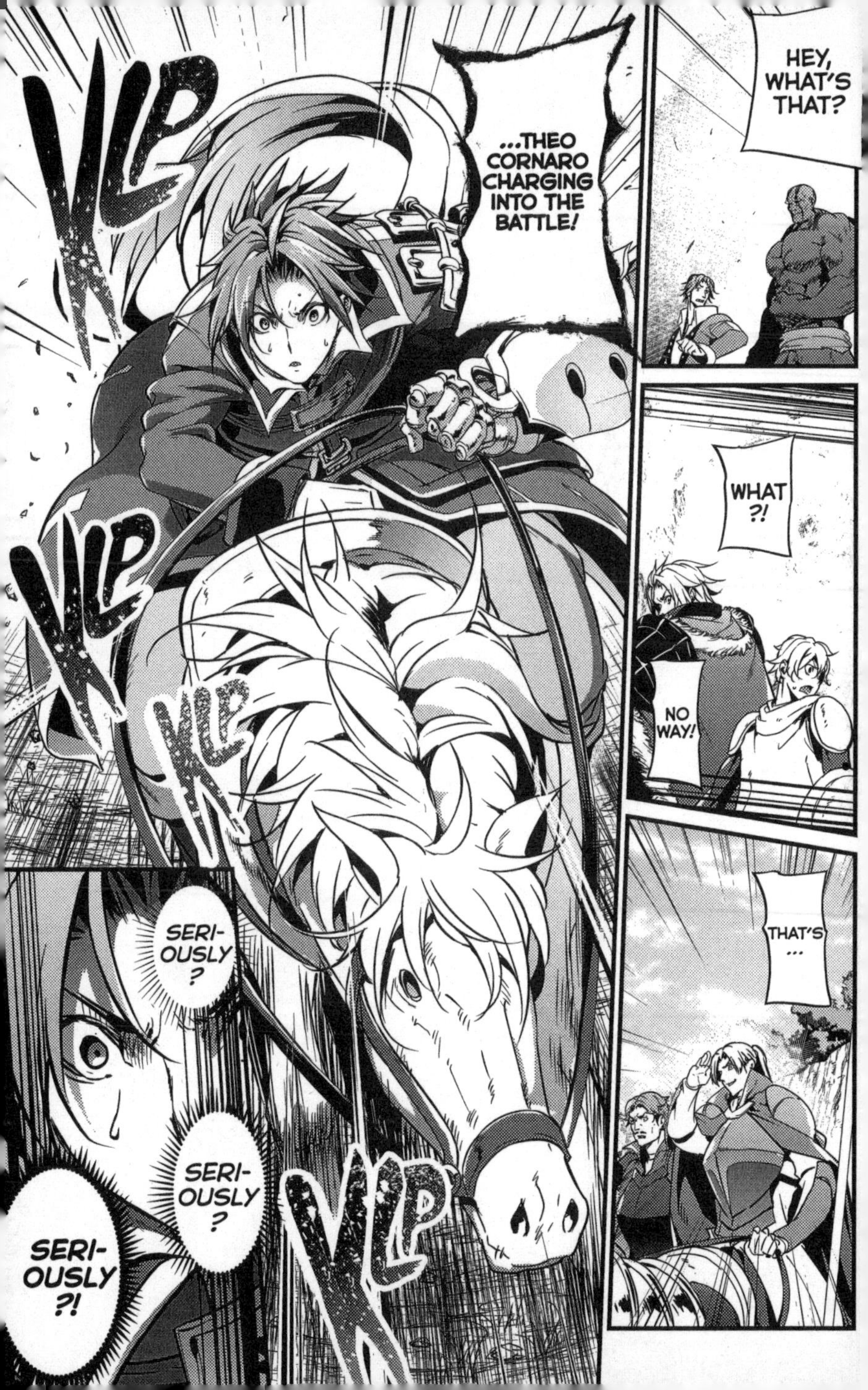
HEY, WHAT'S THAT?
WHAT ?!
NO WAY!
THAT'S ...
...THEO CORNARO CHARGING INTO THE BATTLE!
SERI-OUSLY ?
SERI-OUSLY ?
SERI-OUSLY ?!

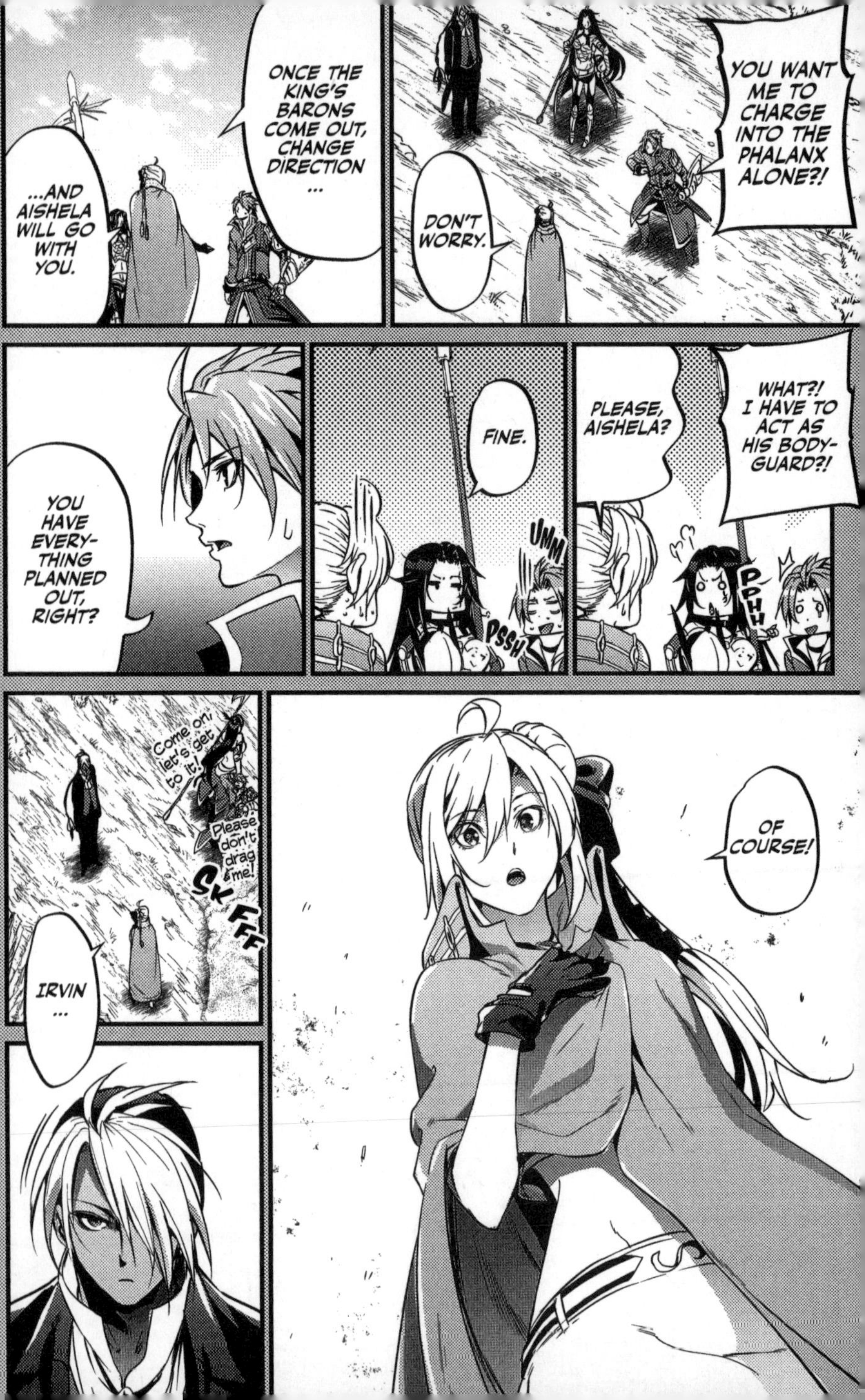
YOU WANT ME TO CHARGE INTO THE PHALANX ALONE?!
DON'T WORRY.
ONCE THE KING'S BARONS COME OUT, CHANGE DIRECTION ...
...AND AISHELA WILL GO WITH YOU.
WHAT?! I HAVE TO ACT AS HIS BODY-GUARD?!
PLEASE, AISHELA?
PPHH
FINE.
UMM
PSSH
YOU HAVE EVERY-THING PLANNED OUT, RIGHT?
OF COURSE!
Come on, let's get to it!
Please don't drag me!
SKFFF
IRVIN ...

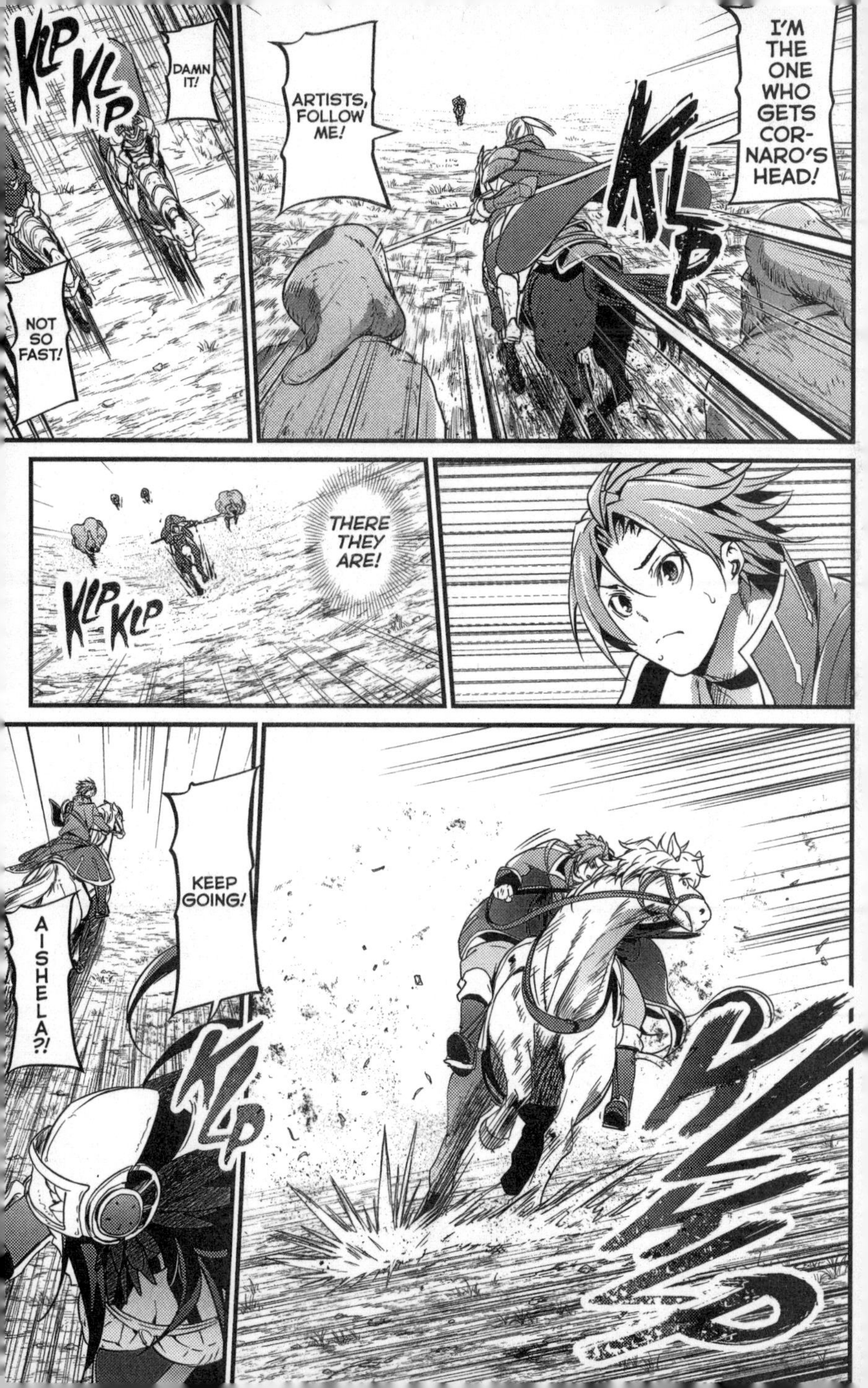
I'M THE ONE WHO GETS COR-NARO'S HEAD!
KLAP
ARTISTS, FOLLOW ME!
DAMN IT!
KLP KLP
NOT SO FAST!
THERE THEY ARE!
KLP KLP
KEEP GOING!
AISHELA?!
KLAP

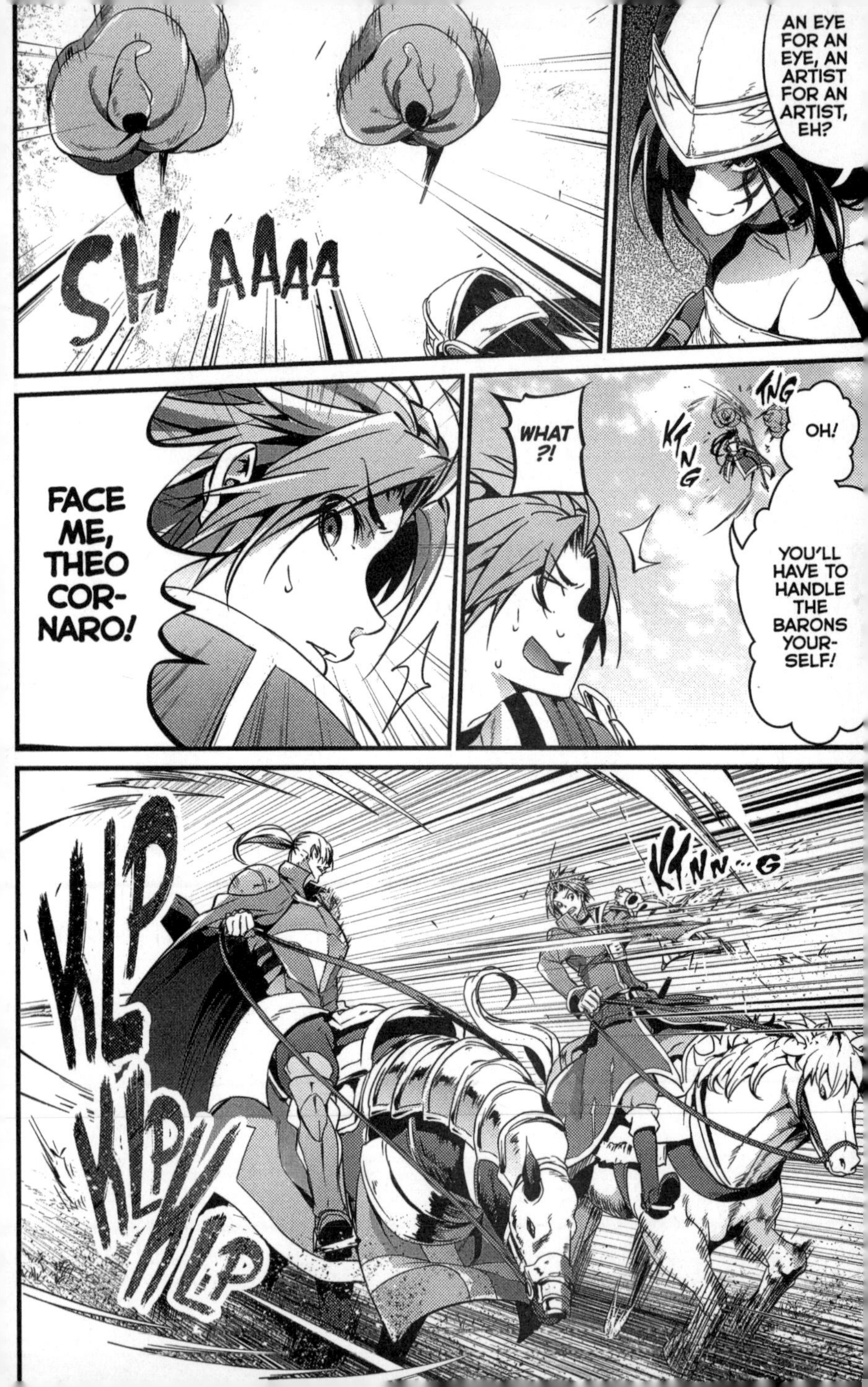
AN EYE FOR AN EYE, AN ARTIST FOR AN ARTIST, EH?
SH AAAA
TNG
KING
OH!
YOU'LL HAVE TO HANDLE THE BARONS YOURSELF!
WHAT ?!
FACE ME, THEO CORNARO!
KINN..G
KLP KLP KLP KLP

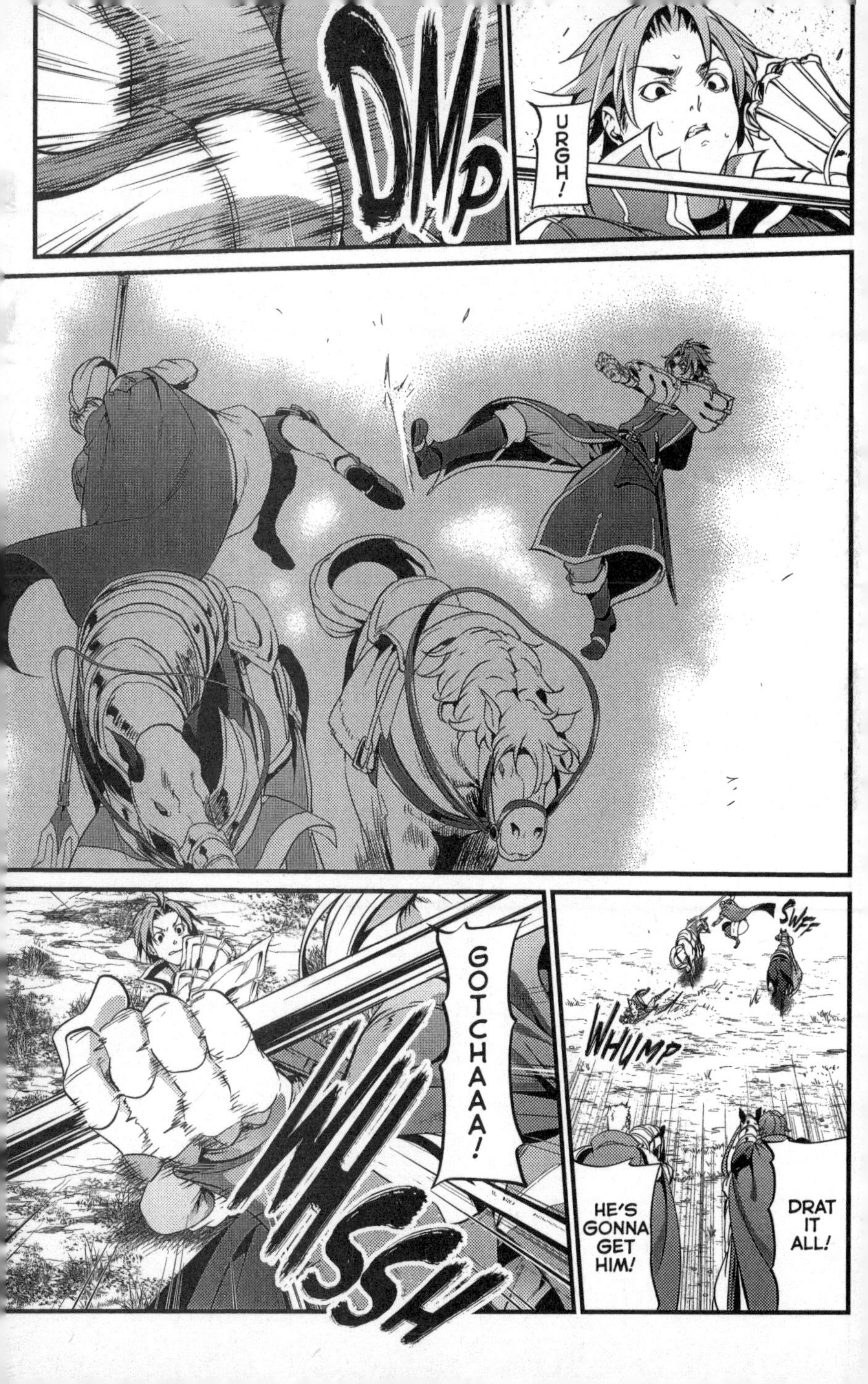
URGH!
DMP
SWFF
WHUMP
DRAT IT ALL!
HE'S GONNA GET HIM!
GOTCHAAA!
WHSH

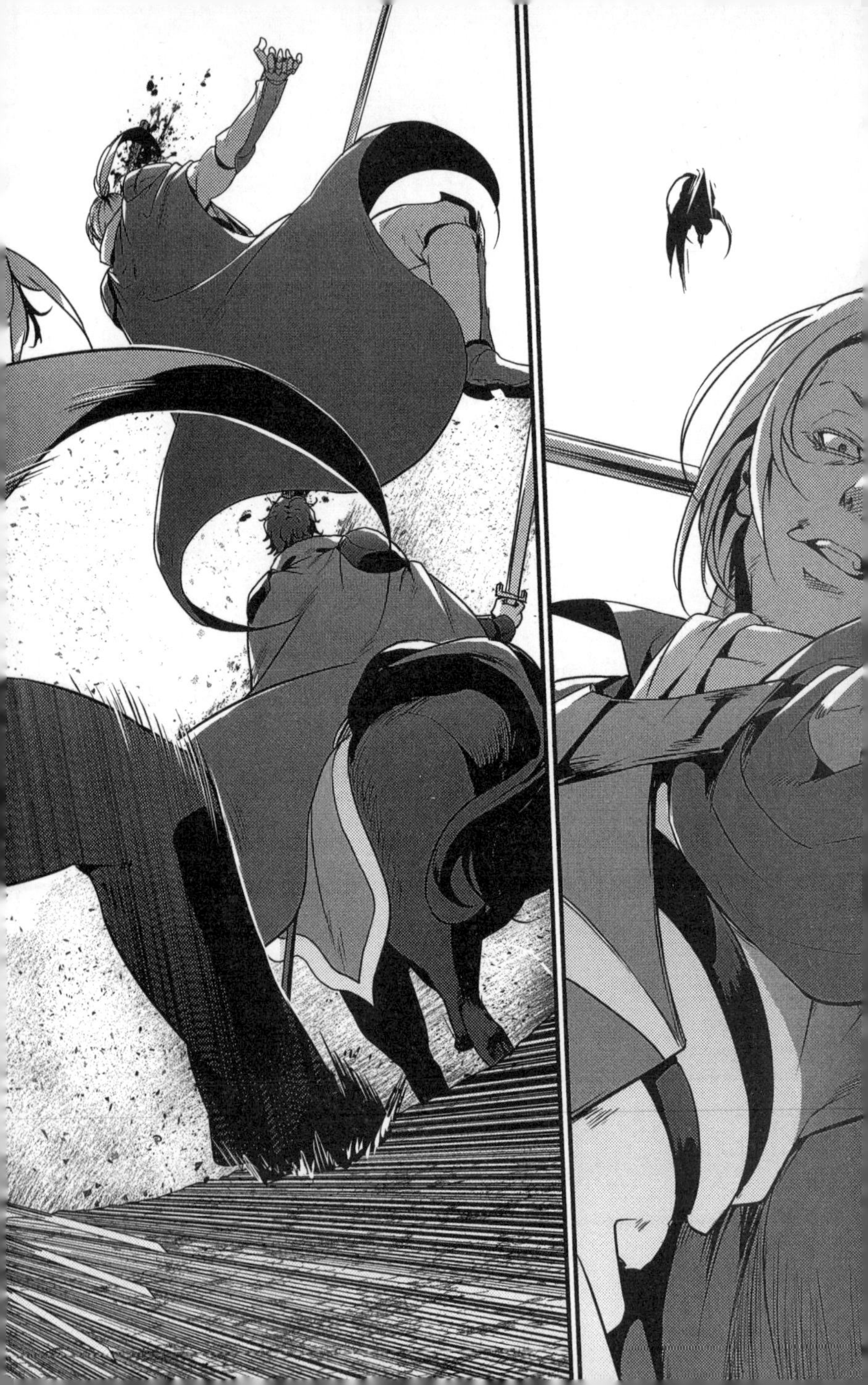

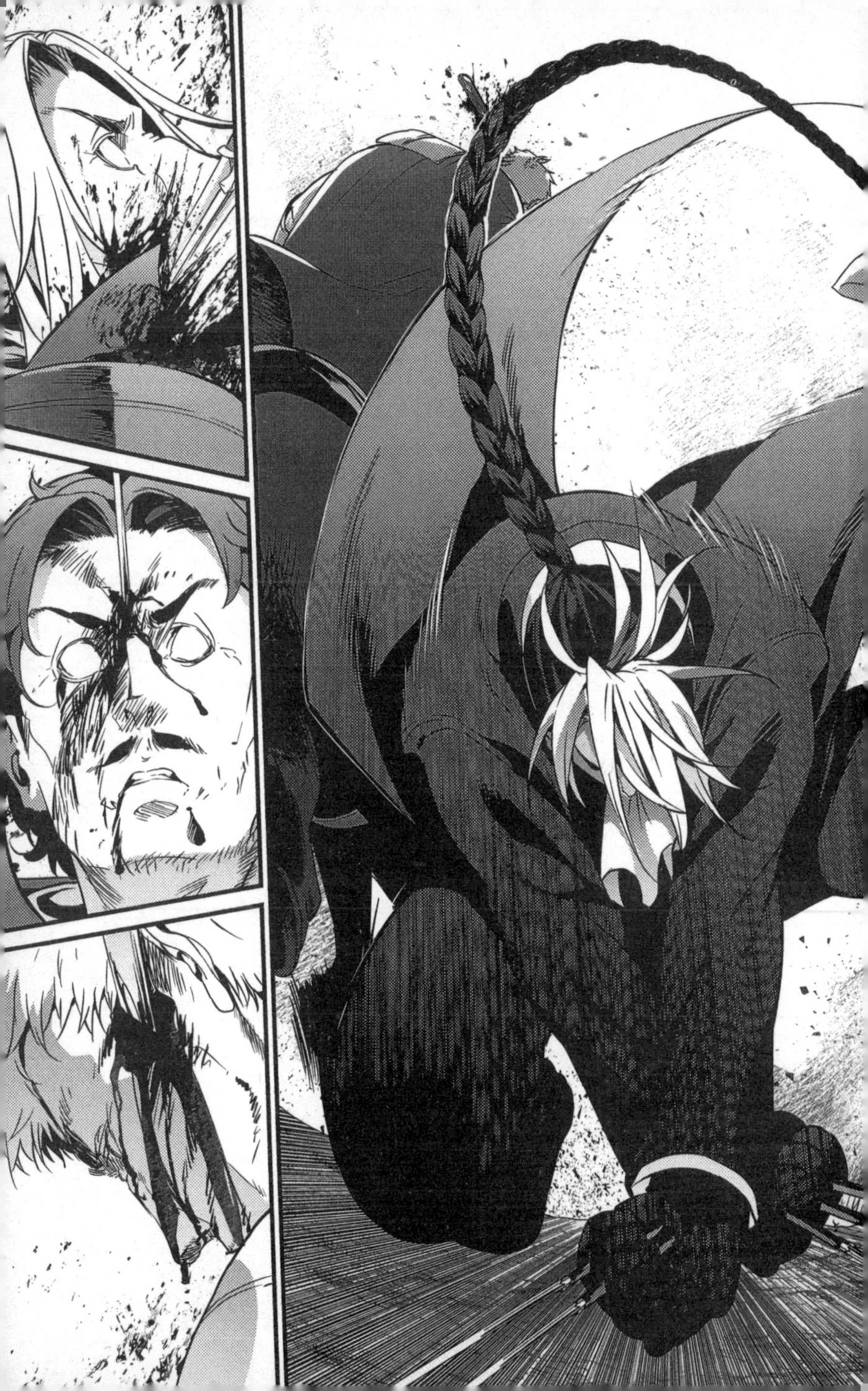

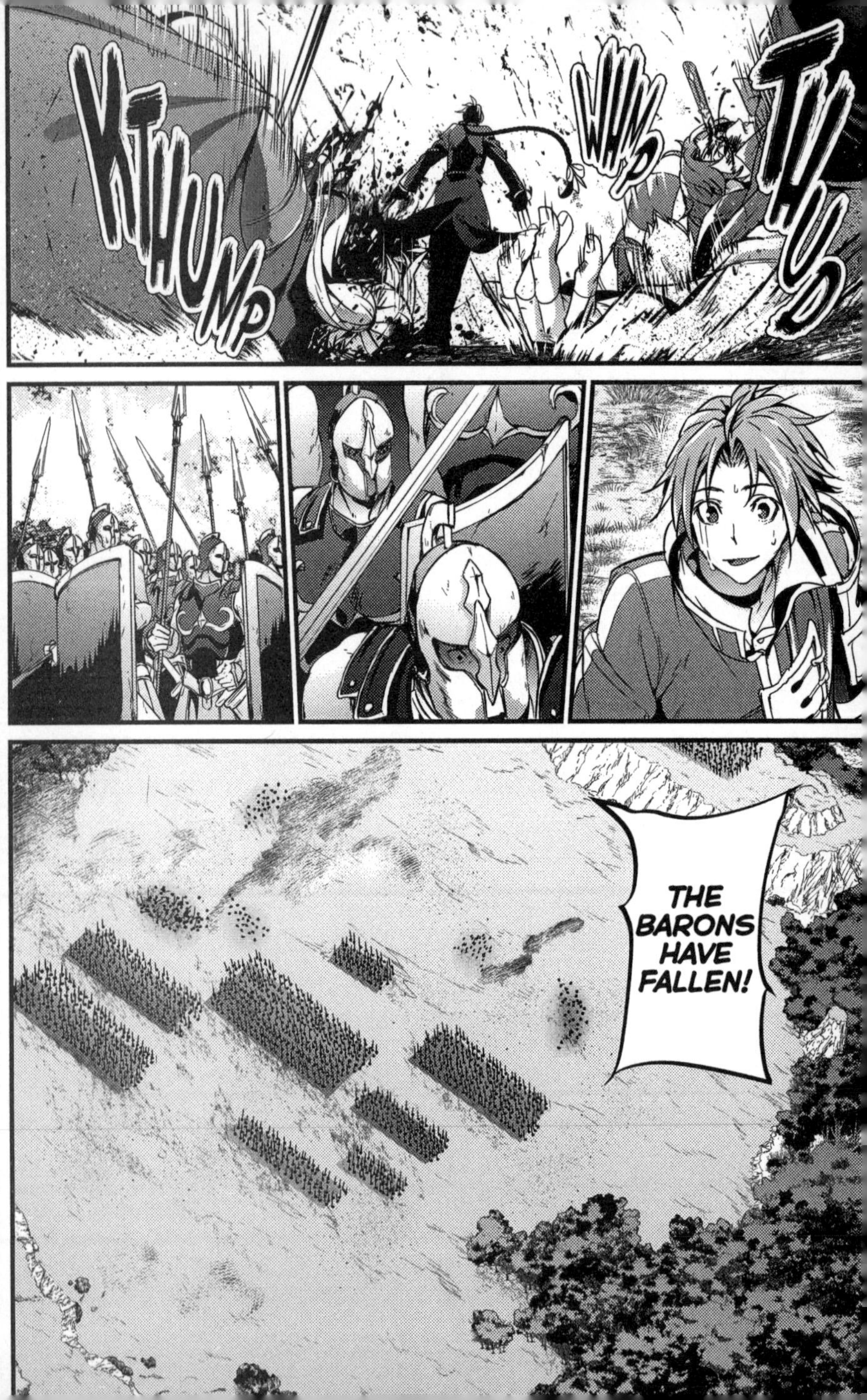
THUD
WHAP
KATHUMP
THE BARONS HAVE FALLEN!

RECORD OF
GRANCREST
WAR

RECORD OF
GRANCREST
WAR

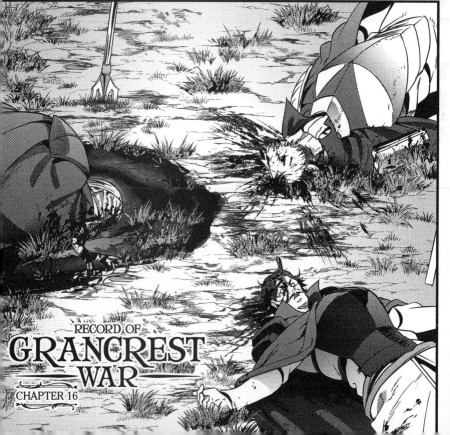

RECORD OF GRANCREST WAR

CHAPTER 16

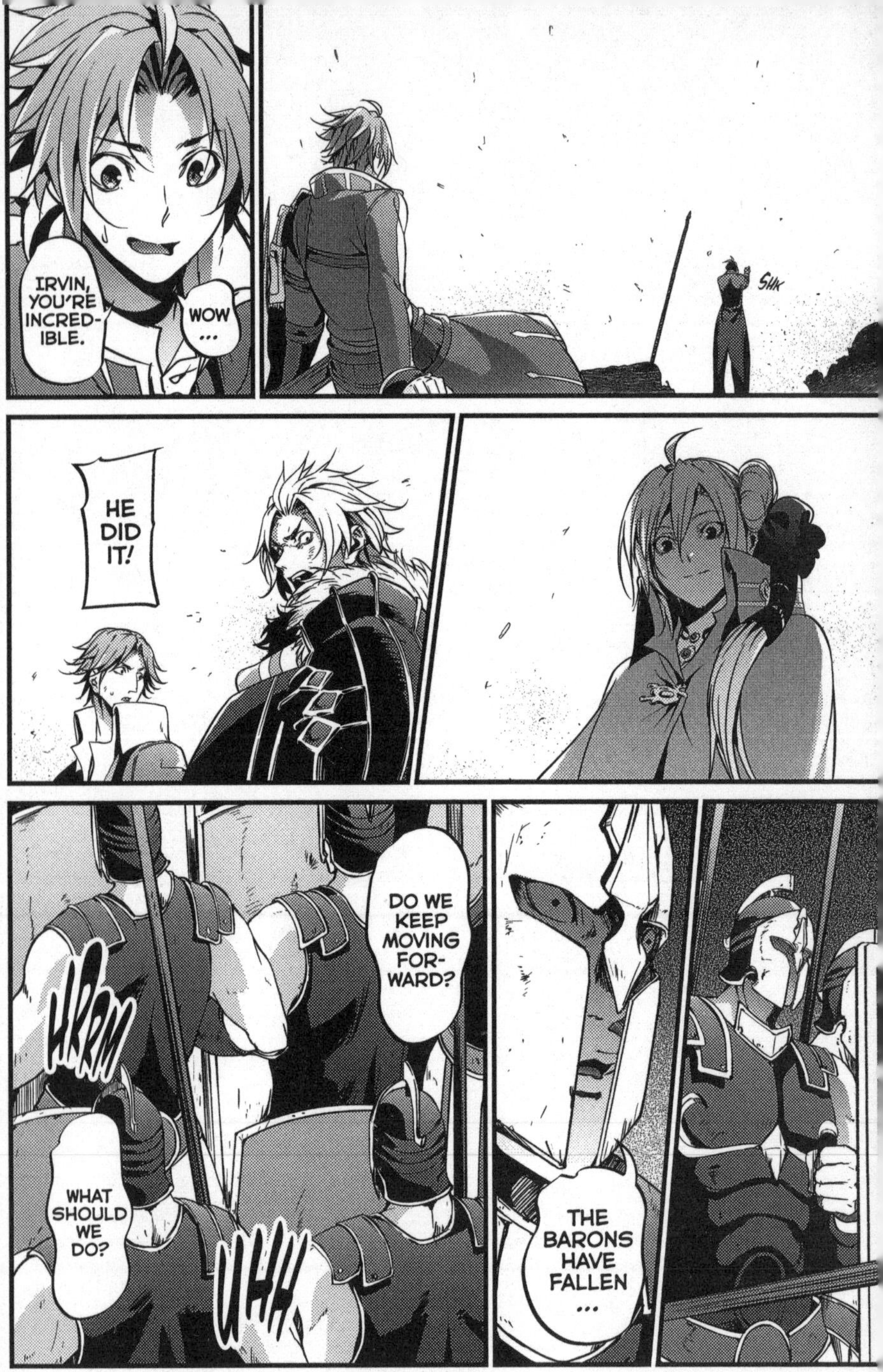
SHK
WOW...
IRVIN, YOU'RE INCREDIBLE.
HE DID IT!
THE BARONS HAVE FALLEN...
DO WE KEEP MOVING FORWARD?
HRRM
WHAT SHOULD WE DO?
UHH

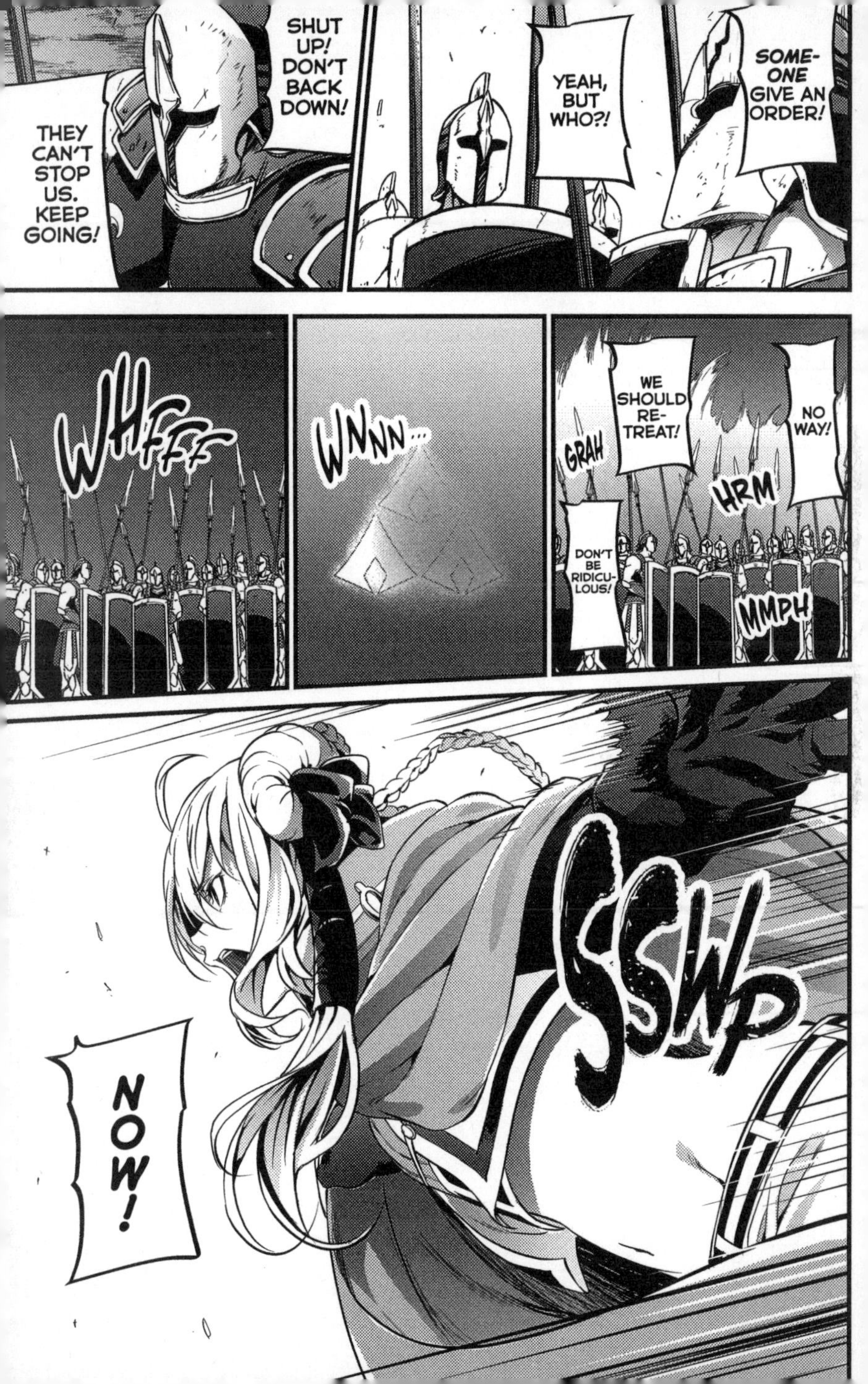
SOME-ONE GIVE AN ORDER!
YEAH, BUT WHO?!
SHUT UP! DON'T BACK DOWN!
THEY CAN'T STOP US. KEEP GOING!
NO WAY!
WE SHOULD RE-TREAT!
HRM
GRAH
DON'T BE RIDICU-LOUS!
MMPH
WNNN...
WHFFF
SSWP
NOW!

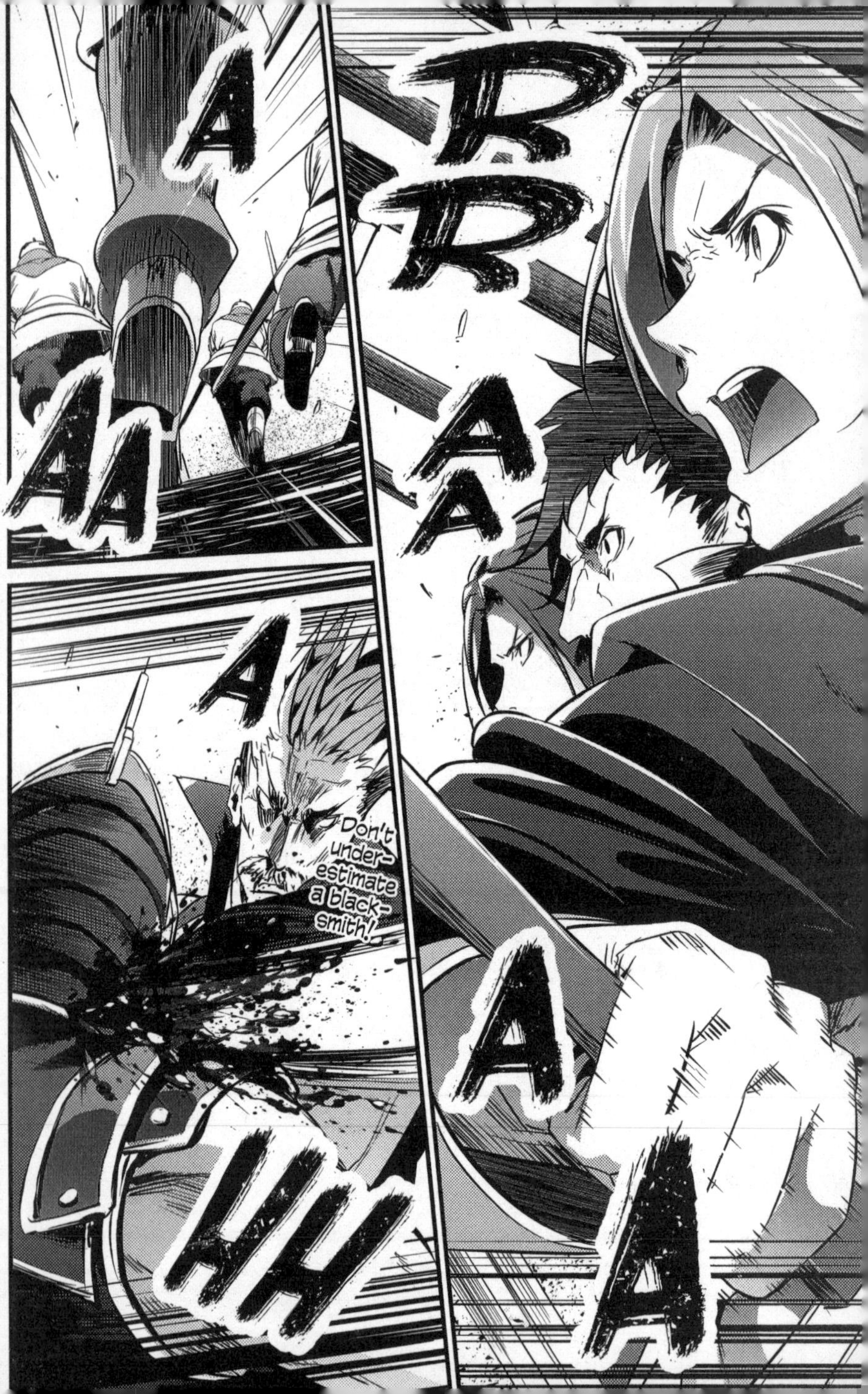

RR!AAAAA
AAA
A
Don't underestimate a blacksmith!
HH

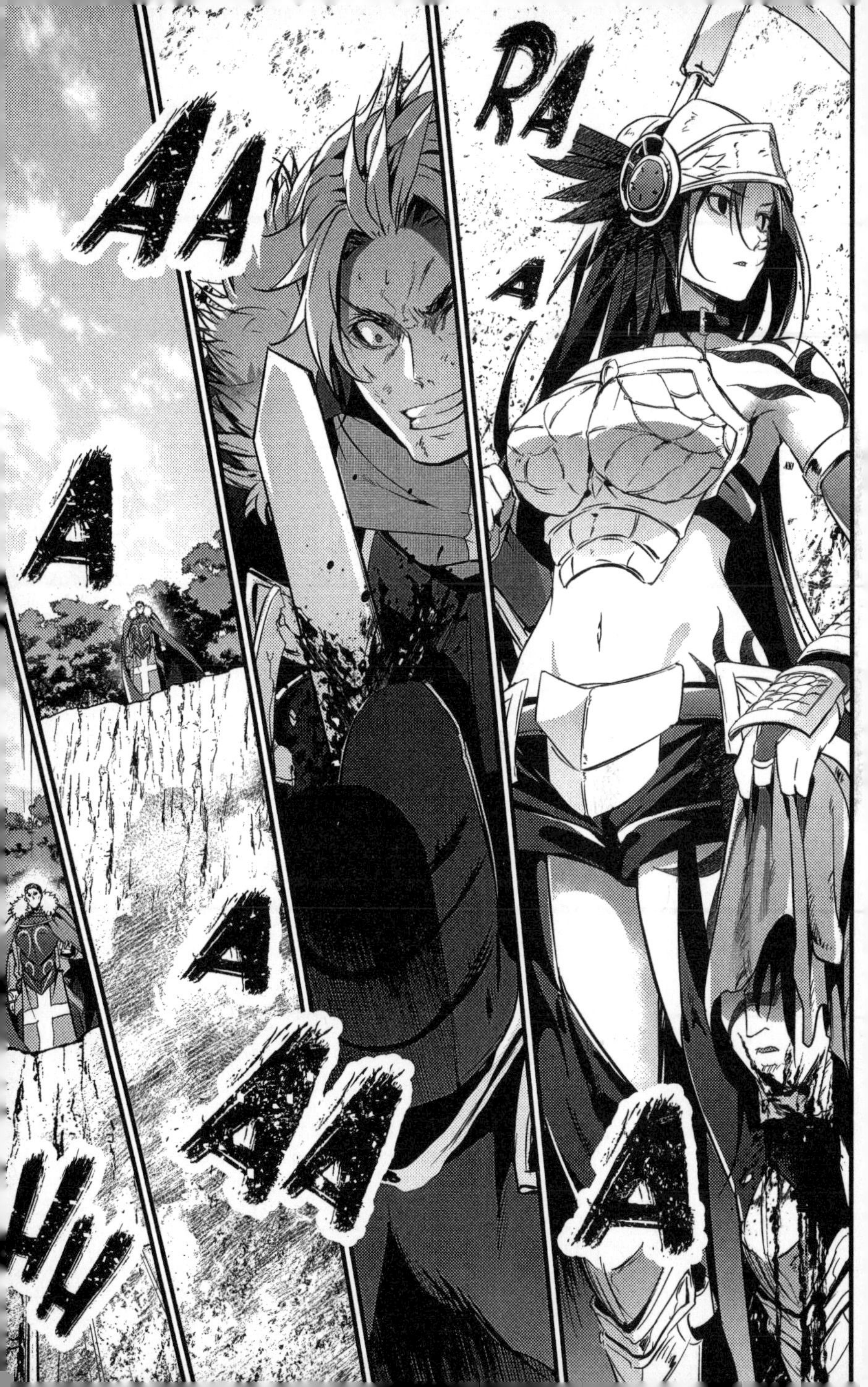
RA
A
A
A
AAA
AA
A
HH

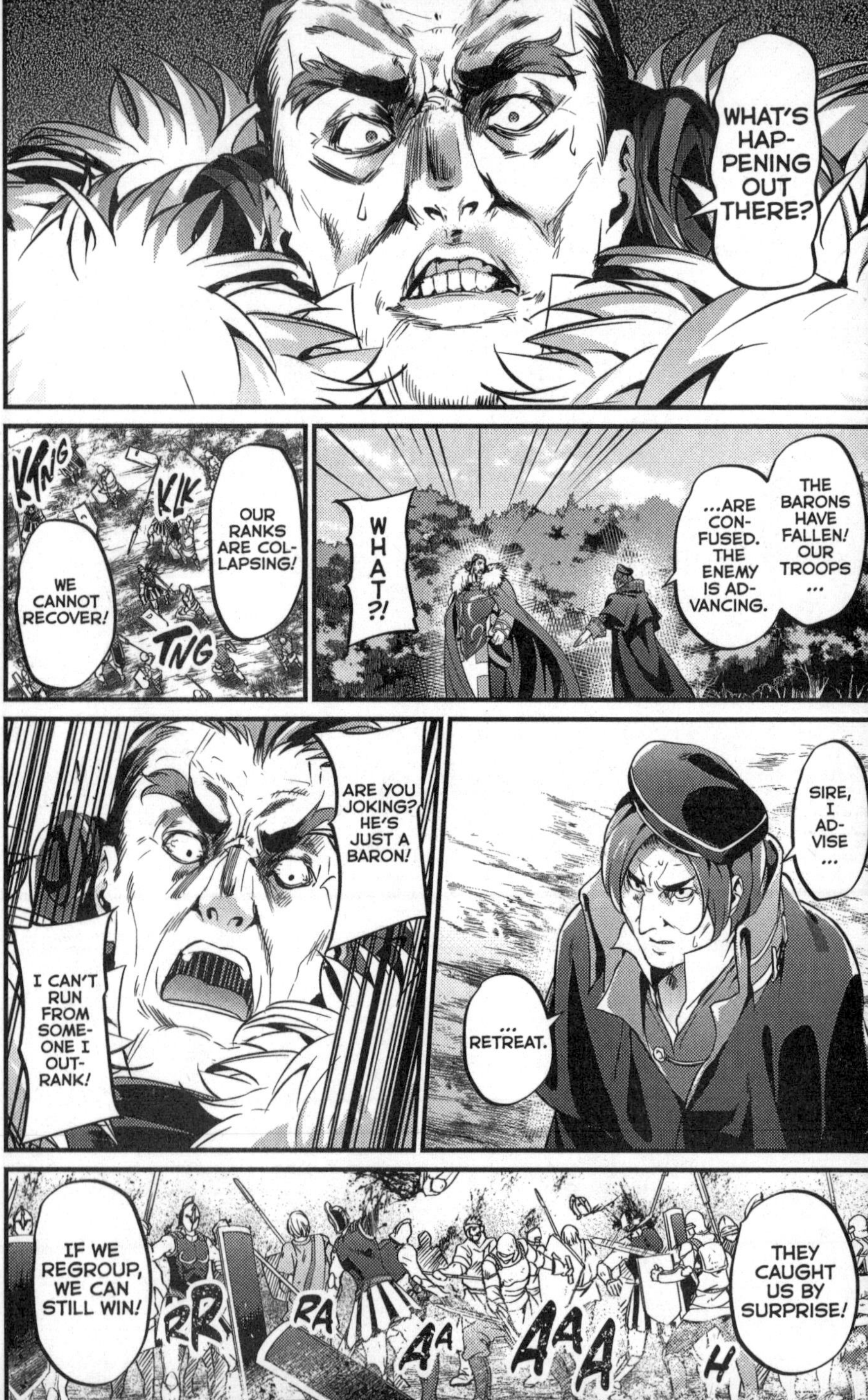
WHAT'S HAPPENING OUT THERE?
THE BARONS HAVE FALLEN! OUR TROOPS ...
...ARE CONFUSED. THE ENEMY IS ADVANCING.
WHAT?!
OUR RANKS ARE COLLAPSING!
KLK
KTNG
WE CANNOT RECOVER!
TNG
SIRE, I ADVISE ...
... RETREAT.
ARE YOU JOKING? HE'S JUST A BARON!
I CAN'T RUN FROM SOMEONE I OUTRANK!
THEY CAUGHT US BY SURPRISE!
IF WE REGROUP, WE CAN STILL WIN!
RR RA AA AAA H

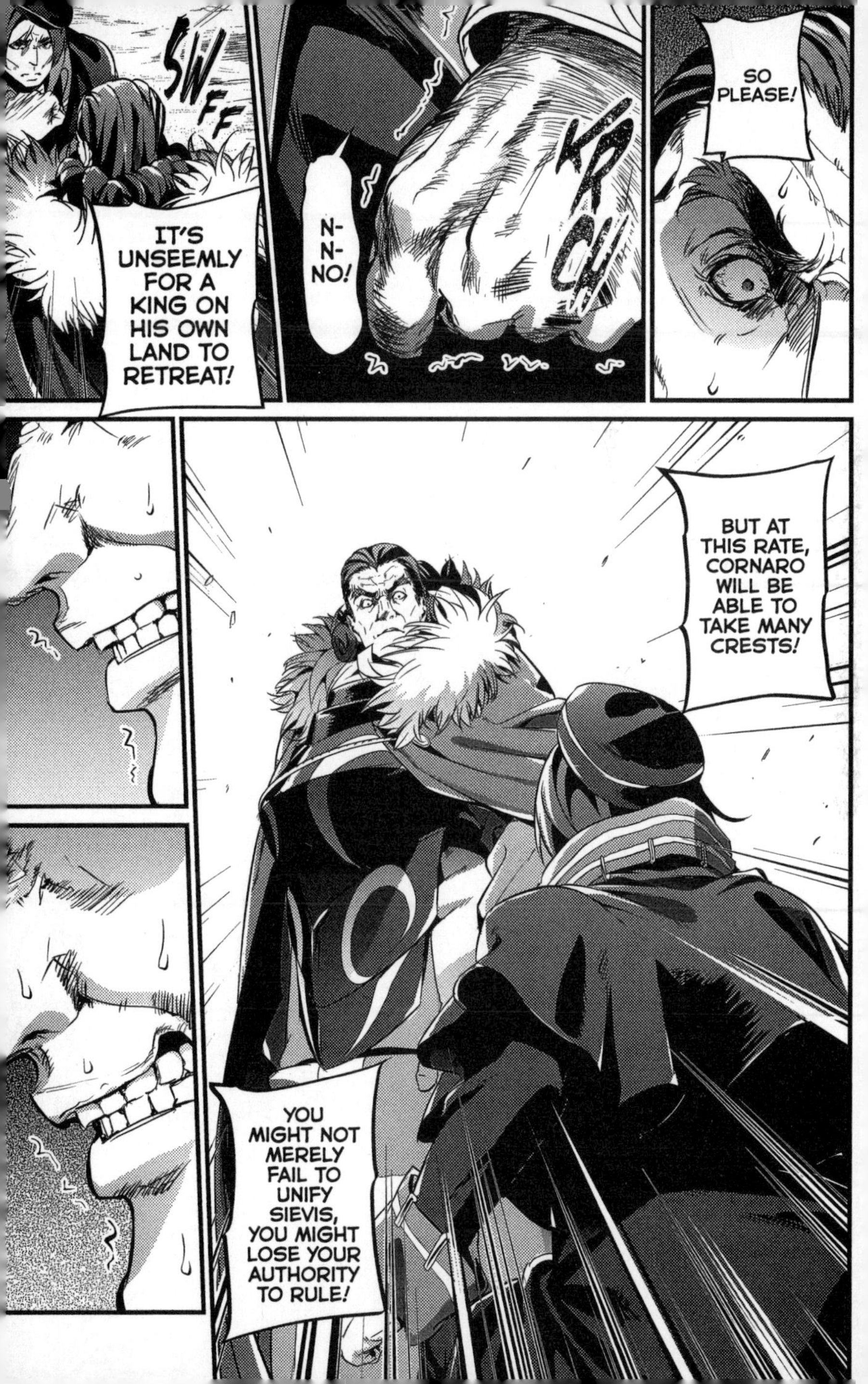
SO PLEASE!
KRCH
N-N-NO!
SWFF
IT'S UNSEEMLY FOR A KING ON HIS OWN LAND TO RETREAT!
BUT AT THIS RATE, CORNARO WILL BE ABLE TO TAKE MANY CRESTS!
YOU MIGHT NOT MERELY FAIL TO UNIFY SIEVIS, YOU MIGHT LOSE YOUR AUTHORITY TO RULE!

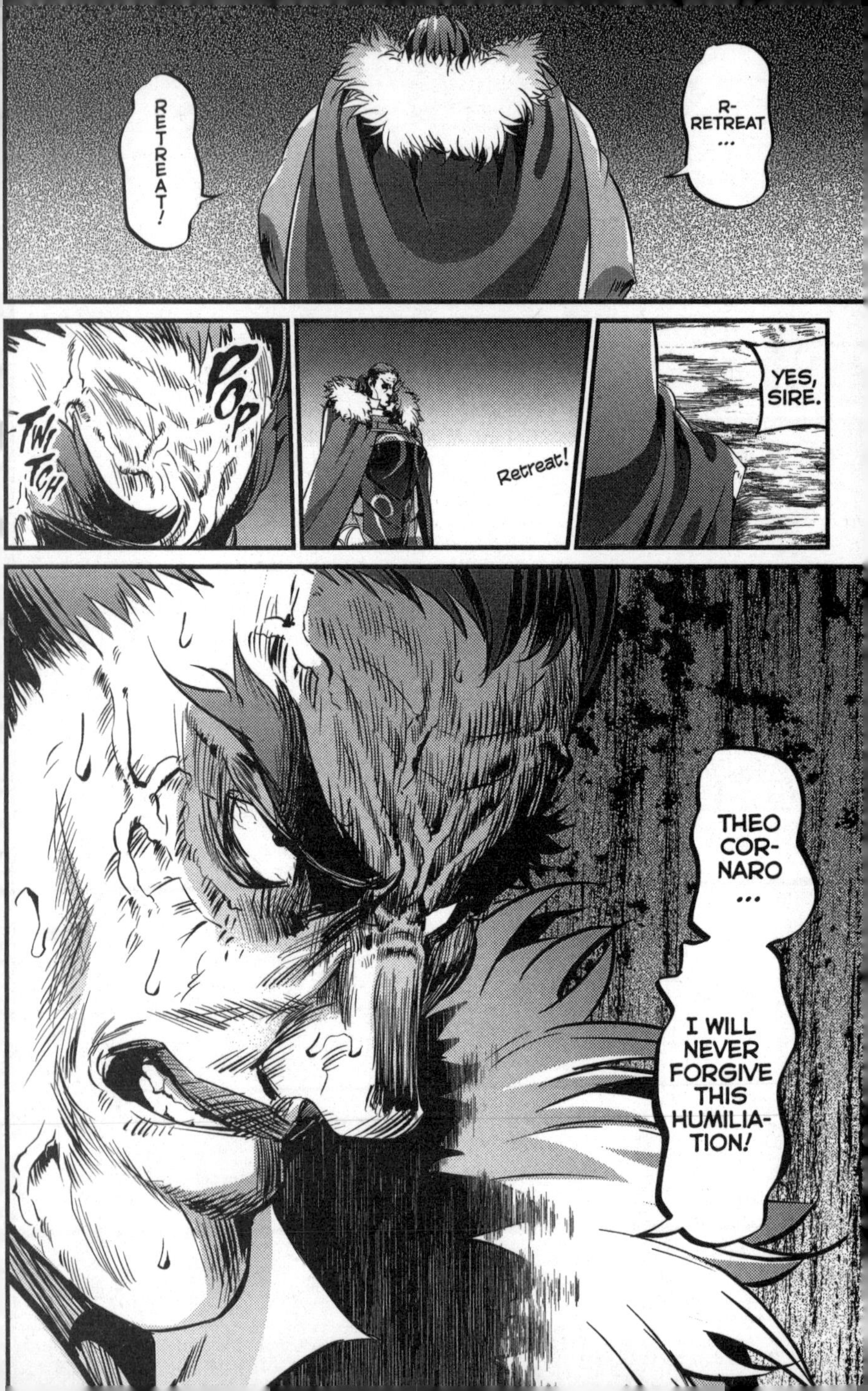
R-RETREAT...
RETREAT!
YES, SIRE.
Retreat!
POP
TWITCH
THEO CORNARO...
I WILL NEVER FORGIVE THIS HUMILIATION!

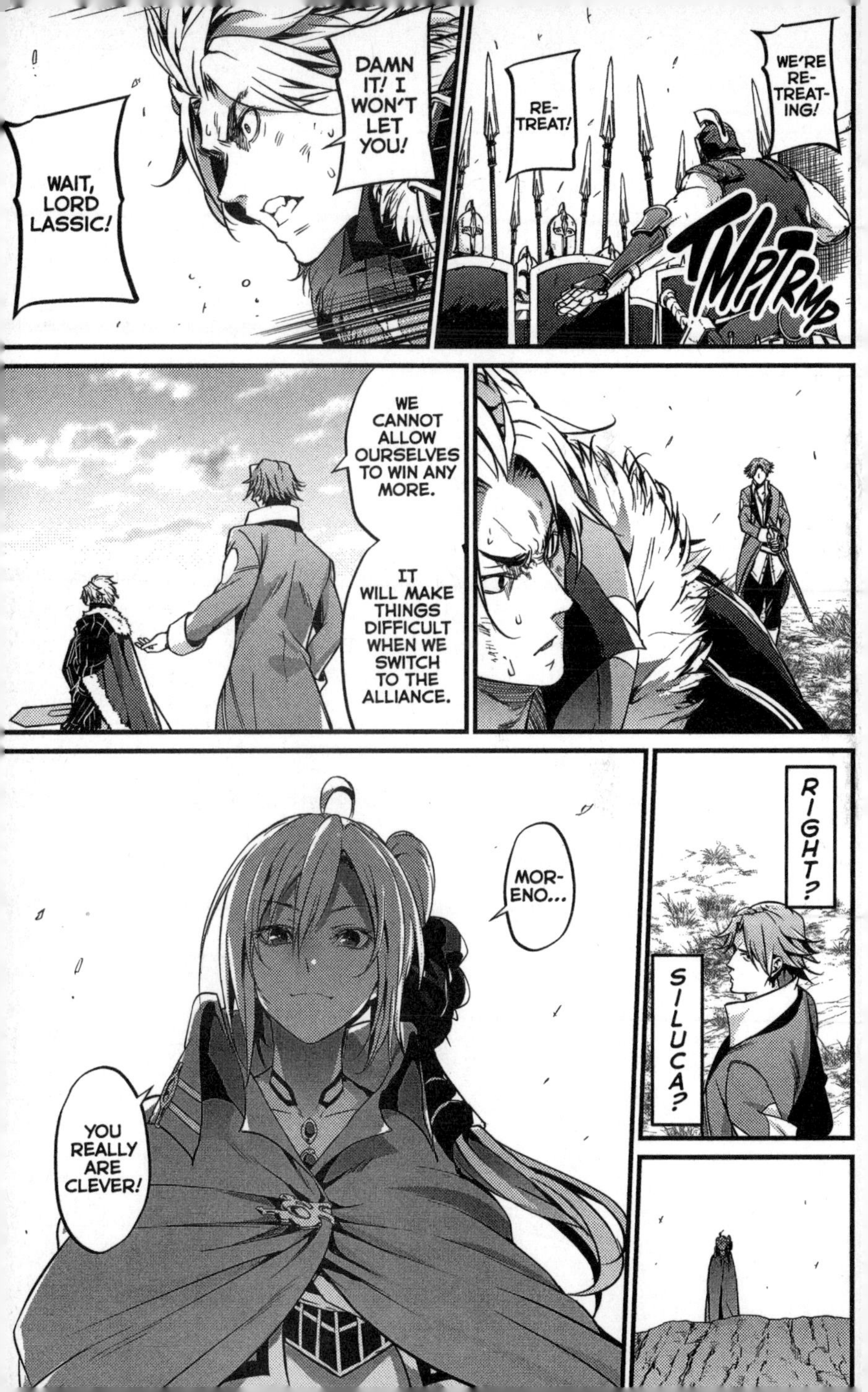
WE'RE RE-TREATING!
RE-TREAT!
TMPTRMP
DAMN IT! I WON'T LET YOU!
WAIT, LORD LASSIC!
WE CANNOT ALLOW OURSELVES TO WIN ANY MORE.
IT WILL MAKE THINGS DIFFICULT WHEN WE SWITCH TO THE ALLIANCE.
RIGHT?
SILUCA?
MOR-ENO...
YOU REALLY ARE CLEVER!

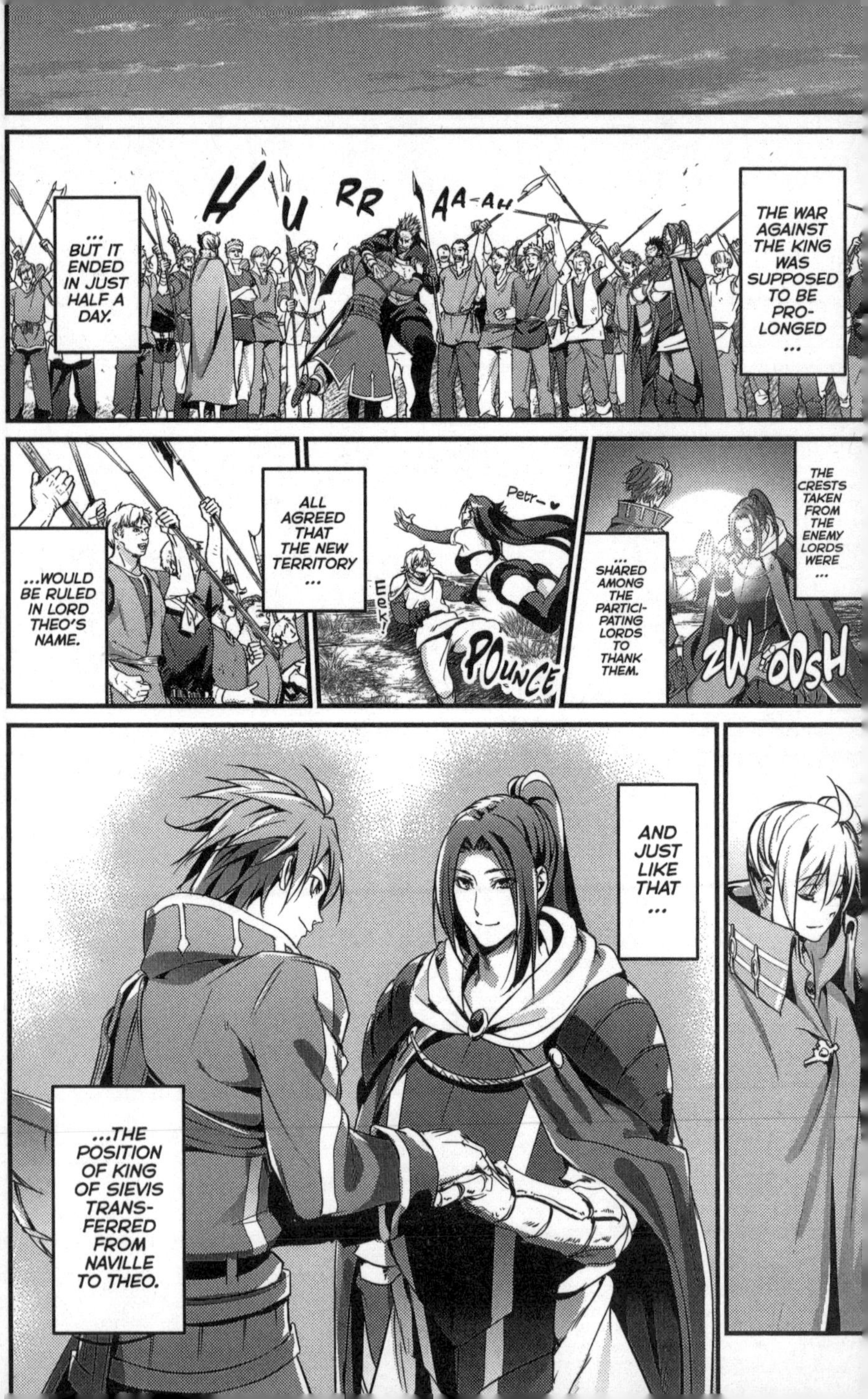
THE WAR AGAINST THE KING WAS SUPPOSED TO BE PRO-LONGED ...
HURRAAAH
... BUT IT ENDED IN JUST HALF A DAY.
THE CRESTS TAKEN FROM THE ENEMY LORDS WERE ...
... SHARED AMONG THE PARTICI-PATING LORDS TO THANK THEM.
ZWOOSH
ALL AGREED THAT THE NEW TERRITORY ...
Petr-♥
Eek!
POUNCE
...WOULD BE RULED IN LORD THEO'S NAME.
AND JUST LIKE THAT ...
...THE POSITION OF KING OF SIEVIS TRANS-FERRED FROM NAVILLE TO THEO.

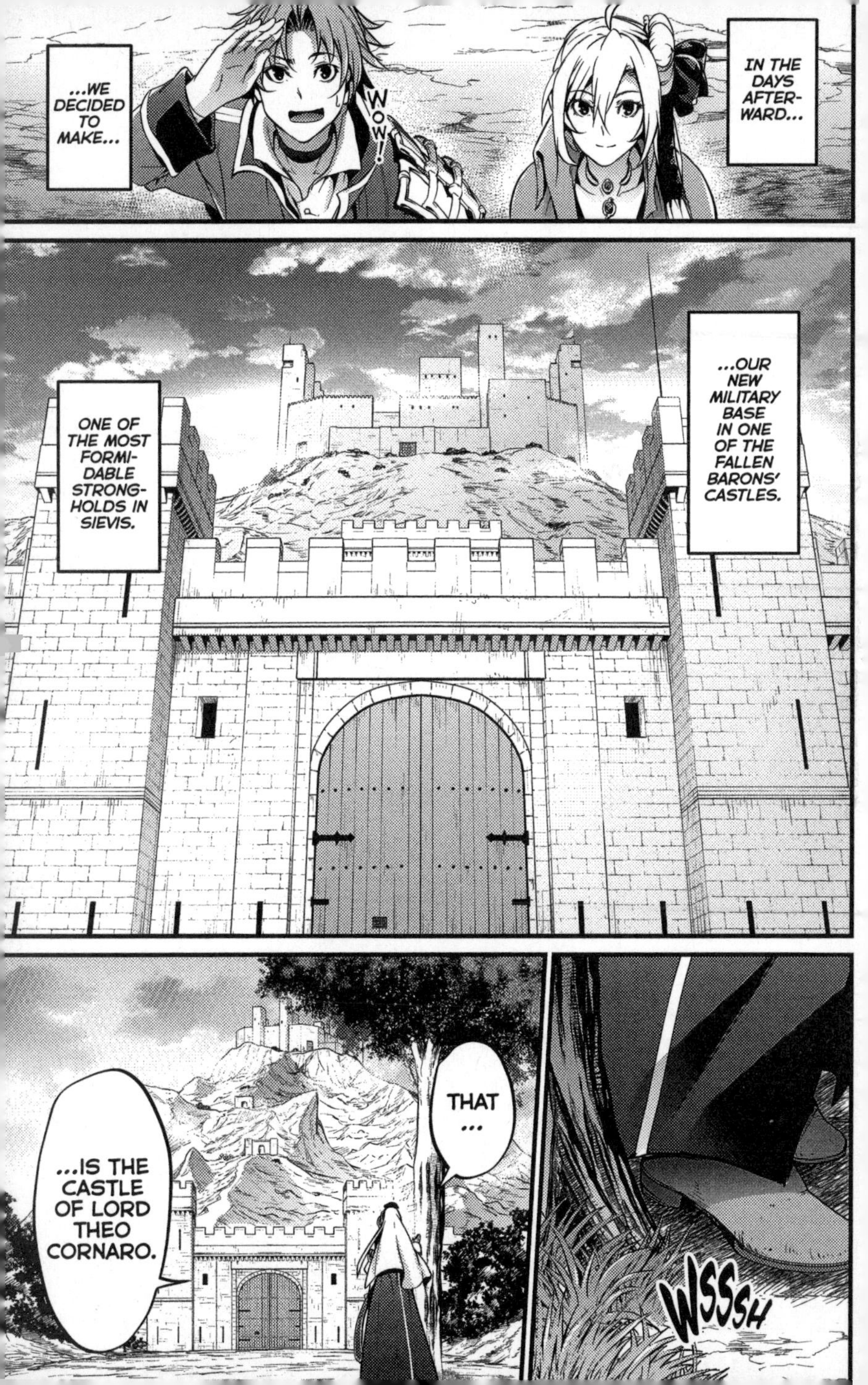
IN THE DAYS AFTER-WARD...
WOW!
...WE DECIDED TO MAKE...
...OUR NEW MILITARY BASE IN ONE OF THE FALLEN BARONS' CASTLES.
ONE OF THE MOST FORMI-DABLE STRONG-HOLDS IN SIEVIS.
WSSSH
THAT ...
...IS THE CASTLE OF LORD THEO CORNARO.

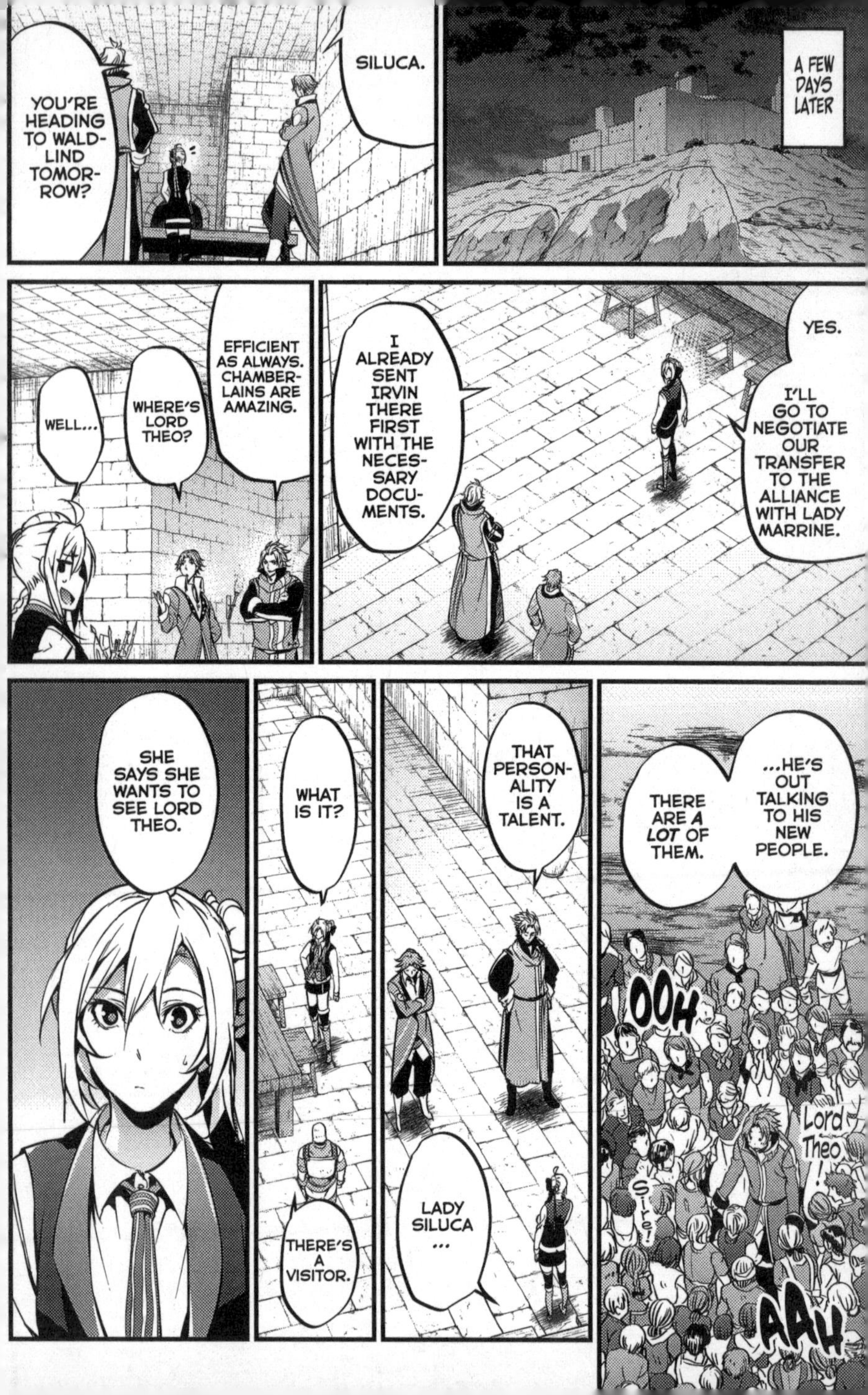
A FEW DAYS LATER
SILUCA.
YOU'RE HEADING TO WALDLIND TOMORROW?
YES.
I'LL GO TO NEGOTIATE OUR TRANSFER TO THE ALLIANCE WITH LADY MARRINE.
I ALREADY SENT IRVIN THERE FIRST WITH THE NECESSARY DOCUMENTS.
EFFICIENT AS ALWAYS. CHAMBERLAINS ARE AMAZING.
WHERE'S LORD THEO?
WELL...
...HE'S OUT TALKING TO HIS NEW PEOPLE.
THERE ARE A *LOT* OF THEM.
OOH
Lord Theo!
Sire!
AAH
THAT PERSONALITY IS A TALENT.
LADY SILUCA...
WHAT IS IT?
THERE'S A VISITOR.
SHE SAYS SHE WANTS TO SEE LORD THEO.

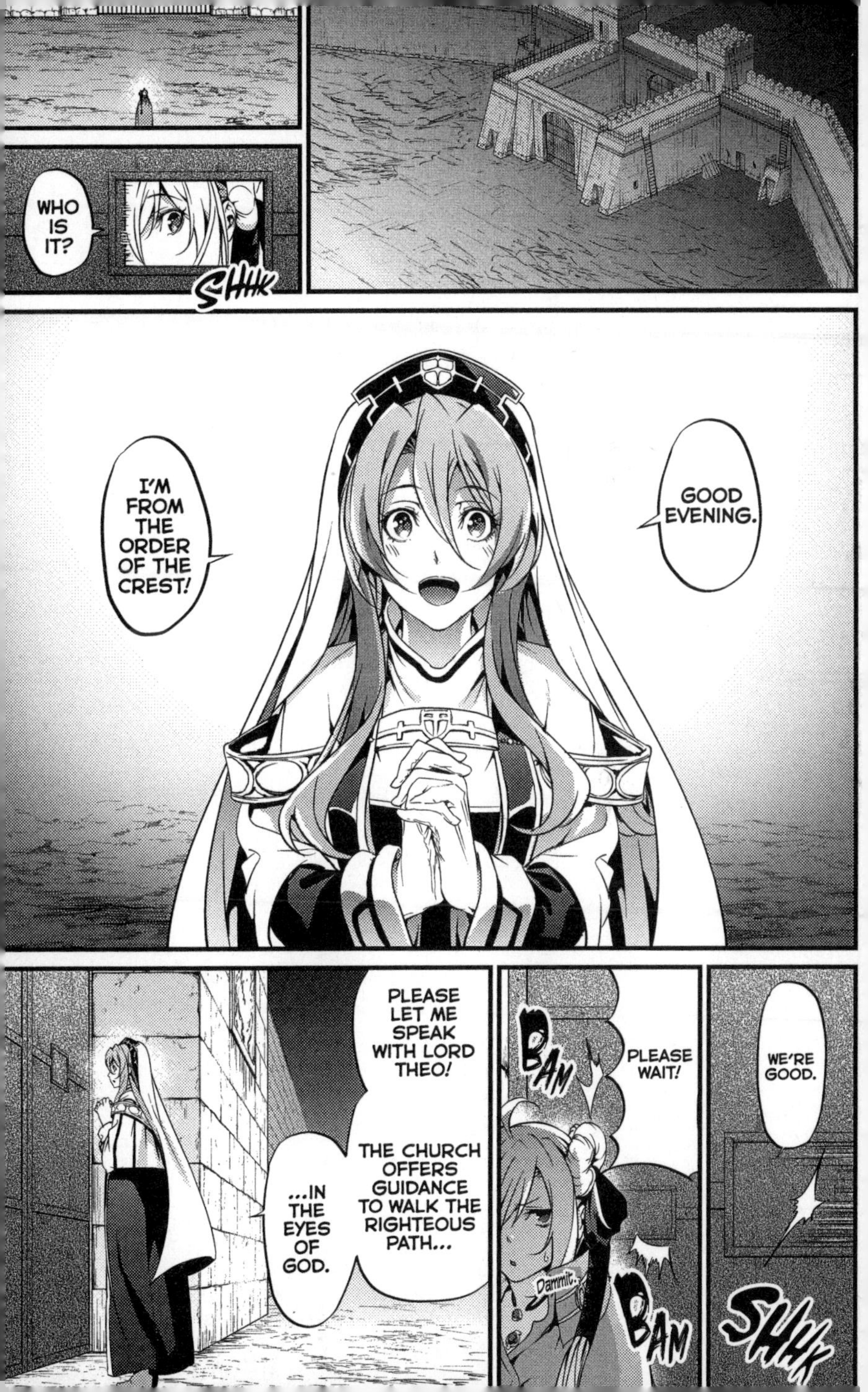
WHO IS IT?
SHHK
GOOD EVENING.
I'M FROM THE ORDER OF THE CREST!
WE'RE GOOD.
SHHK
PLEASE WAIT!
BAM
Dammit.
BAM
PLEASE LET ME SPEAK WITH LORD THEO!
THE CHURCH OFFERS GUIDANCE TO WALK THE RIGHTEOUS PATH...
...IN THE EYES OF GOD.

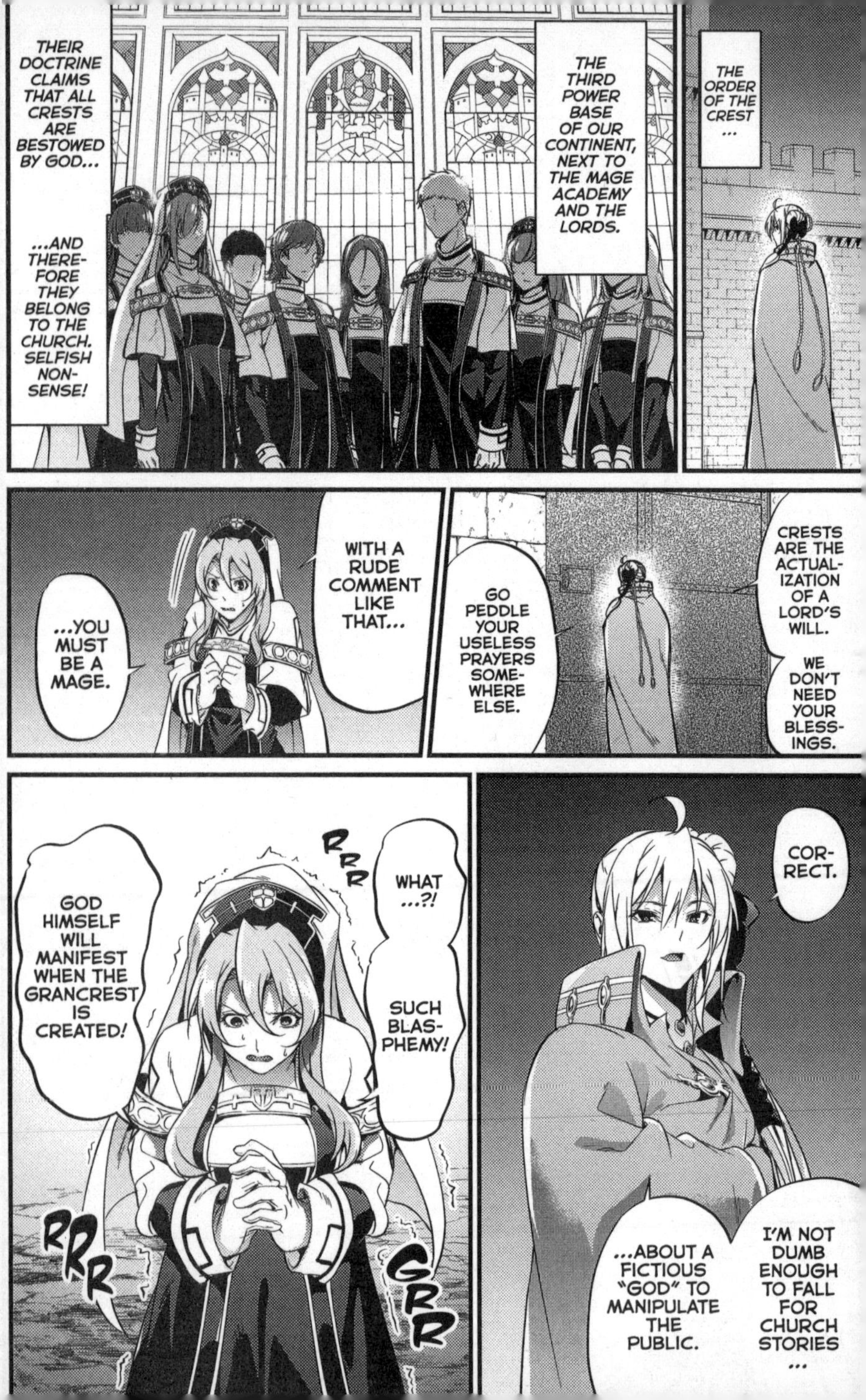
THE ORDER OF THE CREST ...
THE THIRD POWER BASE OF OUR CONTINENT, NEXT TO THE MAGE ACADEMY AND THE LORDS.
THEIR DOCTRINE CLAIMS THAT ALL CRESTS ARE BESTOWED BY GOD...
...AND THEREFORE THEY BELONG TO THE CHURCH. SELFISH NONSENSE!
CRESTS ARE THE ACTUALIZATION OF A LORD'S WILL.
WE DON'T NEED YOUR BLESSINGS.
GO PEDDLE YOUR USELESS PRAYERS SOMEWHERE ELSE.
WITH A RUDE COMMENT LIKE THAT...
...YOU MUST BE A MAGE.
CORRECT.
I'M NOT DUMB ENOUGH TO FALL FOR CHURCH STORIES ...
...ABOUT A FICTIOUS "GOD" TO MANIPULATE THE PUBLIC.
RRR
WHAT ...?!
SUCH BLASPHEMY!
GOD HIMSELF WILL MANIFEST WHEN THE GRANCREST IS CREATED!
RRR
GRR

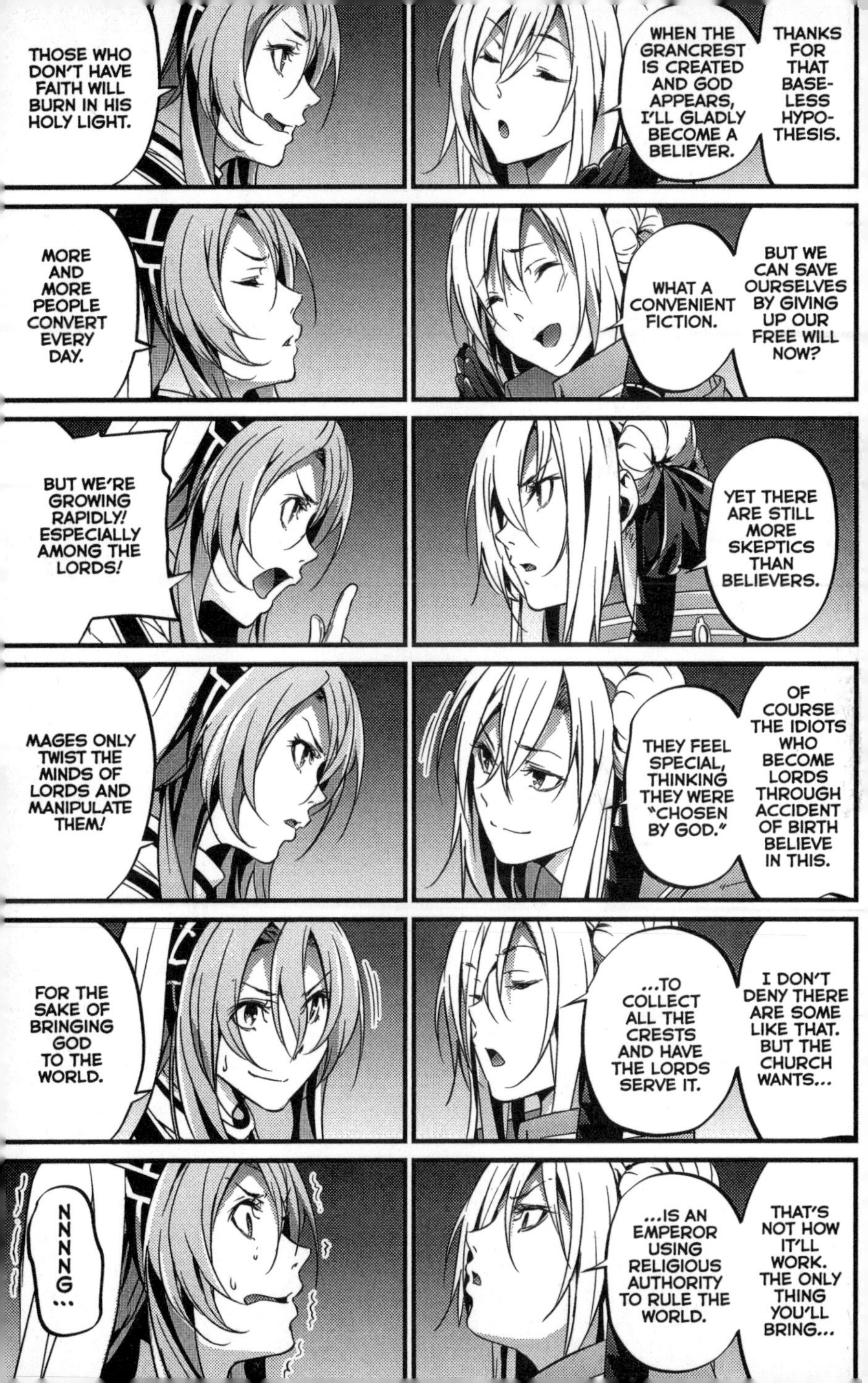
THANKS FOR THAT BASELESS HYPOTHESIS.
WHEN THE GRANCREST IS CREATED AND GOD APPEARS, I'LL GLADLY BECOME A BELIEVER.
THOSE WHO DON'T HAVE FAITH WILL BURN IN HIS HOLY LIGHT.
BUT WE CAN SAVE OURSELVES BY GIVING UP OUR FREE WILL NOW?
WHAT A CONVENIENT FICTION.
MORE AND MORE PEOPLE CONVERT EVERY DAY.
YET THERE ARE STILL MORE SKEPTICS THAN BELIEVERS.
BUT WE'RE GROWING RAPIDLY! ESPECIALLY AMONG THE LORDS!
OF COURSE THE IDIOTS WHO BECOME LORDS THROUGH ACCIDENT OF BIRTH BELIEVE IN THIS.
THEY FEEL SPECIAL, THINKING THEY WERE "CHOSEN BY GOD."
MAGES ONLY TWIST THE MINDS OF LORDS AND MANIPULATE THEM!
I DON'T DENY THERE ARE SOME LIKE THAT. BUT THE CHURCH WANTS...
...TO COLLECT ALL THE CRESTS AND HAVE THE LORDS SERVE IT.
FOR THE SAKE OF BRINGING GOD TO THE WORLD.
THAT'S NOT HOW IT'LL WORK. THE ONLY THING YOU'LL BRING...
...IS AN EMPEROR USING RELIGIOUS AUTHORITY TO RULE THE WORLD.
NNNNG...

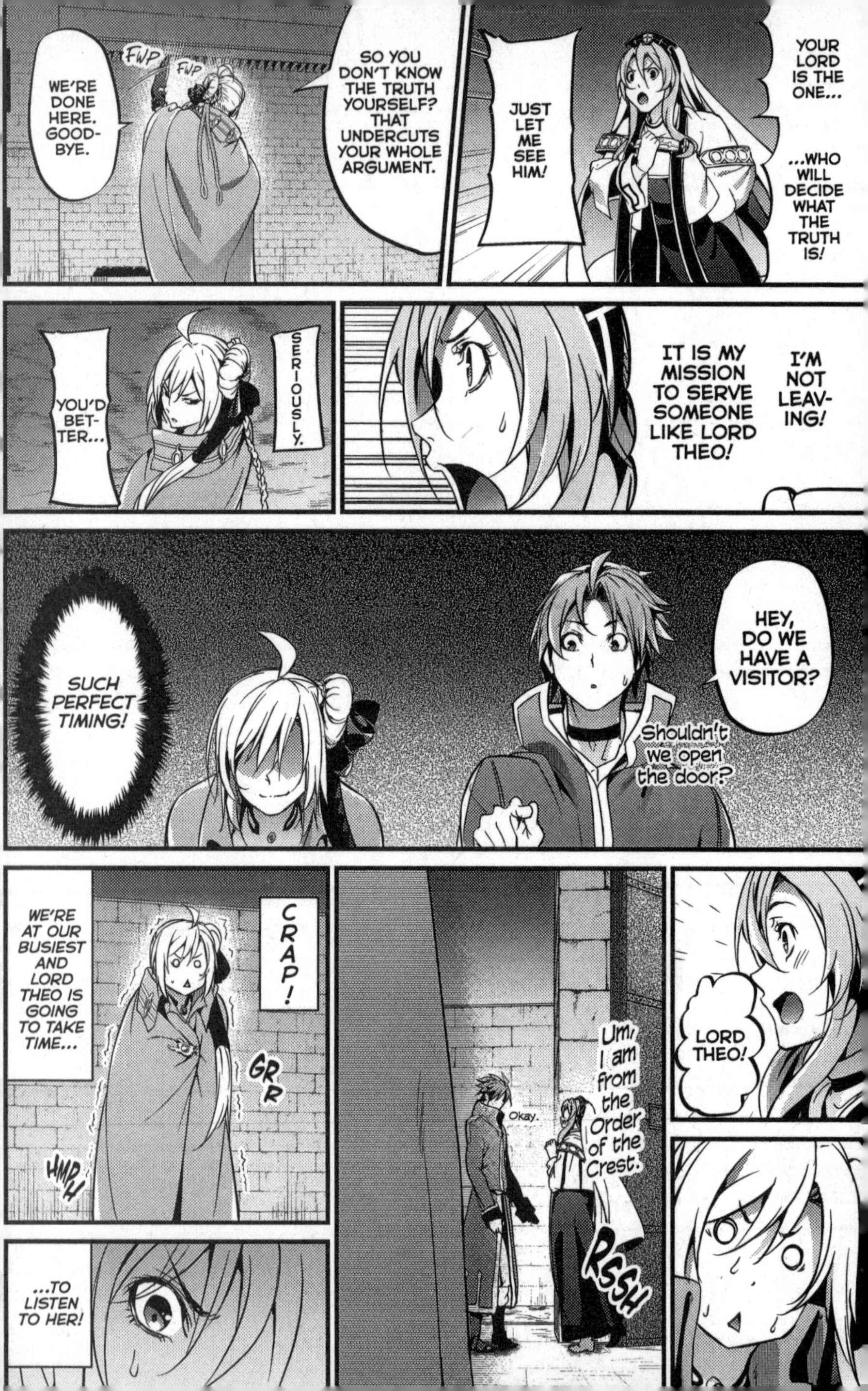
YOUR LORD IS THE ONE...
...WHO WILL DECIDE WHAT THE TRUTH IS!
JUST LET ME SEE HIM!
SO YOU DON'T KNOW THE TRUTH YOURSELF? THAT UNDERCUTS YOUR WHOLE ARGUMENT.
FWP
FWP
WE'RE DONE HERE. GOOD-BYE.
I'M NOT LEAVING!
IT IS MY MISSION TO SERVE SOMEONE LIKE LORD THEO!
SERIOUSLY.
YOU'D BET-TER...
HEY, DO WE HAVE A VISITOR?
Shouldn't we open the door?
SUCH PERFECT TIMING!
LORD THEO!
Um, I am from the Order of the Crest.
Okay.
RSSH
CRAP!
WE'RE AT OUR BUSIEST AND LORD THEO IS GOING TO TAKE TIME...
GRR
HMPH
...TO LISTEN TO HER!

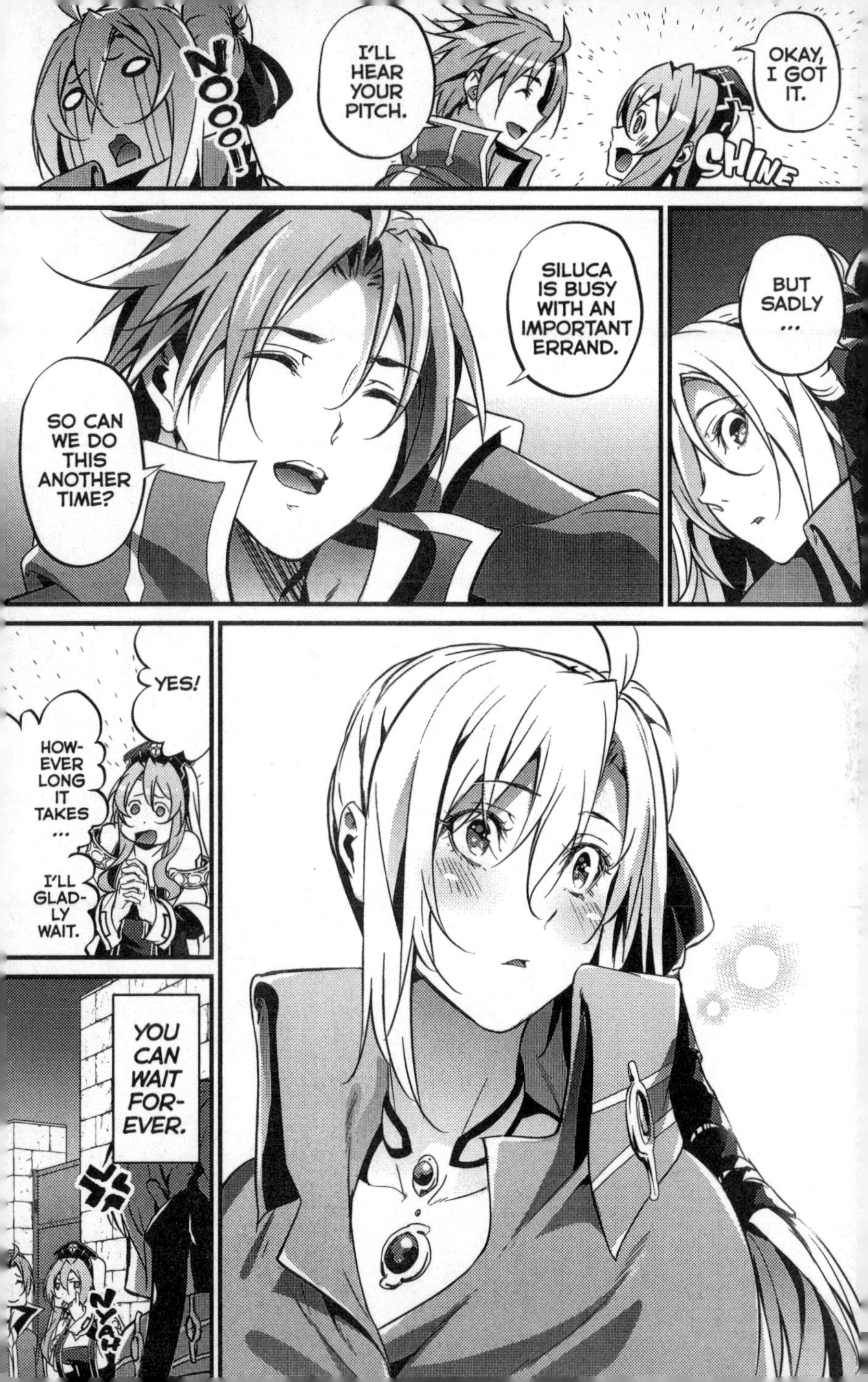
OKAY, I GOT IT.
SHINE
I'LL HEAR YOUR PITCH.
NOOO!!
BUT SADLY ...
SILUCA IS BUSY WITH AN IMPORTANT ERRAND.
SO CAN WE DO THIS ANOTHER TIME?
YES!
HOW-EVER LONG IT TAKES ...
I'LL GLAD-LY WAIT.
YOU CAN WAIT FOR-EVER.
NYAH

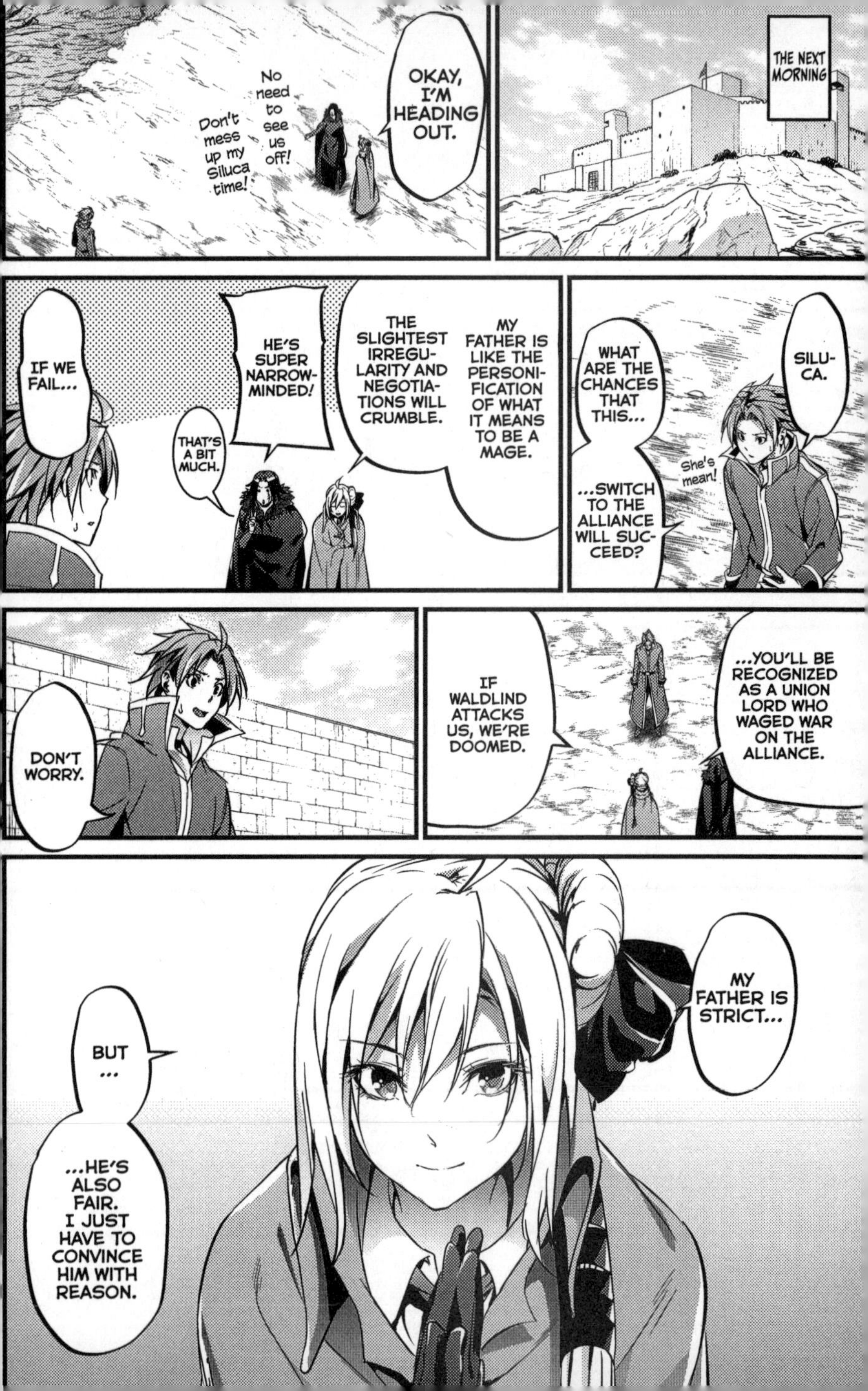
THE NEXT MORNING
OKAY, I'M HEADING OUT.
No need to see us off!
Don't mess up my Siluca time!
SILUCA.
She's mean!
WHAT ARE THE CHANCES THAT THIS...
...SWITCH TO THE ALLIANCE WILL SUCCEED?
MY FATHER IS LIKE THE PERSONIFICATION OF WHAT IT MEANS TO BE A MAGE.
THE SLIGHTEST IRREGULARITY AND NEGOTIATIONS WILL CRUMBLE.
HE'S SUPER NARROW-MINDED!
THAT'S A BIT MUCH.
IF WE FAIL...
...YOU'LL BE RECOGNIZED AS A UNION LORD WHO WAGED WAR ON THE ALLIANCE.
IF WALDLIND ATTACKS US, WE'RE DOOMED.
DON'T WORRY.
MY FATHER IS STRICT...
BUT...
...HE'S ALSO FAIR. I JUST HAVE TO CONVINCE HIM WITH REASON.

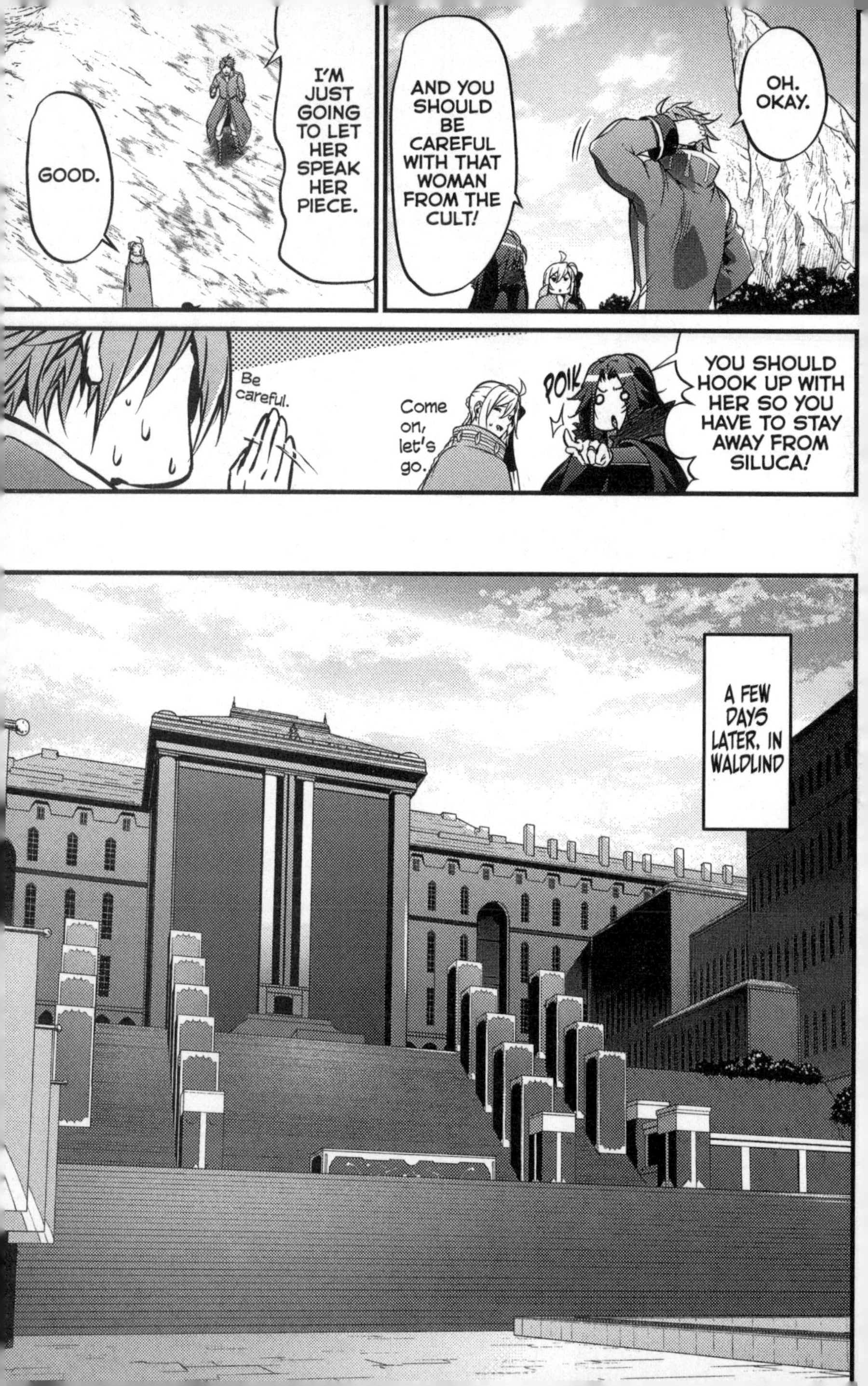
OH. OKAY.
AND YOU SHOULD BE CAREFUL WITH THAT WOMAN FROM THE CULT!
I'M JUST GOING TO LET HER SPEAK HER PIECE.
GOOD.
YOU SHOULD HOOK UP WITH HER SO YOU HAVE TO STAY AWAY FROM SILUCA!
POIK
Come on, let's go.
Be careful.
A FEW DAYS LATER, IN WALDLIND

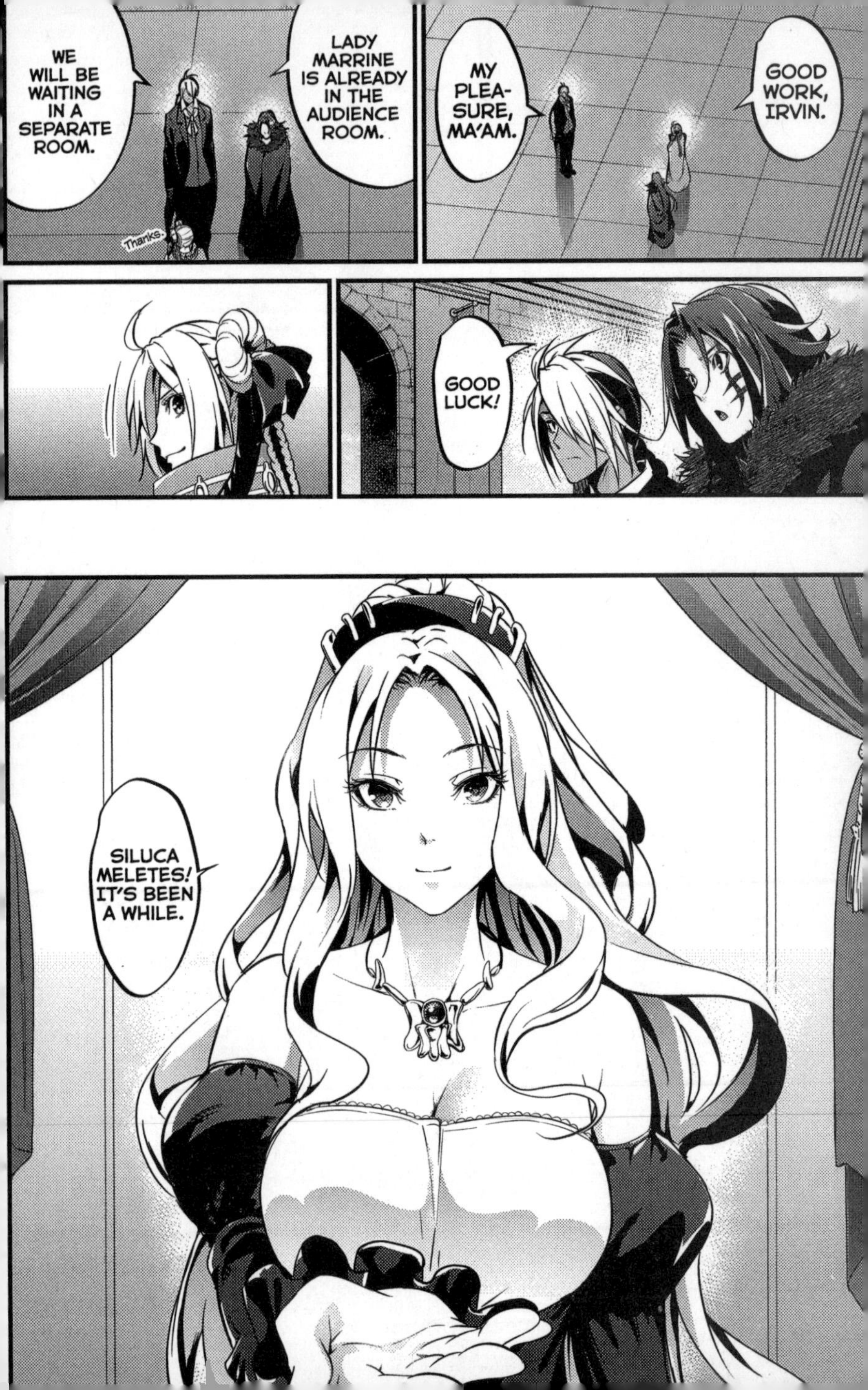
GOOD WORK, IRVIN.
MY PLEASURE, MA'AM.
LADY MARRINE IS ALREADY IN THE AUDIENCE ROOM.
WE WILL BE WAITING IN A SEPARATE ROOM.
Thanks.
GOOD LUCK!
SILUCA MELETES! IT'S BEEN A WHILE.

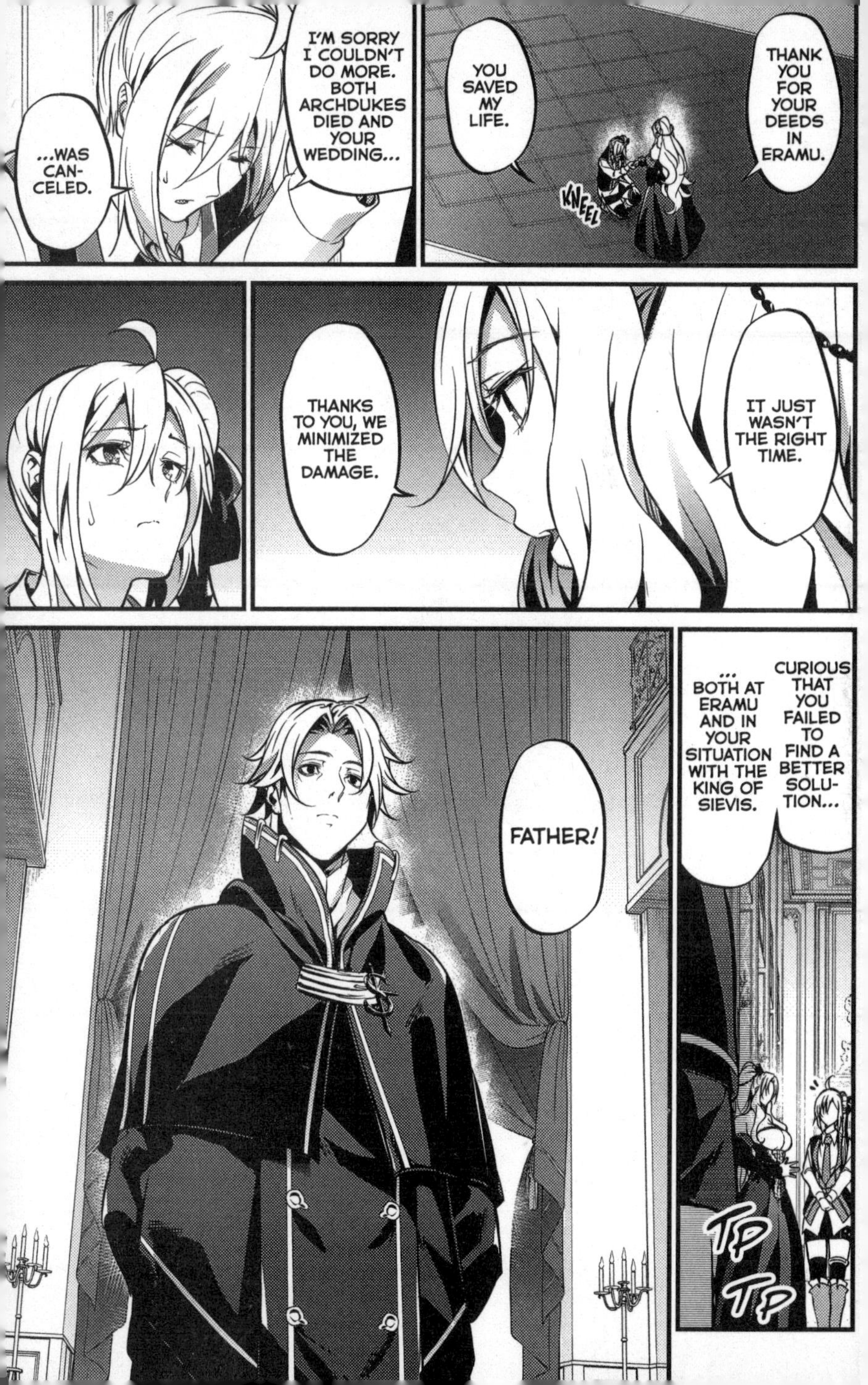
THANK YOU FOR YOUR DEEDS IN ERAMU.
YOU SAVED MY LIFE.
KNEEL
I'M SORRY I COULDN'T DO MORE. BOTH ARCHDUKES DIED AND YOUR WEDDING...
...WAS CANCELED.
IT JUST WASN'T THE RIGHT TIME.
THANKS TO YOU, WE MINIMIZED THE DAMAGE.
CURIOUS THAT YOU FAILED TO FIND A BETTER SOLUTION...
...BOTH AT ERAMU AND IN YOUR SITUATION WITH THE KING OF SIEVIS.
TP
TP
FATHER!

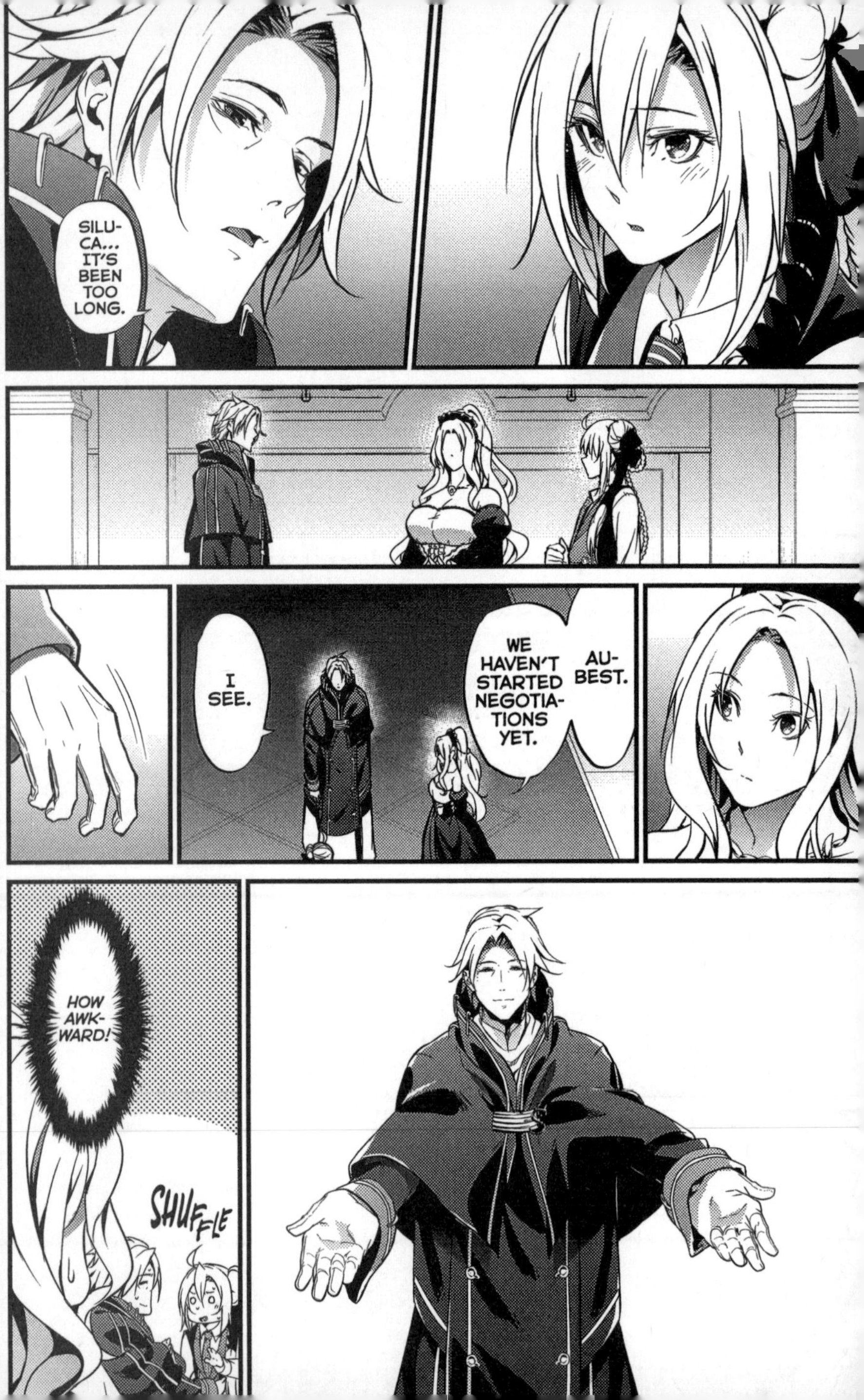
SILUCA... IT'S BEEN TOO LONG.
AUBEST.
WE HAVEN'T STARTED NEGOTIATIONS YET.
I SEE.
HOW AWKWARD!
SHUFFLE

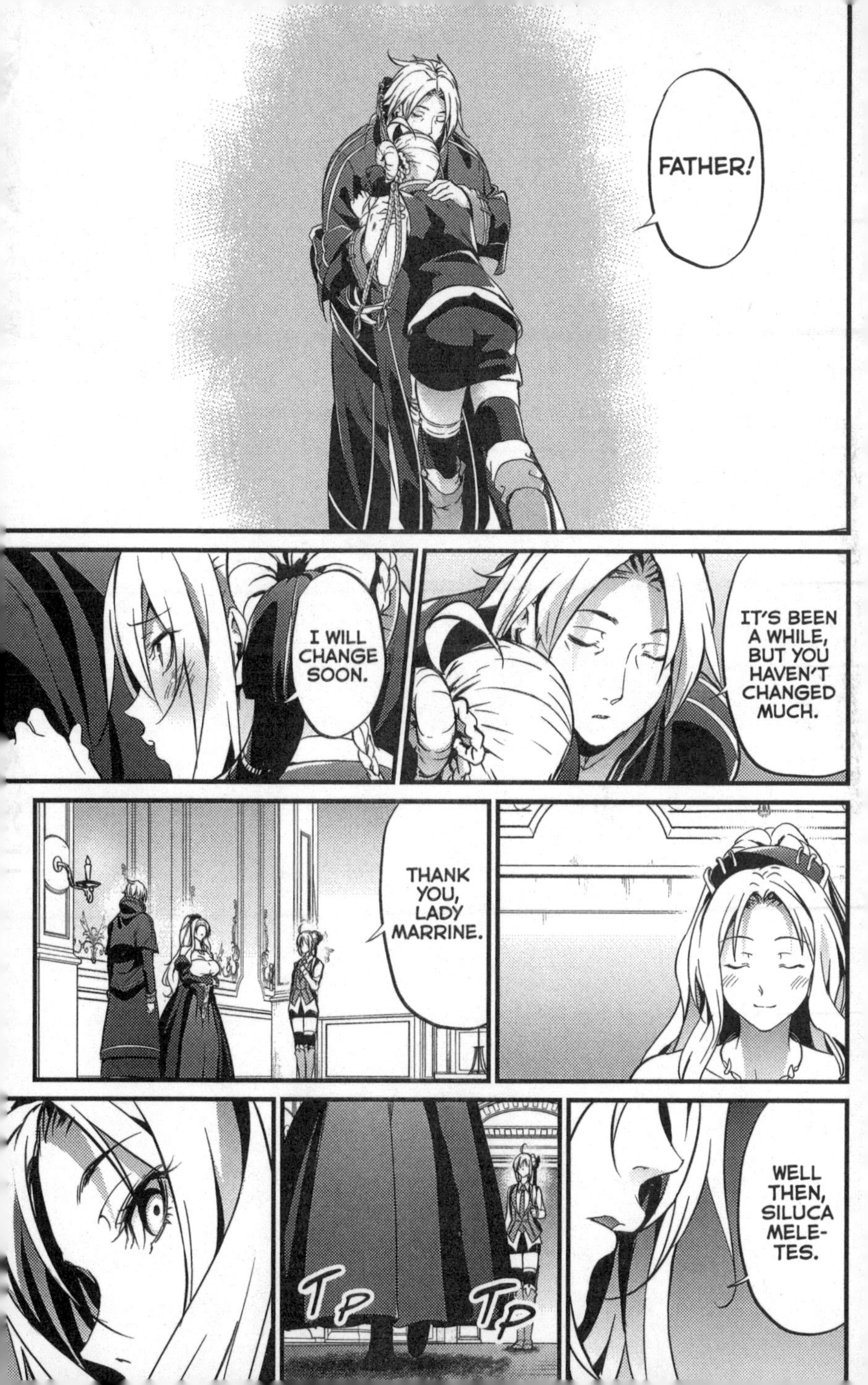
FATHER!
IT'S BEEN A WHILE, BUT YOU HAVEN'T CHANGED MUCH.
I WILL CHANGE SOON.
THANK YOU, LADY MARRINE.
WELL THEN, SILUCA MELETES.
TP
TP

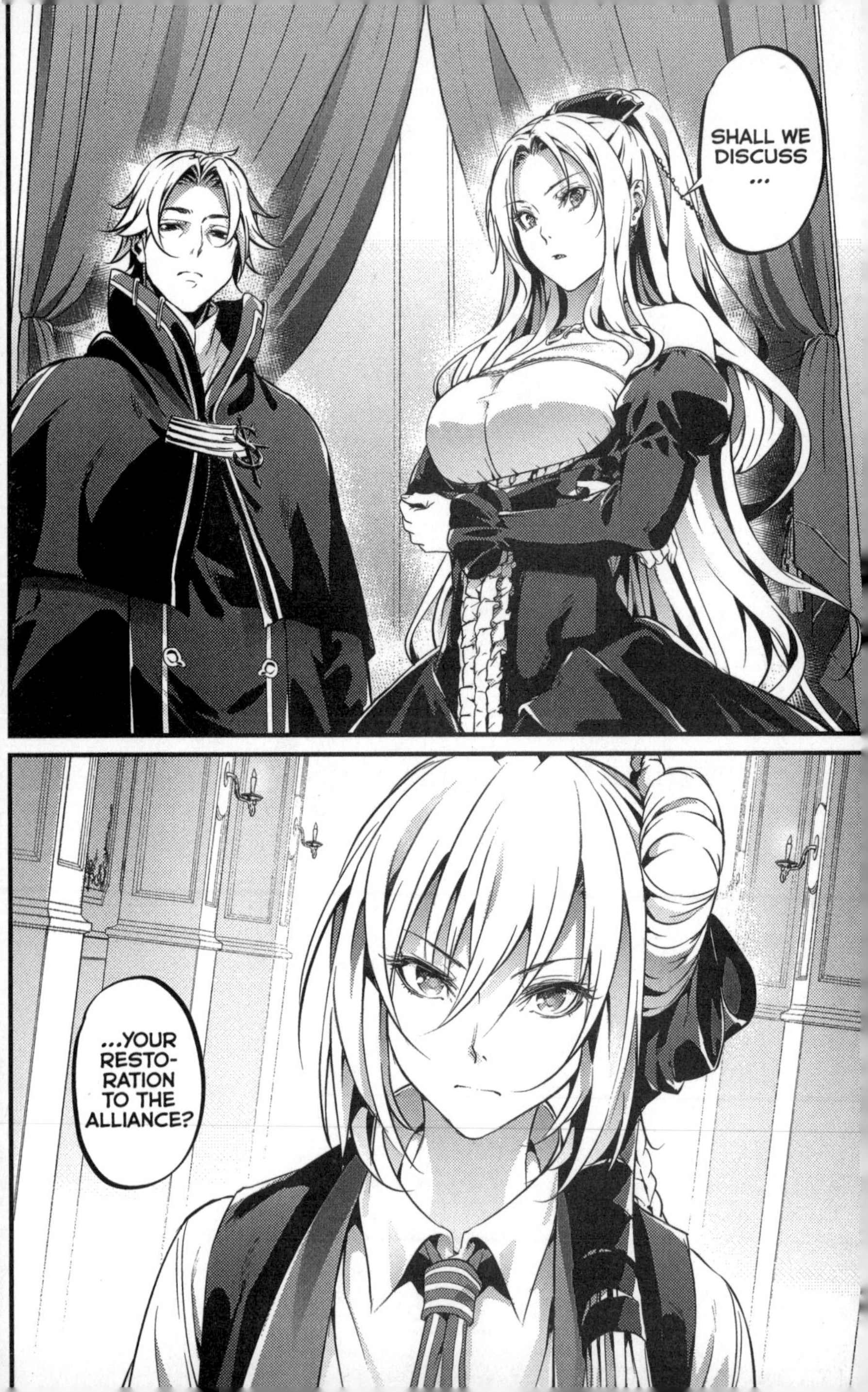
SHALL WE DISCUSS ...
...YOUR RESTO-RATION TO THE ALLIANCE?

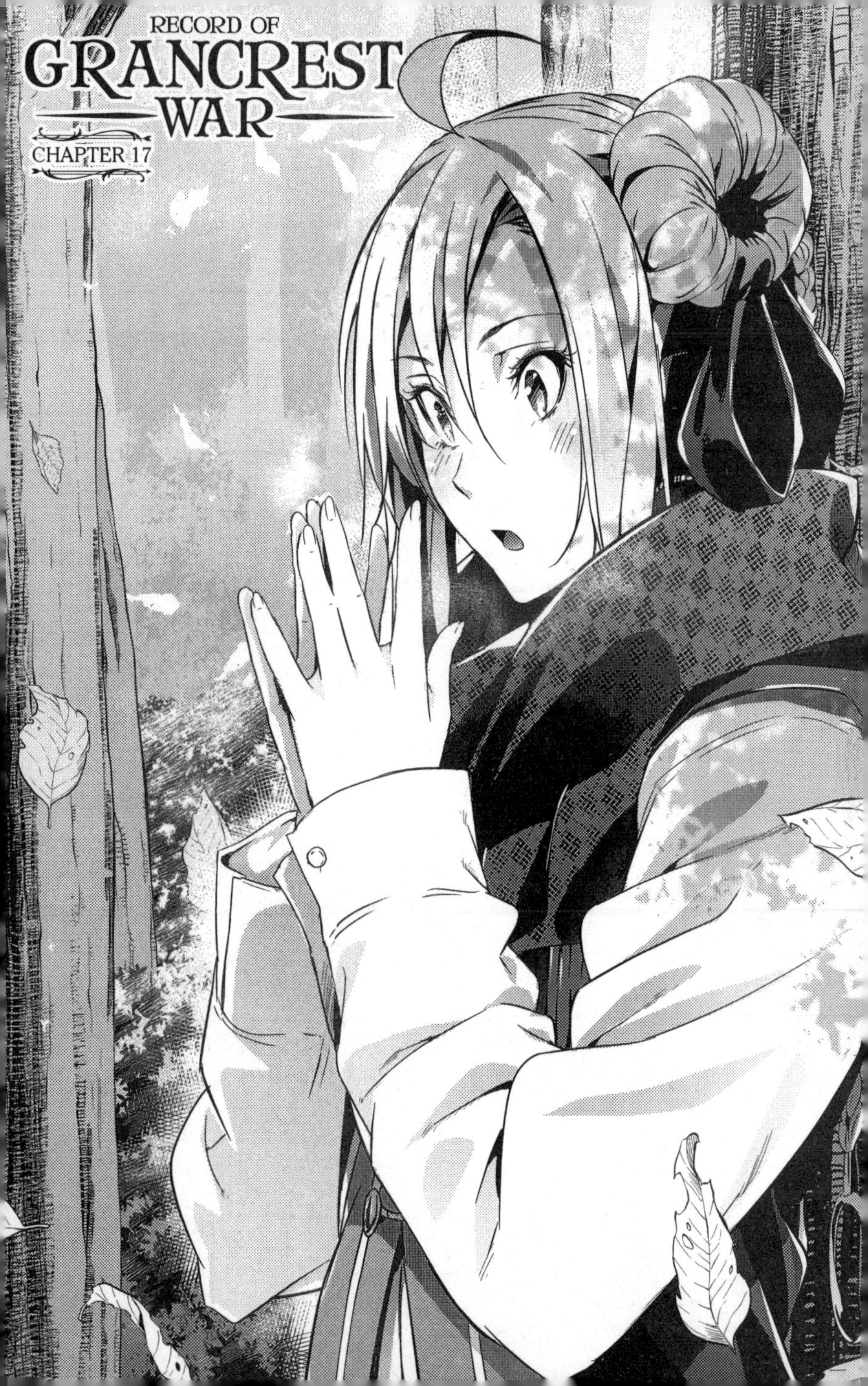
RECORD OF
GRANCREST
WAR
CHAPTER 17

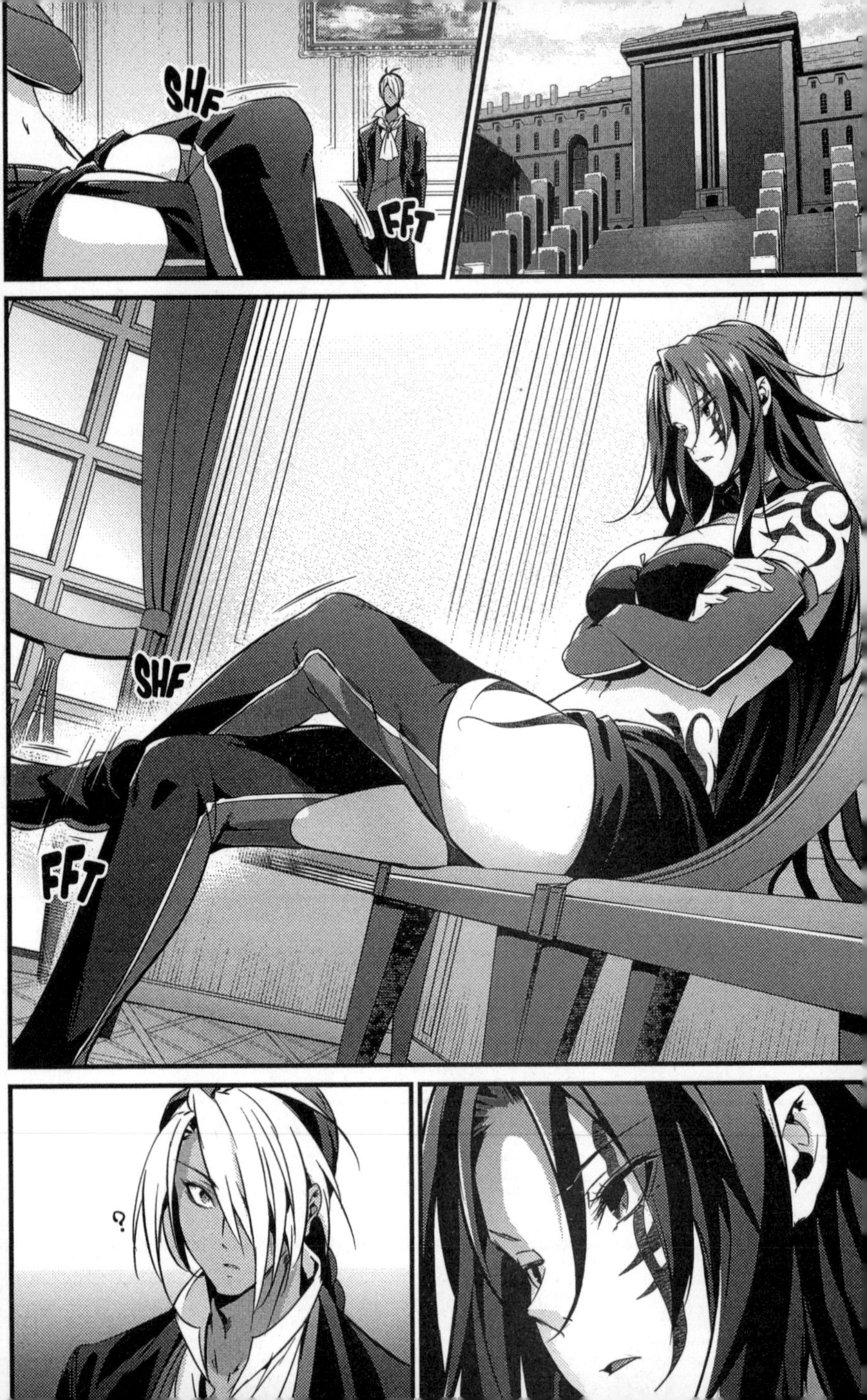
SHF
FFT
SHF
FFT
?

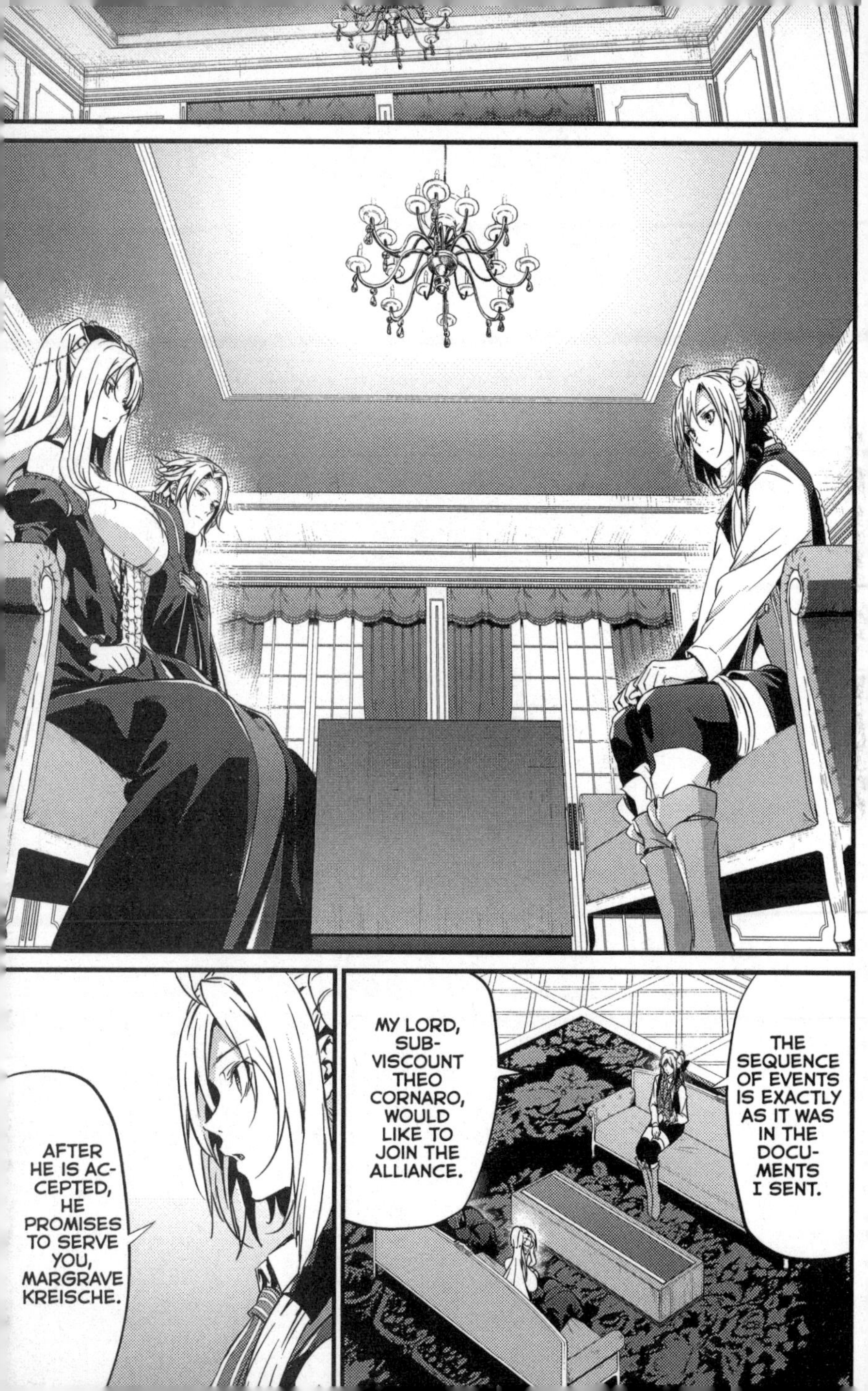
THE SEQUENCE OF EVENTS IS EXACTLY AS IT WAS IN THE DOCU-MENTS I SENT.
MY LORD, SUB-VISCOUNT THEO CORNARO, WOULD LIKE TO JOIN THE ALLIANCE.
AFTER HE IS AC-CEPTED, HE PROMISES TO SERVE YOU, MARGRAVE KREISCHE.

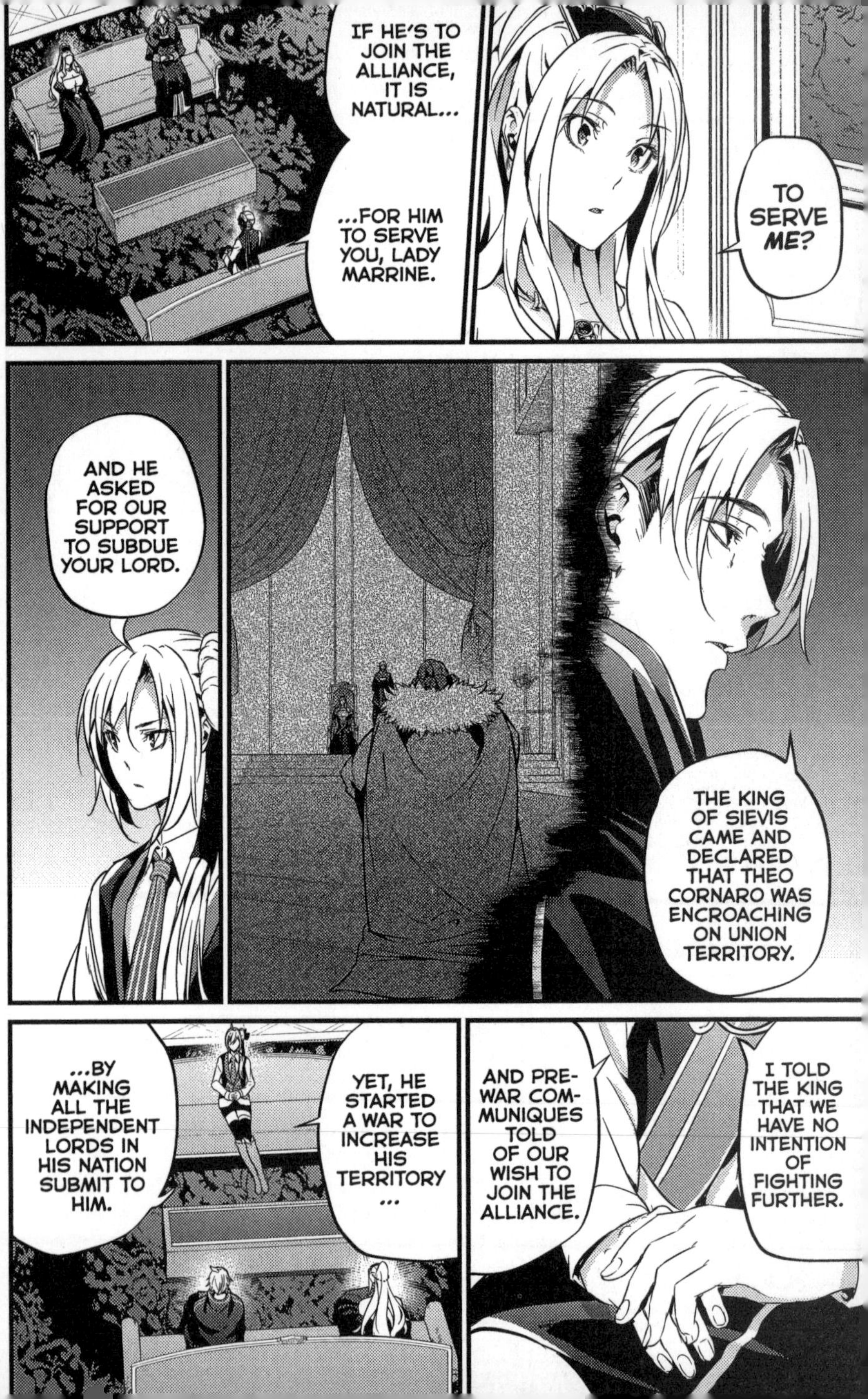
TO SERVE *ME*?
IF HE'S TO JOIN THE ALLIANCE, IT IS NATURAL...
...FOR HIM TO SERVE YOU, LADY MARRINE.
THE KING OF SIEVIS CAME AND DECLARED THAT THEO CORNARO WAS ENCROACHING ON UNION TERRITORY.
AND HE ASKED FOR OUR SUPPORT TO SUBDUE YOUR LORD.
I TOLD THE KING THAT WE HAVE NO INTENTION OF FIGHTING FURTHER.
AND PRE-WAR COM-MUNIQUES TOLD OF OUR WISH TO JOIN THE ALLIANCE.
YET, HE STARTED A WAR TO INCREASE HIS TERRITORY...
...BY MAKING ALL THE INDEPENDENT LORDS IN HIS NATION SUBMIT TO HIM.

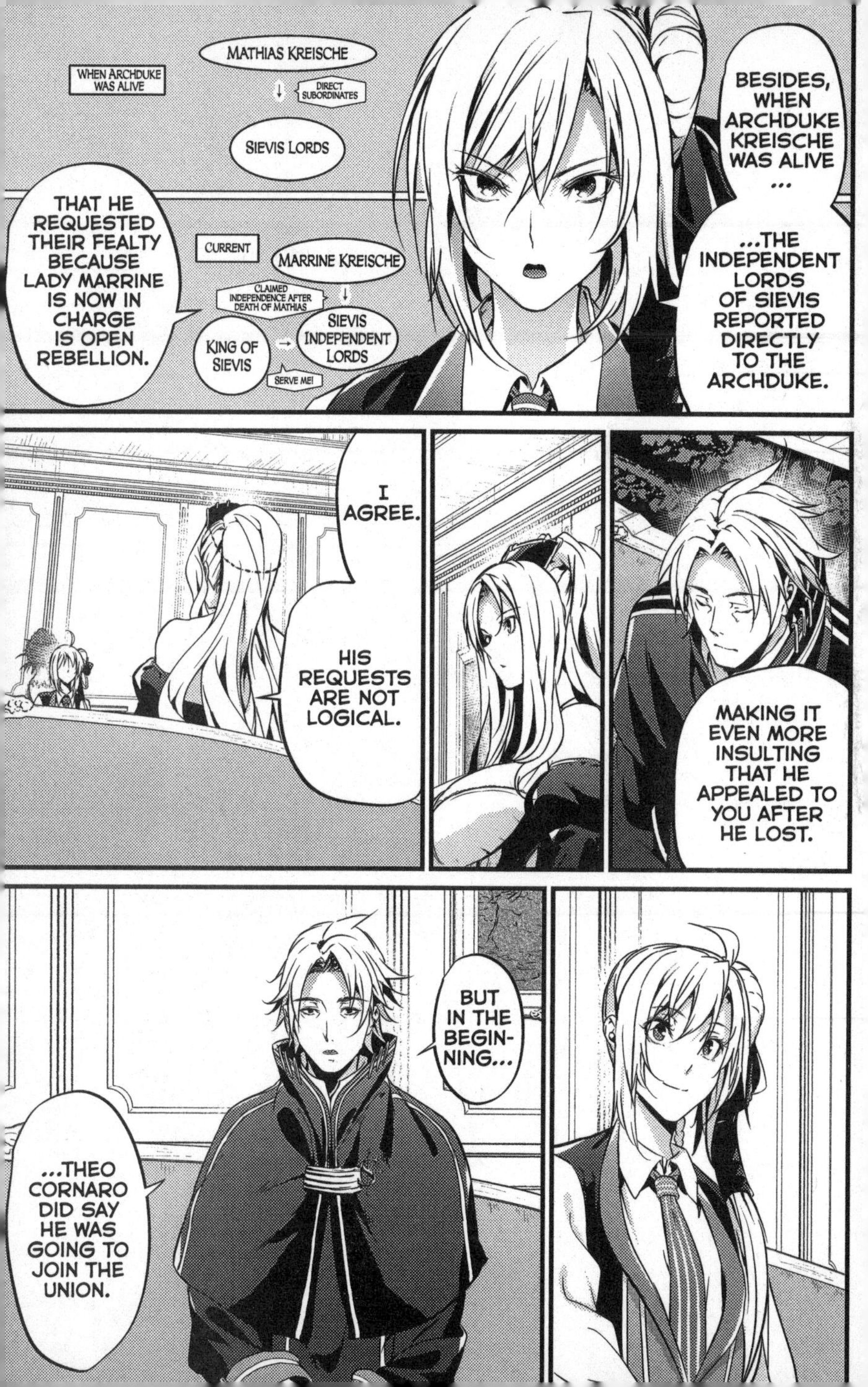
BESIDES, WHEN ARCHDUKE KREISCHE WAS ALIVE...
...THE INDEPENDENT LORDS OF SIEVIS REPORTED DIRECTLY TO THE ARCHDUKE.
WHEN ARCHDUKE WAS ALIVE
MATHIAS KREISCHE
DIRECT SUBORDINATES
SIEVIS LORDS
CURRENT
MARRINE KREISCHE
CLAIMED INDEPENDENCE AFTER DEATH OF MATHIAS
SIEVIS INDEPENDENT LORDS
KING OF SIEVIS
SERVE ME!
THAT HE REQUESTED THEIR FEALTY BECAUSE LADY MARRINE IS NOW IN CHARGE IS OPEN REBELLION.
MAKING IT EVEN MORE INSULTING THAT HE APPEALED TO YOU AFTER HE LOST.
I AGREE.
HIS REQUESTS ARE NOT LOGICAL.
BUT IN THE BEGIN-NING...
...THEO CORNARO DID SAY HE WAS GOING TO JOIN THE UNION.

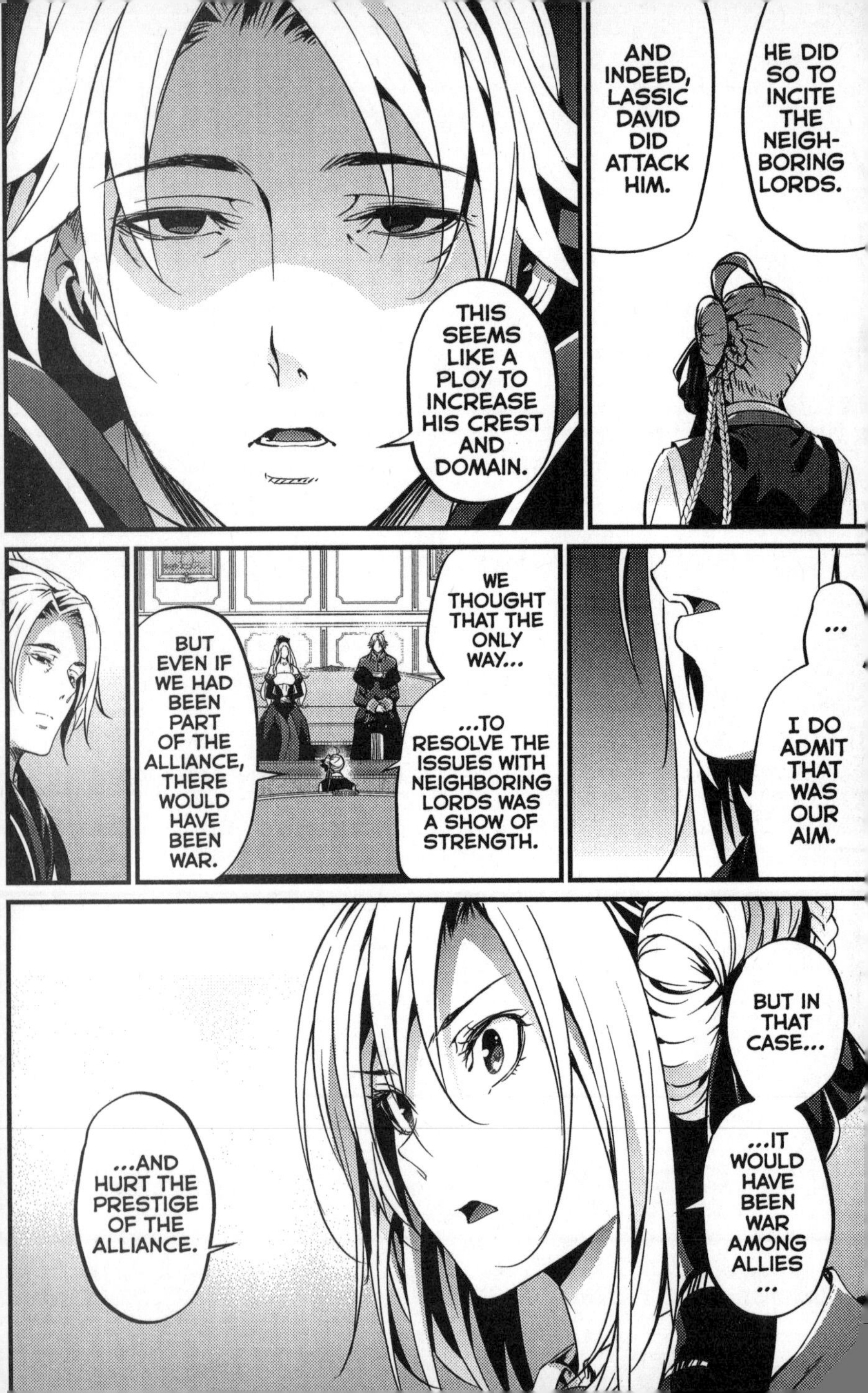
HE DID SO TO INCITE THE NEIGHBORING LORDS.
AND INDEED, LASSIC DAVID DID ATTACK HIM.
THIS SEEMS LIKE A PLOY TO INCREASE HIS CREST AND DOMAIN.
...
I DO ADMIT THAT WAS OUR AIM.
WE THOUGHT THAT THE ONLY WAY...
...TO RESOLVE THE ISSUES WITH NEIGHBORING LORDS WAS A SHOW OF STRENGTH.
BUT EVEN IF WE HAD BEEN PART OF THE ALLIANCE, THERE WOULD HAVE BEEN WAR.
BUT IN THAT CASE...
...IT WOULD HAVE BEEN WAR AMONG ALLIES...
...AND HURT THE PRESTIGE OF THE ALLIANCE.

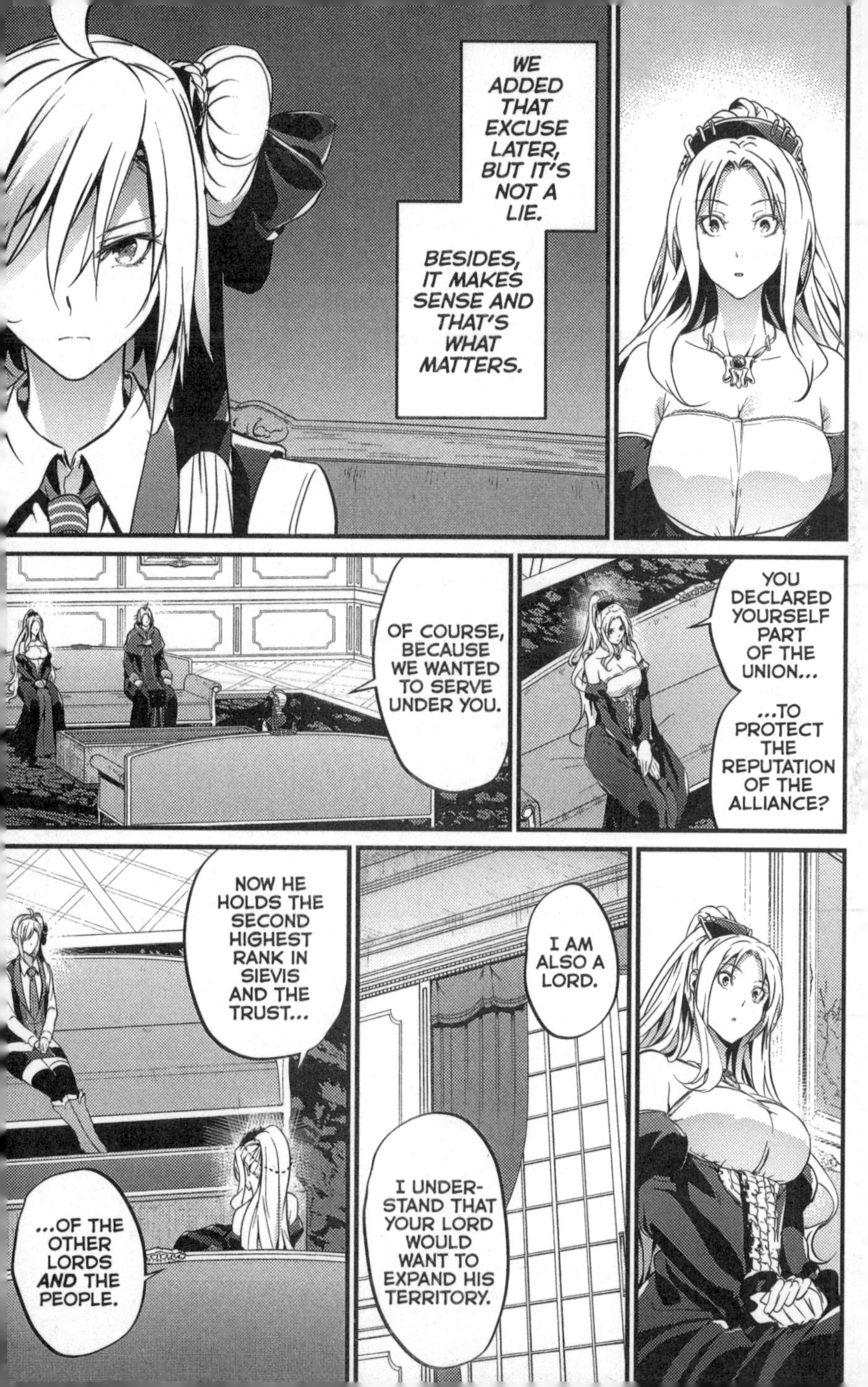
WE ADDED THAT EXCUSE LATER, BUT IT'S NOT A LIE.
BESIDES, IT MAKES SENSE AND THAT'S WHAT MATTERS.
YOU DECLARED YOURSELF PART OF THE UNION...
...TO PROTECT THE REPUTATION OF THE ALLIANCE?
OF COURSE, BECAUSE WE WANTED TO SERVE UNDER YOU.
I AM ALSO A LORD.
I UNDER-STAND THAT YOUR LORD WOULD WANT TO EXPAND HIS TERRITORY.
NOW HE HOLDS THE SECOND HIGHEST RANK IN SIEVIS AND THE TRUST...
...OF THE OTHER LORDS *AND* THE PEOPLE.

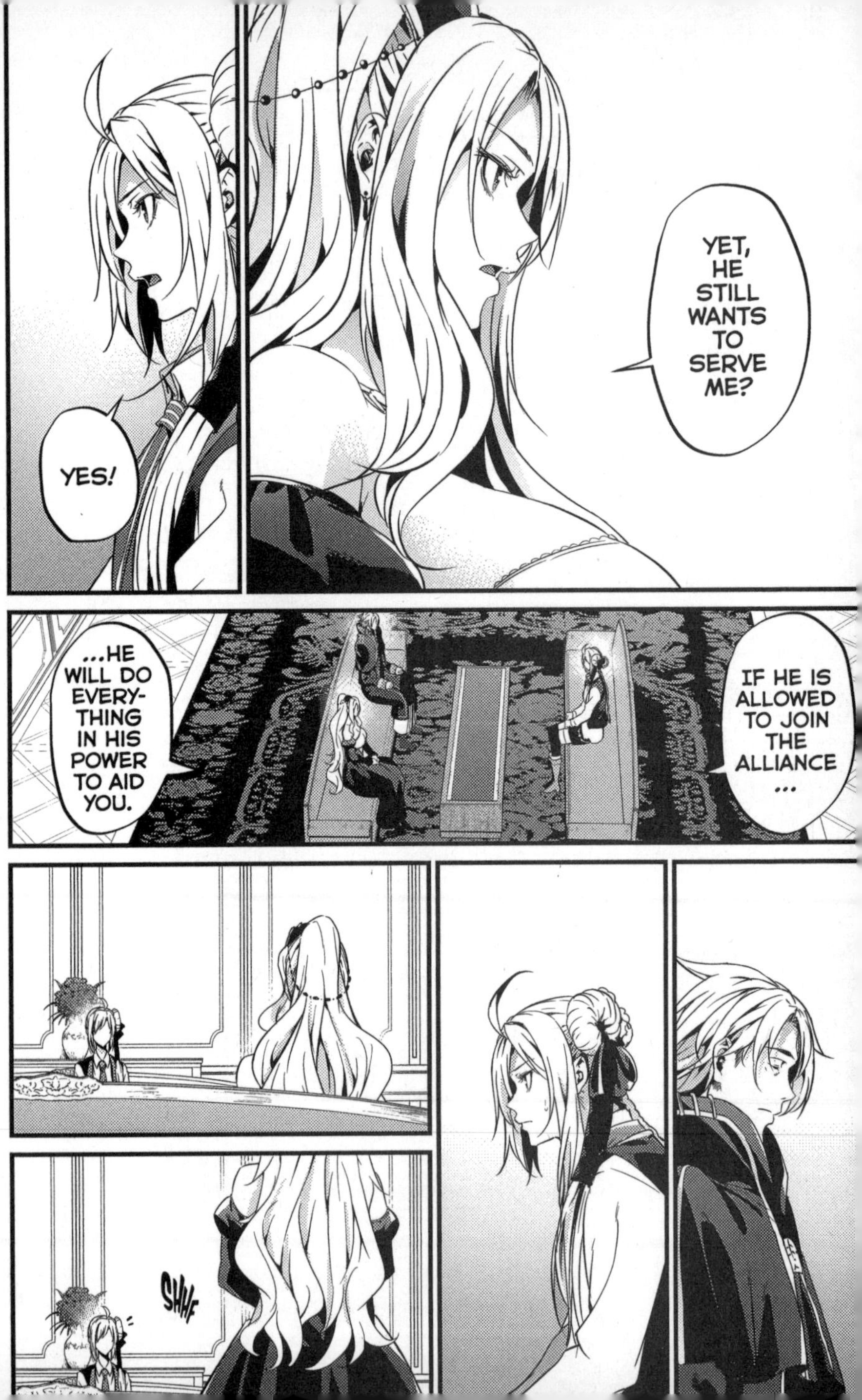
YET, HE STILL WANTS TO SERVE ME?
YES!
IF HE IS ALLOWED TO JOIN THE ALLIANCE...
...HE WILL DO EVERY-THING IN HIS POWER TO AID YOU.
SHHF

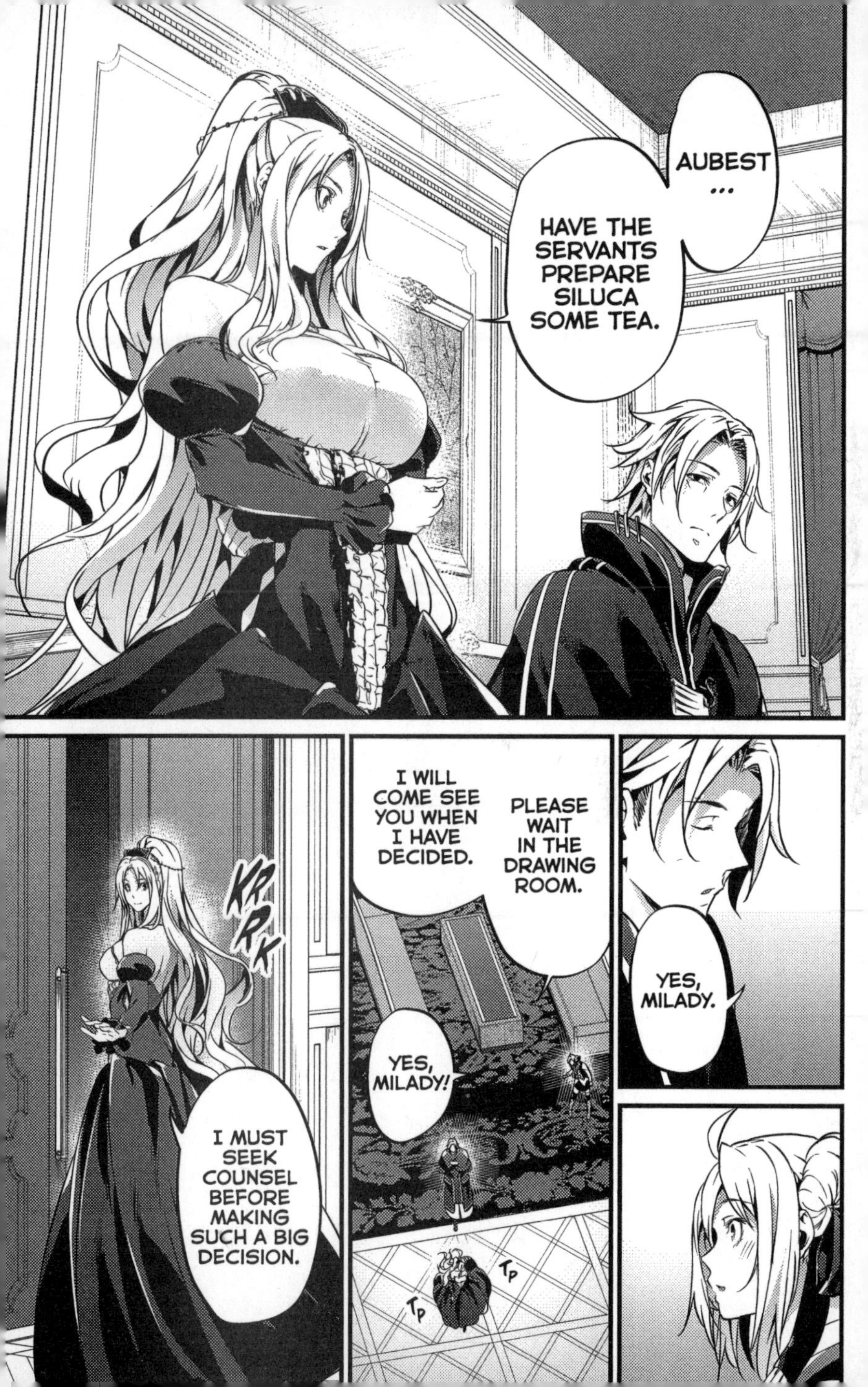
AUBEST ...
HAVE THE SERVANTS PREPARE SILUCA SOME TEA.
YES, MILADY.
PLEASE WAIT IN THE DRAWING ROOM.
I WILL COME SEE YOU WHEN I HAVE DECIDED.
YES, MILADY!
TP
TP
KRRK
I MUST SEEK COUNSEL BEFORE MAKING SUCH A BIG DECISION.

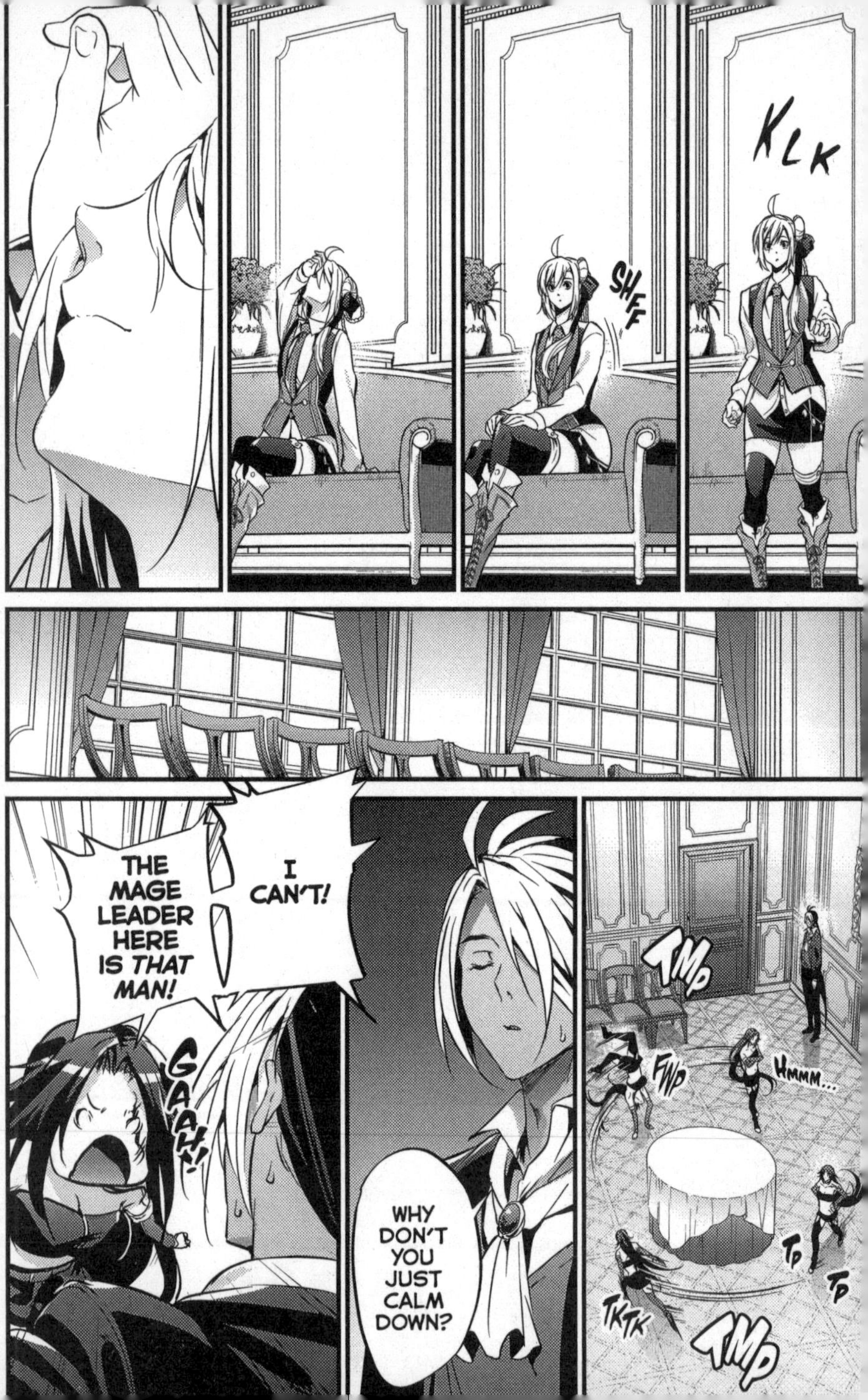
KLK
SHFF
TMP
HMMM...
FWP
TP
TP
TKTK
TMP
WHY DON'T YOU JUST CALM DOWN?
I CAN'T!
THE MAGE LEADER HERE IS *THAT* MAN!
GAAAH!

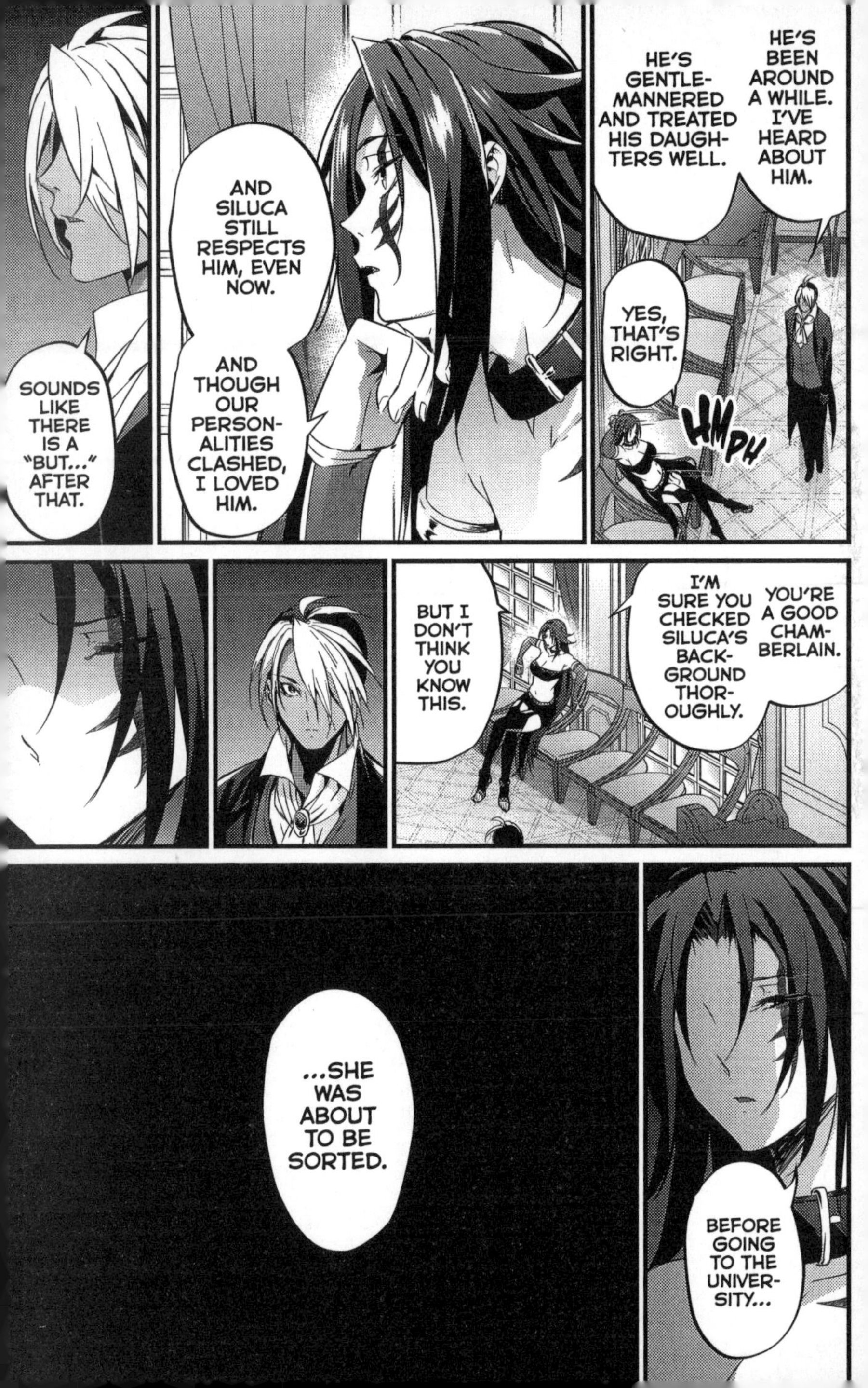
HE'S BEEN AROUND A WHILE. I'VE HEARD ABOUT HIM.
HE'S GENTLE-MANNERED AND TREATED HIS DAUGHTERS WELL.
YES, THAT'S RIGHT.
HMPH
AND SILUCA STILL RESPECTS HIM, EVEN NOW.
AND THOUGH OUR PERSONALITIES CLASHED, I LOVED HIM.
SOUNDS LIKE THERE IS A "BUT..." AFTER THAT.
YOU'RE A GOOD CHAMBERLAIN.
I'M SURE YOU CHECKED SILUCA'S BACKGROUND THOROUGHLY.
BUT I DON'T THINK YOU KNOW THIS.
BEFORE GOING TO THE UNIVERSITY...
...SHE WAS ABOUT TO BE SORTED.

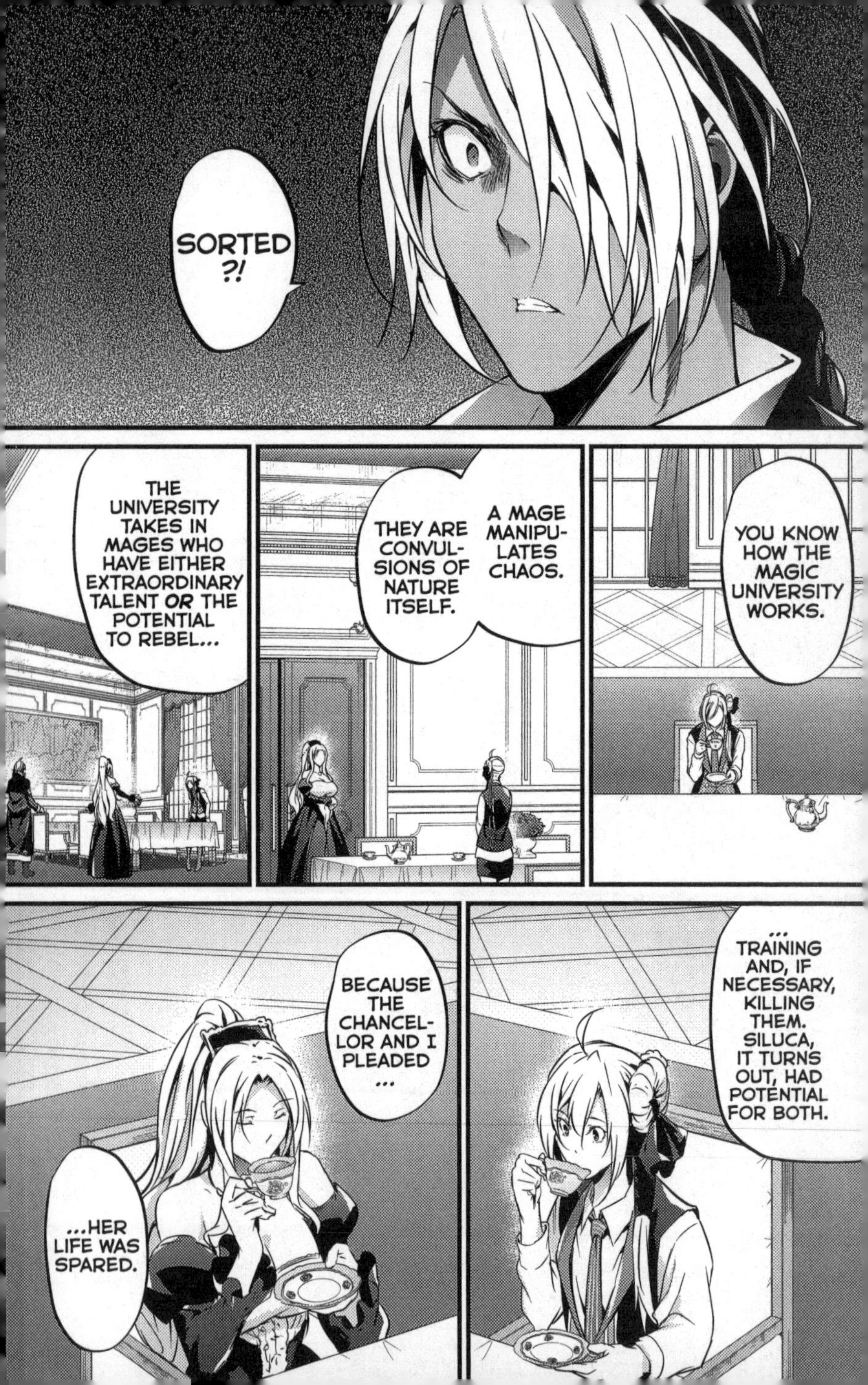
SORTED ?!
YOU KNOW HOW THE MAGIC UNIVERSITY WORKS.
A MAGE MANIPULATES CHAOS.
THEY ARE CONVULSIONS OF NATURE ITSELF.
THE UNIVERSITY TAKES IN MAGES WHO HAVE EITHER EXTRAORDINARY TALENT *OR* THE POTENTIAL TO REBEL...
...TRAINING AND, IF NECESSARY, KILLING THEM. SILUCA, IT TURNS OUT, HAD POTENTIAL FOR BOTH.
BECAUSE THE CHANCELLOR AND I PLEADED...
...HER LIFE WAS SPARED.

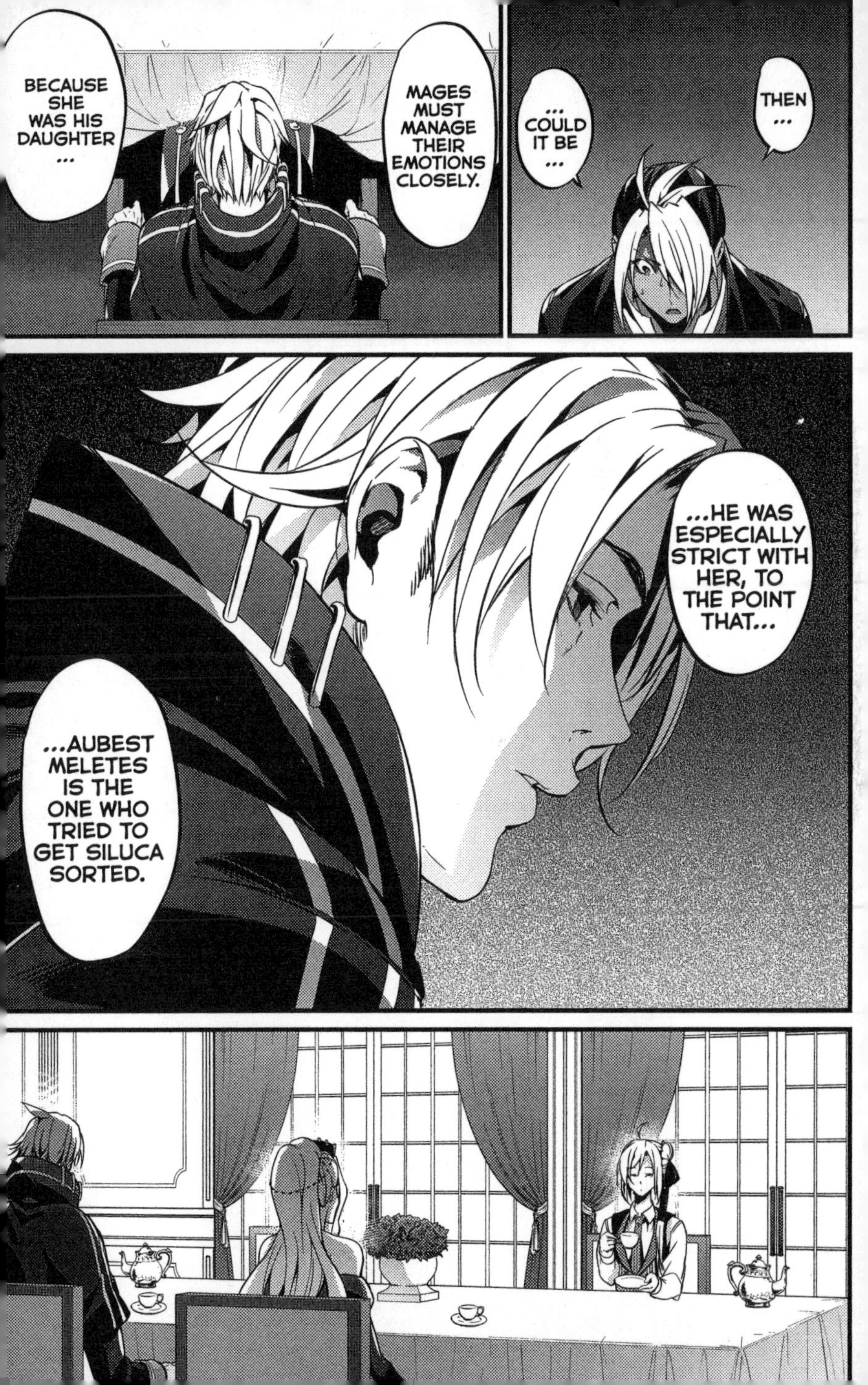
THEN ...
... COULD IT BE ...
MAGES MUST MANAGE THEIR EMOTIONS CLOSELY.
BECAUSE SHE WAS HIS DAUGHTER ...
...HE WAS ESPECIALLY STRICT WITH HER, TO THE POINT THAT...
...AUBEST MELETES IS THE ONE WHO TRIED TO GET SILUCA SORTED.

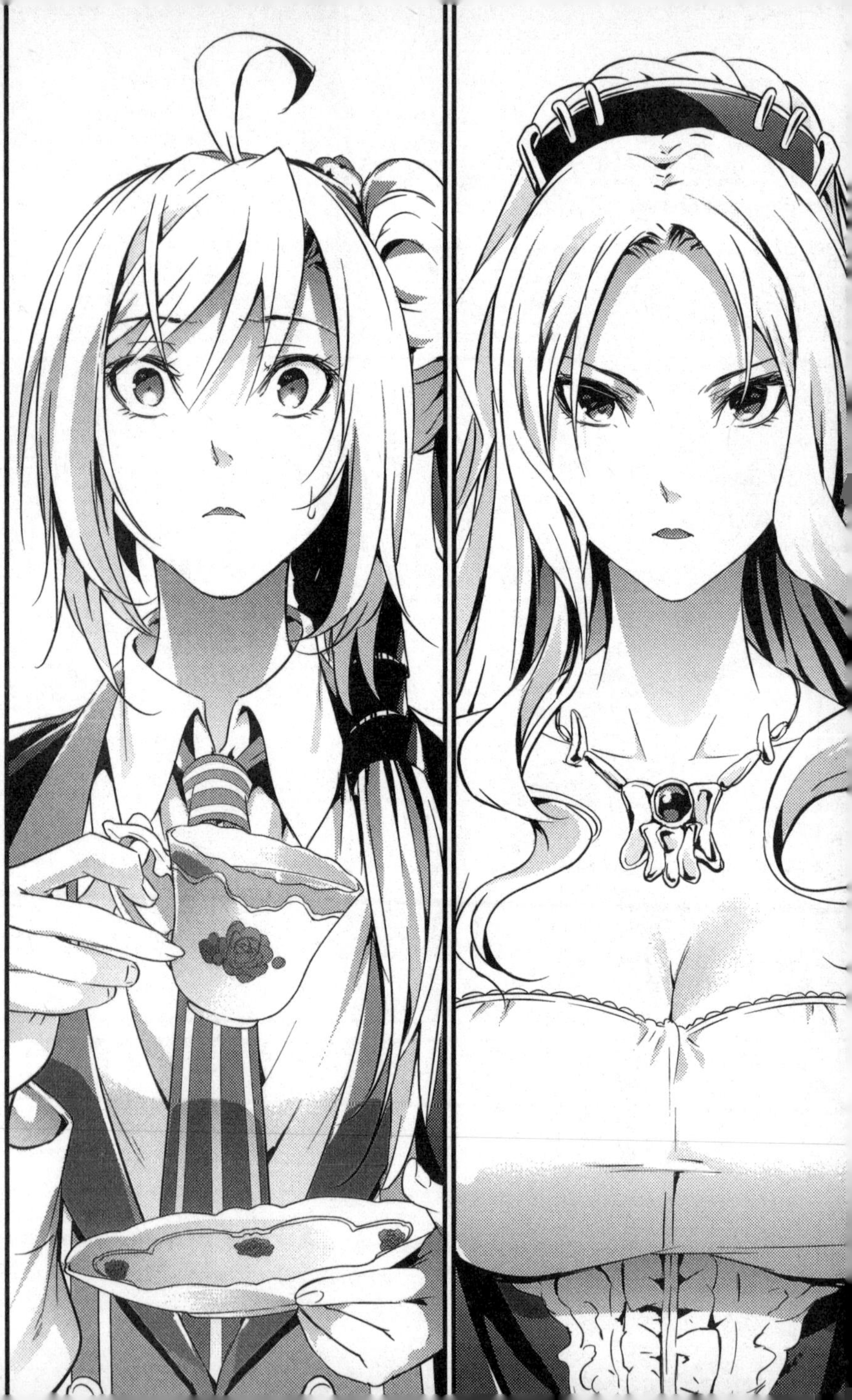

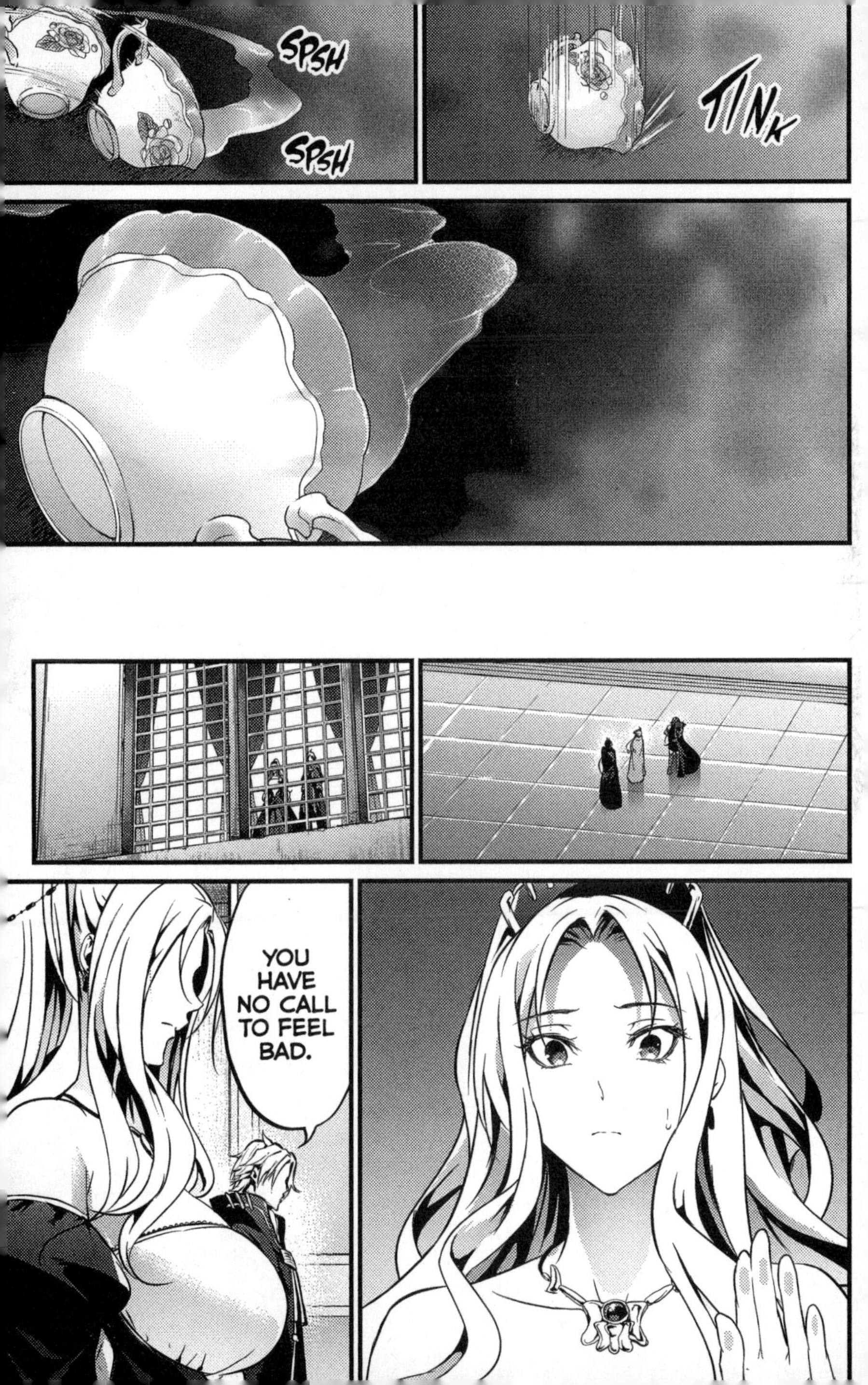
TINK
SPSH
SPSH
YOU HAVE NO CALL TO FEEL BAD.

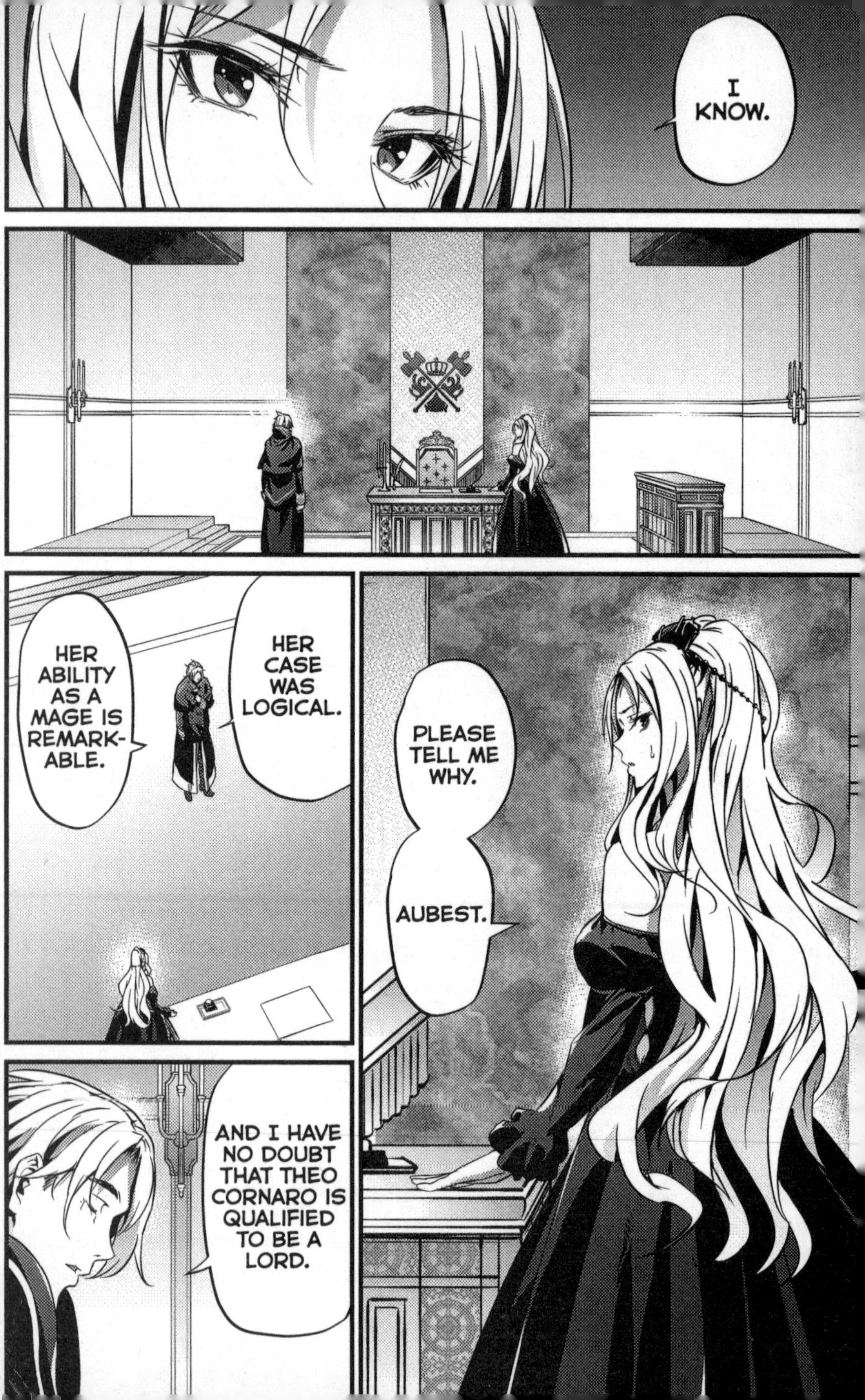
I KNOW.
PLEASE TELL ME WHY.
AUBEST.
HER CASE WAS LOGICAL.
HER ABILITY AS A MAGE IS REMARKABLE.
AND I HAVE NO DOUBT THAT THEO CORNARO IS QUALIFIED TO BE A LORD.

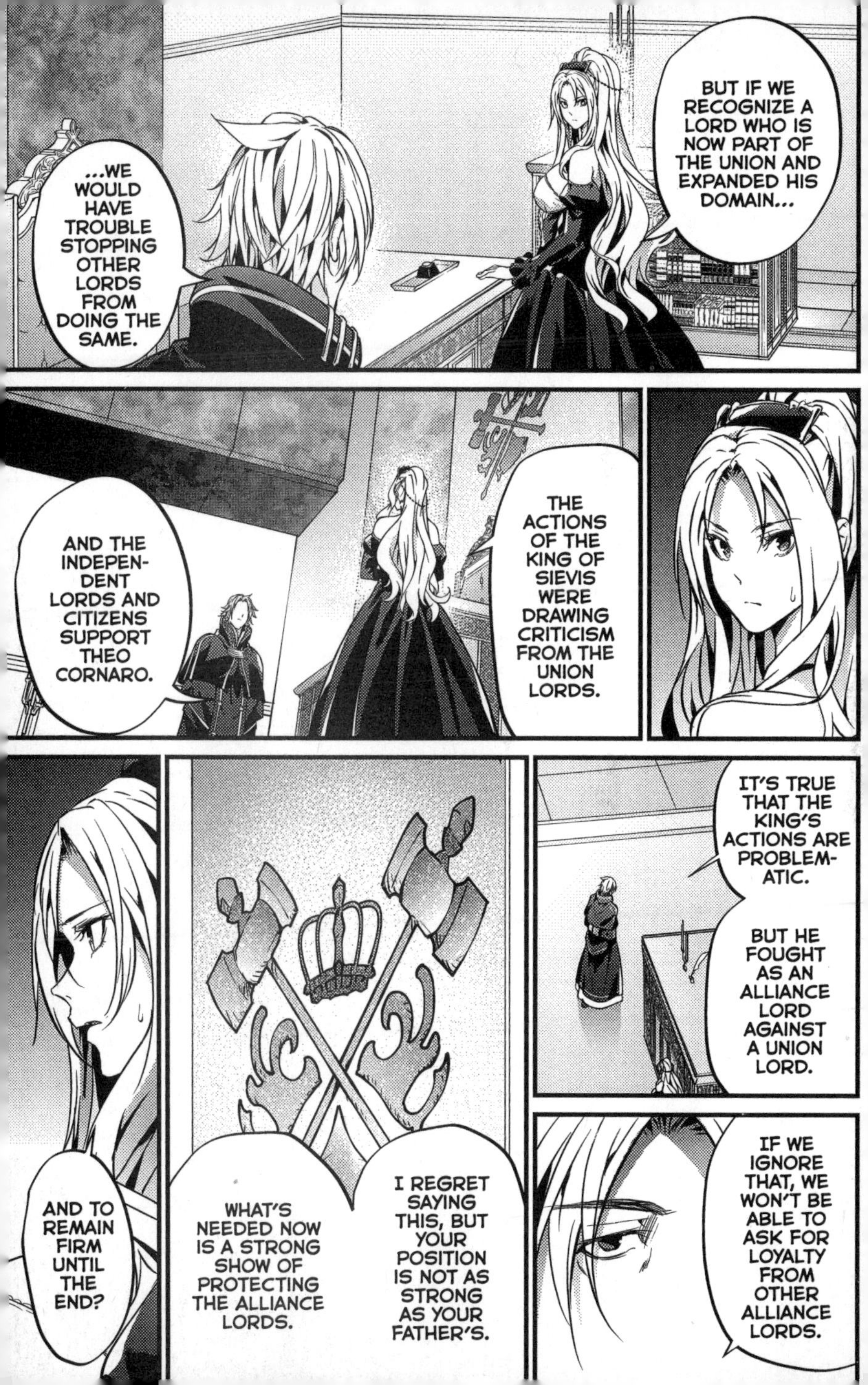
BUT IF WE RECOGNIZE A LORD WHO IS NOW PART OF THE UNION AND EXPANDED HIS DOMAIN...
...WE WOULD HAVE TROUBLE STOPPING OTHER LORDS FROM DOING THE SAME.
THE ACTIONS OF THE KING OF SIEVIS WERE DRAWING CRITICISM FROM THE UNION LORDS.
AND THE INDEPEN-DENT LORDS AND CITIZENS SUPPORT THEO CORNARO.
IT'S TRUE THAT THE KING'S ACTIONS ARE PROBLEM-ATIC.
BUT HE FOUGHT AS AN ALLIANCE LORD AGAINST A UNION LORD.
IF WE IGNORE THAT, WE WON'T BE ABLE TO ASK FOR LOYALTY FROM OTHER ALLIANCE LORDS.
I REGRET SAYING THIS, BUT YOUR POSITION IS NOT AS STRONG AS YOUR FATHER'S.
WHAT'S NEEDED NOW IS A STRONG SHOW OF PROTECTING THE ALLIANCE LORDS.
AND TO REMAIN FIRM UNTIL THE END?

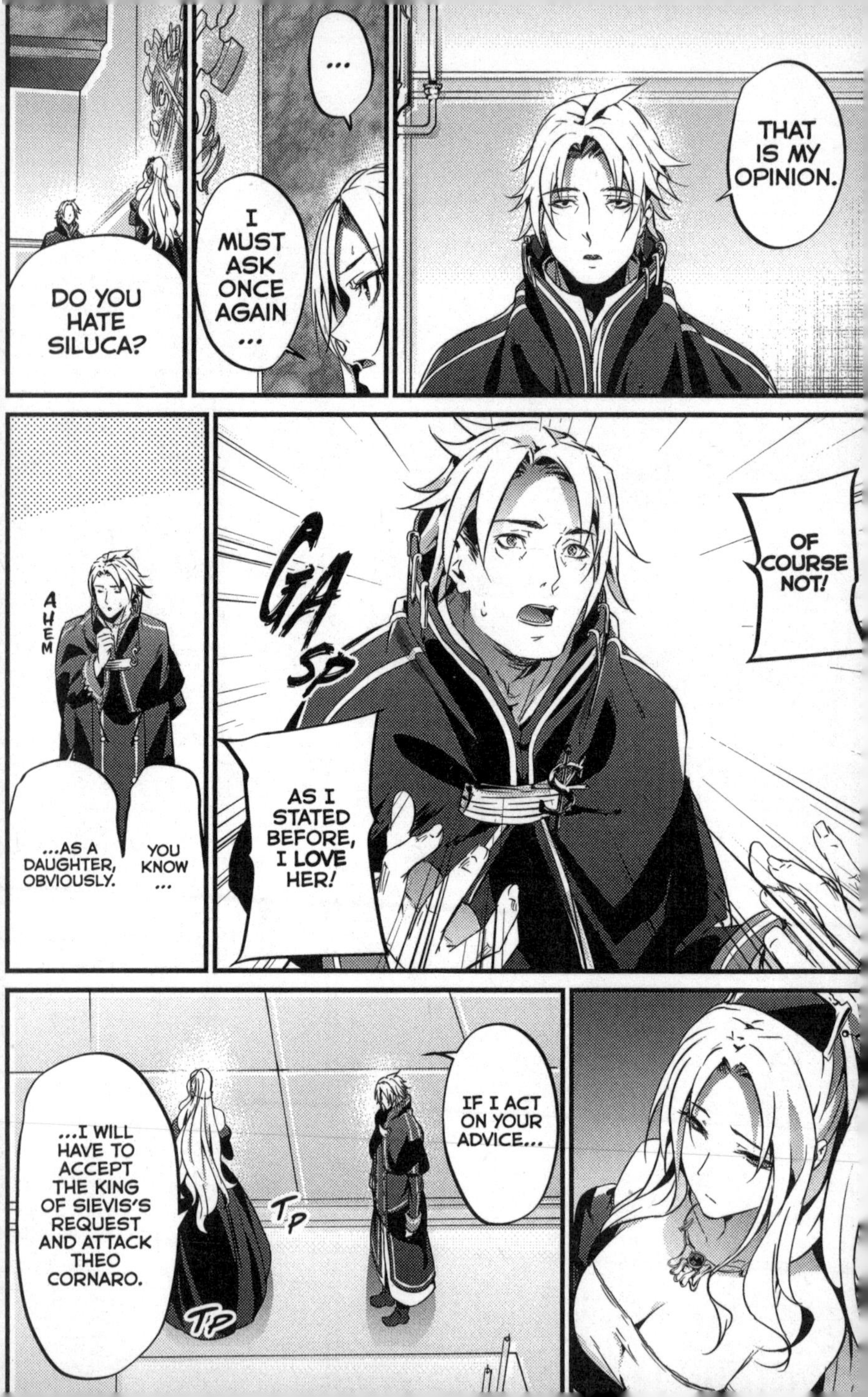
THAT IS MY OPINION.
...
I MUST ASK ONCE AGAIN...
DO YOU HATE SILUCA?
OF COURSE NOT!
GASP
AS I STATED BEFORE, I LOVE HER!
AHEM
YOU KNOW...
...AS A DAUGHTER, OBVIOUSLY.
IF I ACT ON YOUR ADVICE...
TP
...I WILL HAVE TO ACCEPT THE KING OF SIEVIS'S REQUEST AND ATTACK THEO CORNARO.
TP

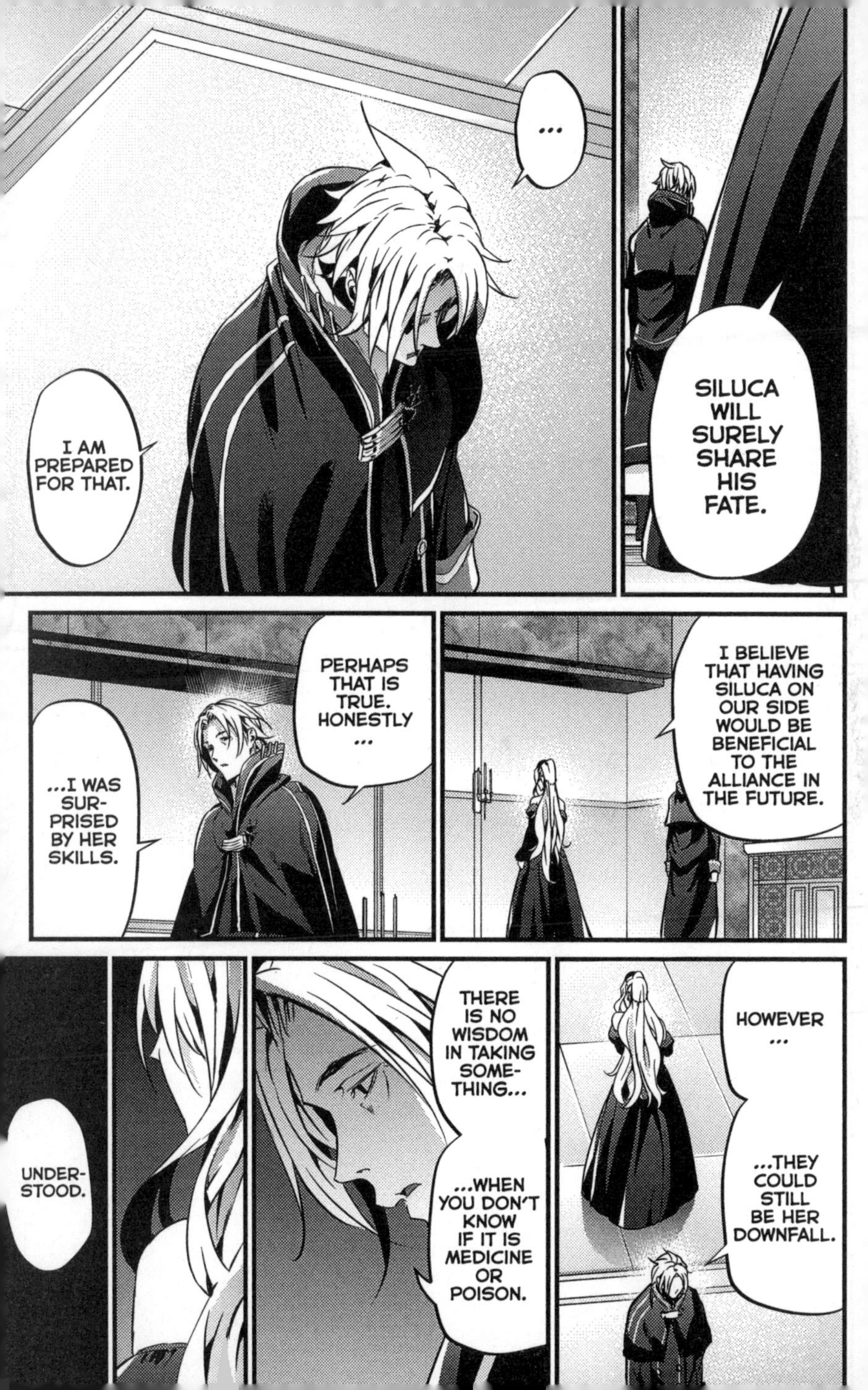
SILUCA WILL SURELY SHARE HIS FATE.
...
I AM PREPARED FOR THAT.
I BELIEVE THAT HAVING SILUCA ON OUR SIDE WOULD BE BENEFICIAL TO THE ALLIANCE IN THE FUTURE.
PERHAPS THAT IS TRUE. HONESTLY...
...I WAS SURPRISED BY HER SKILLS.
HOWEVER...
...THEY COULD STILL BE HER DOWNFALL.
THERE IS NO WISDOM IN TAKING SOMETHING...
...WHEN YOU DON'T KNOW IF IT IS MEDICINE OR POISON.
UNDERSTOOD.

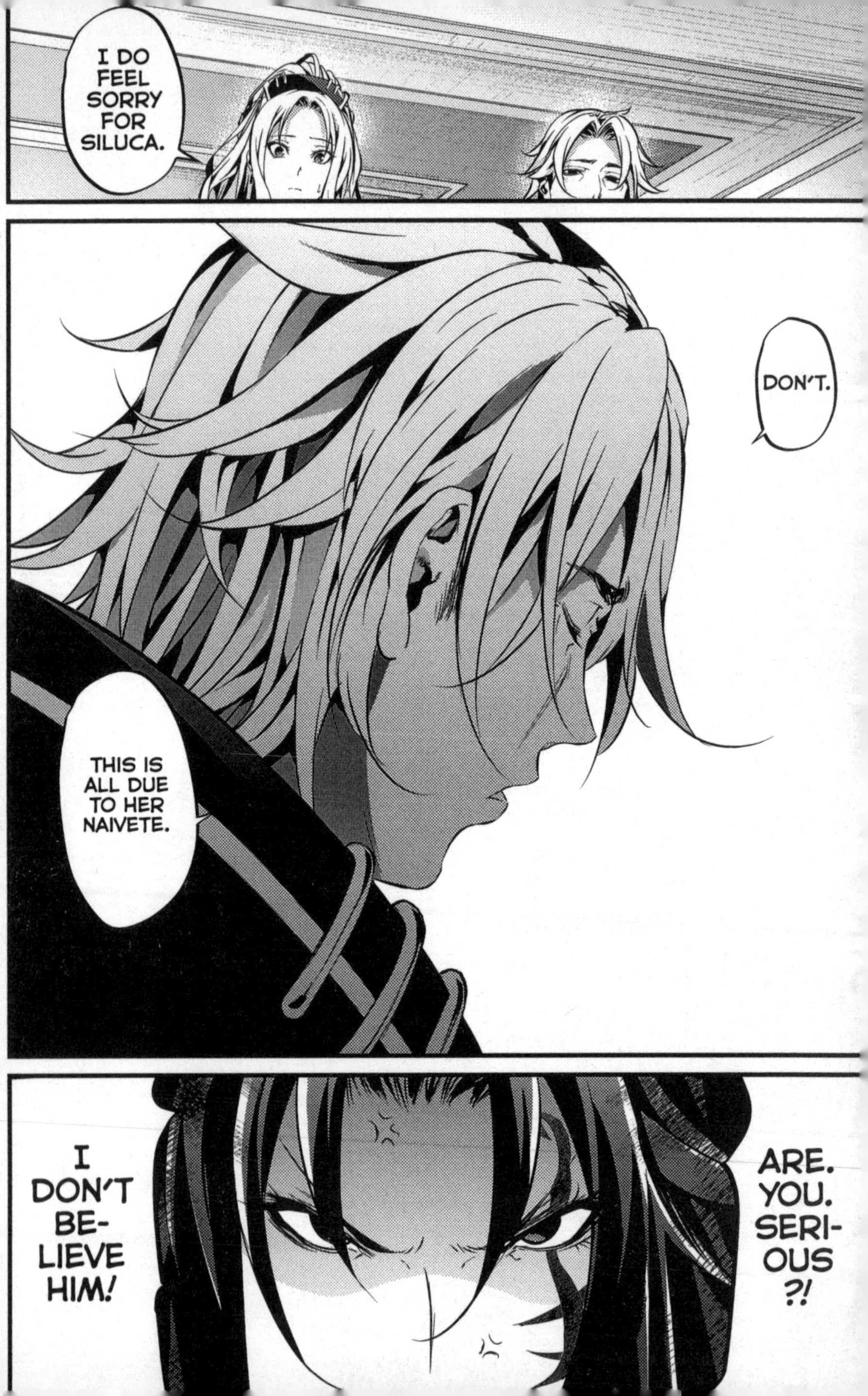
I DO FEEL SORRY FOR SILUCA.
DON'T.
THIS IS ALL DUE TO HER NAIVETE.
ARE. YOU. SERI-OUS ?!
I DON'T BE-LIEVE HIM!

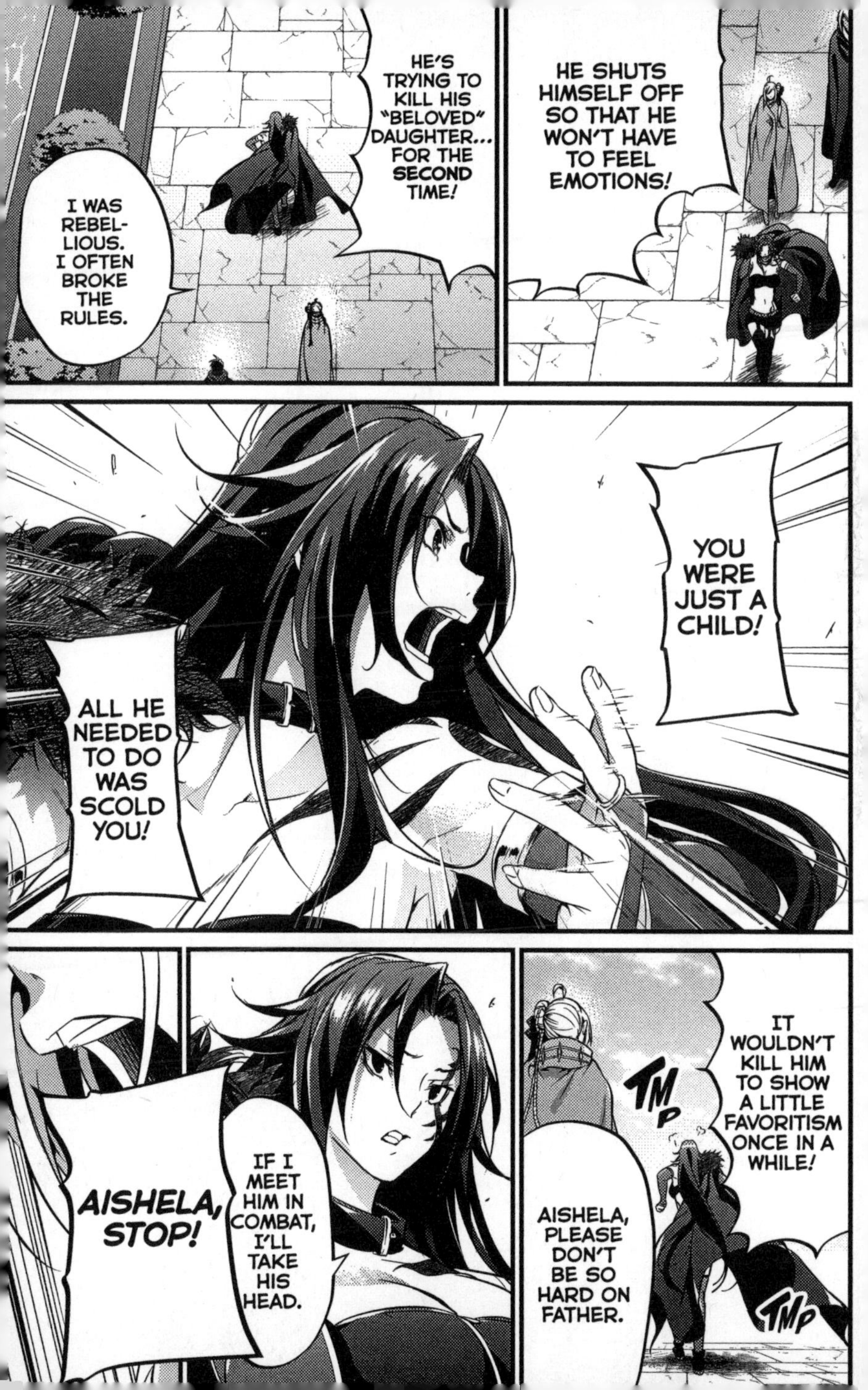
HE SHUTS HIMSELF OFF SO THAT HE WON'T HAVE TO FEEL EMOTIONS!
HE'S TRYING TO KILL HIS "BELOVED" DAUGHTER... FOR THE SECOND TIME!
I WAS REBEL-LIOUS. I OFTEN BROKE THE RULES.
YOU WERE JUST A CHILD!
ALL HE NEEDED TO DO WAS SCOLD YOU!
IT WOULDN'T KILL HIM TO SHOW A LITTLE FAVORITISM ONCE IN A WHILE!
TMP
AISHELA, PLEASE DON'T BE SO HARD ON FATHER.
TMP
IF I MEET HIM IN COMBAT, I'LL TAKE HIS HEAD.
AISHELA, STOP!

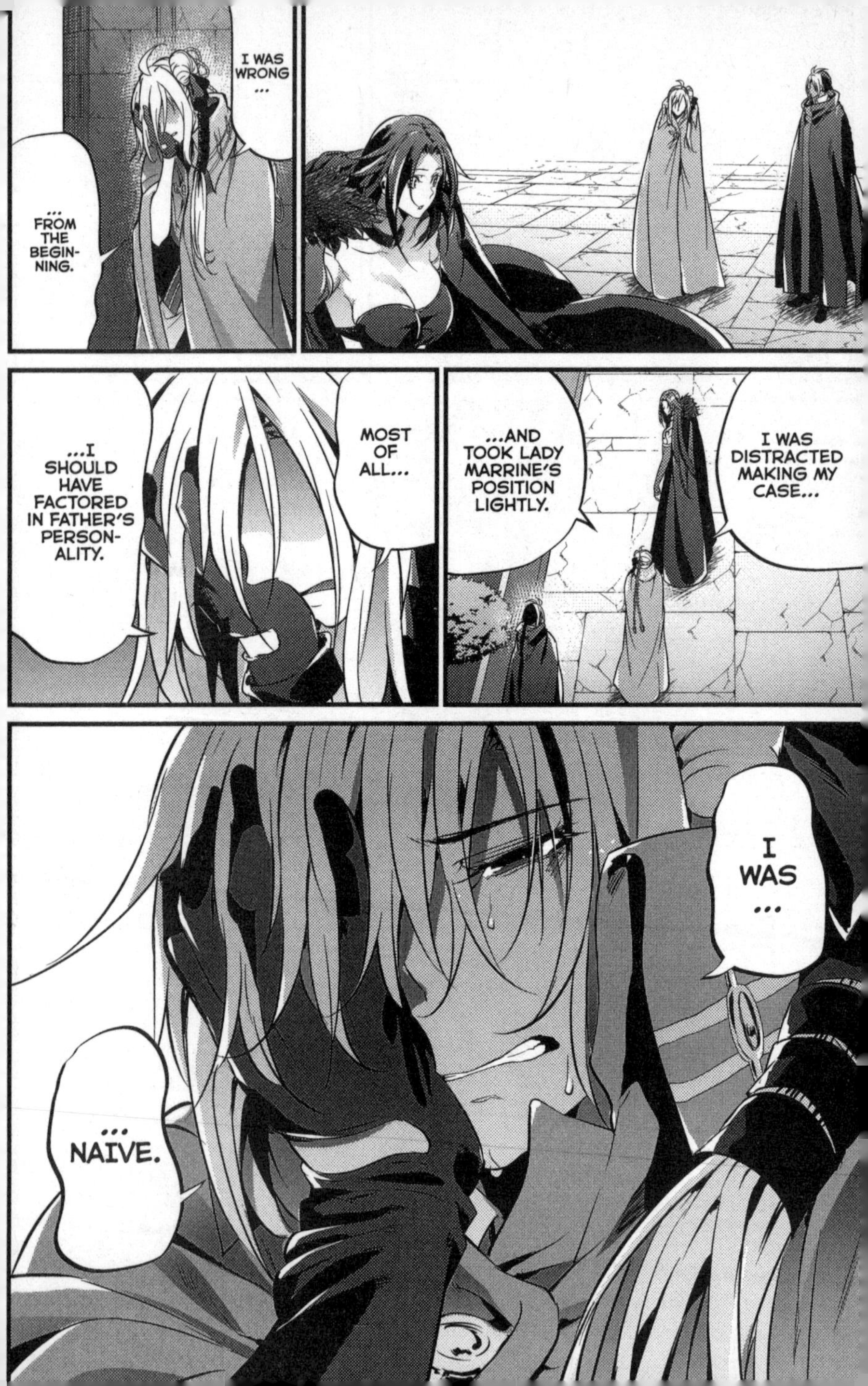
I WAS WRONG ...
... FROM THE BEGIN-NING.
I WAS DISTRACTED MAKING MY CASE...
...AND TOOK LADY MARRINE'S POSITION LIGHTLY.
MOST OF ALL...
...I SHOULD HAVE FACTORED IN FATHER'S PERSON-ALITY.
I WAS ...
... NAIVE.

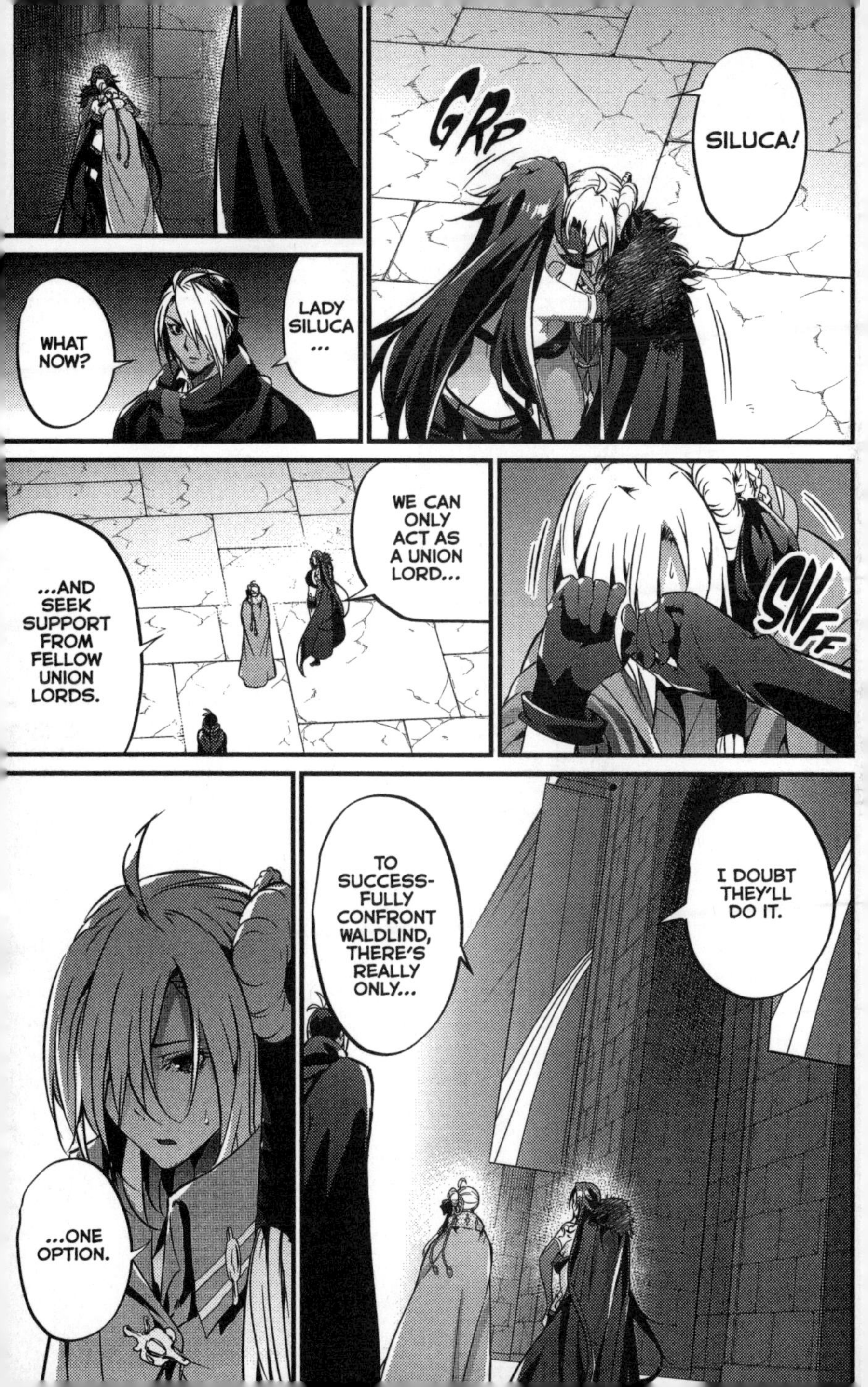
GRP
SILUCA!
LADY SILUCA...
WHAT NOW?
SNFF
WE CAN ONLY ACT AS A UNION LORD...
...AND SEEK SUPPORT FROM FELLOW UNION LORDS.
I DOUBT THEY'LL DO IT.
TO SUCCESS-FULLY CONFRONT WALDLIND, THERE'S REALLY ONLY...
...ONE OPTION.

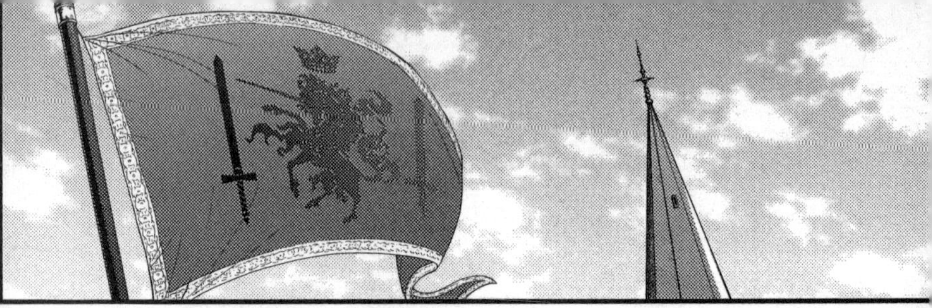
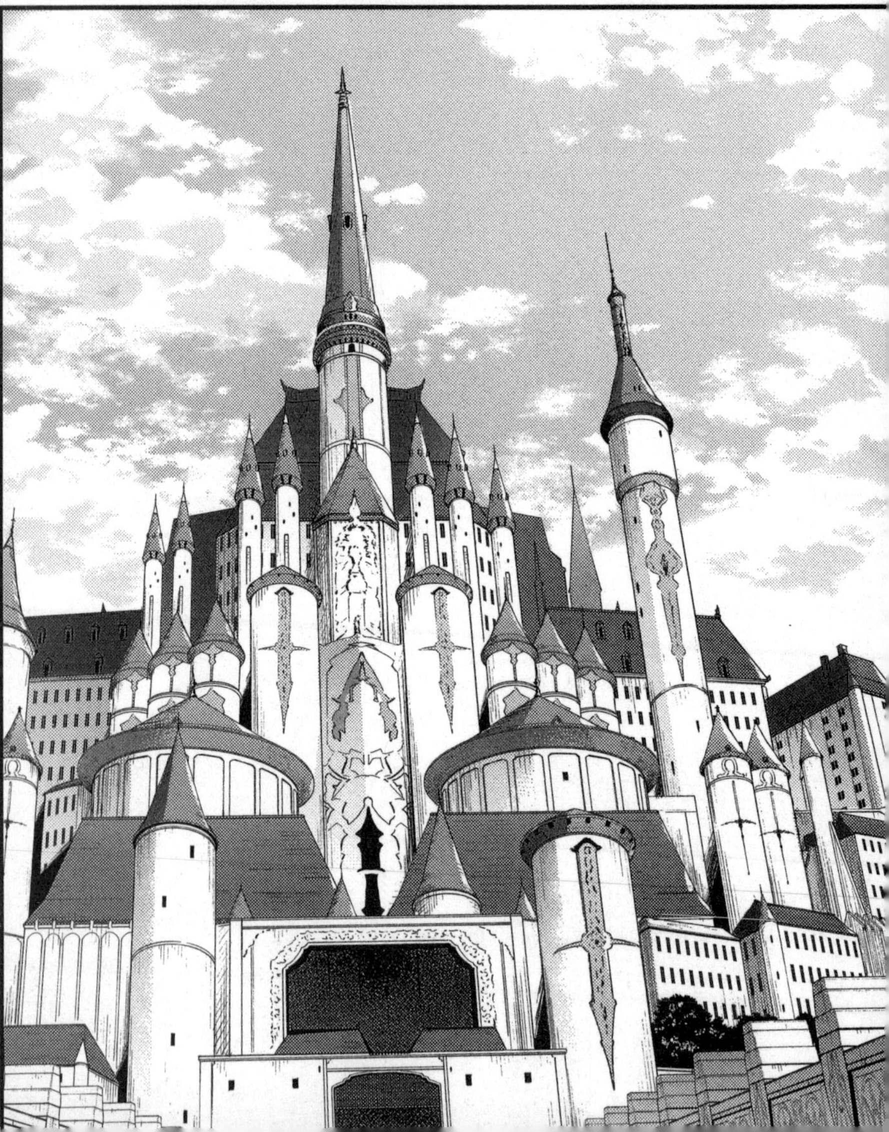

RECORD OF
GRANCREST WAR

RECORD OF
GRANCREST
WAR

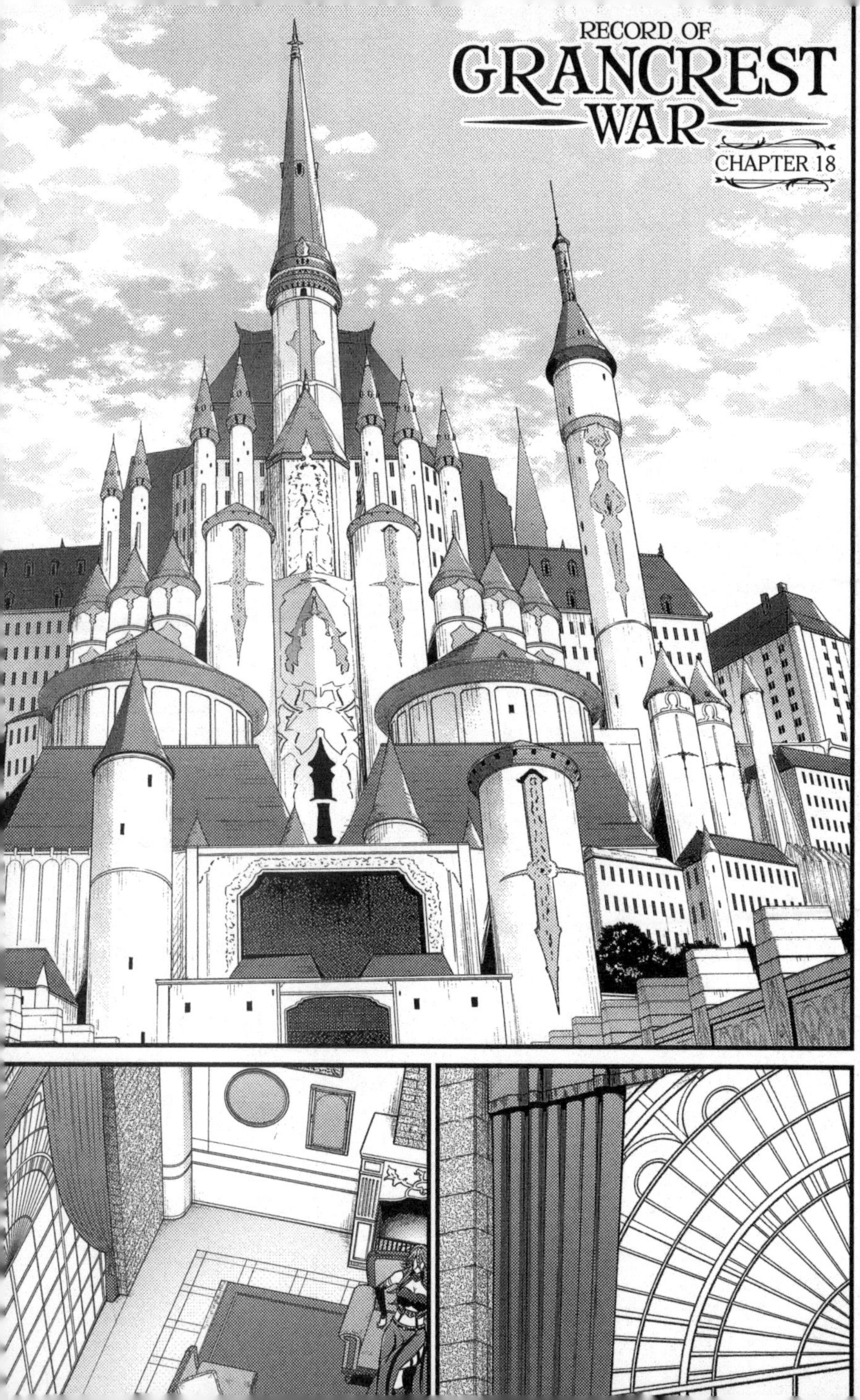
RECORD OF
GRANCREST
WAR
CHAPTER 18

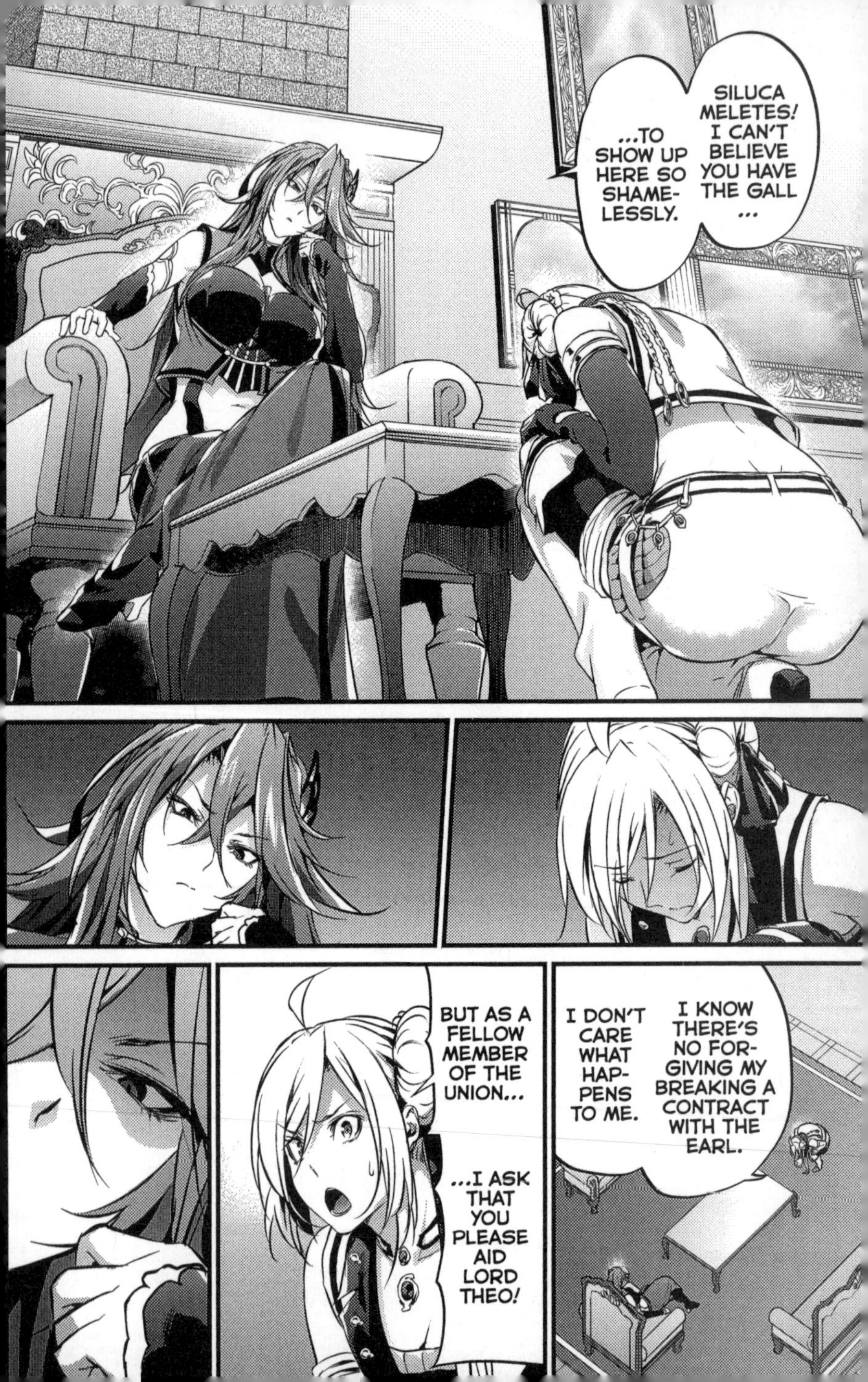
SILUCA MELETES! I CAN'T BELIEVE YOU HAVE THE GALL...
...TO SHOW UP HERE SO SHAMELESSLY.
I KNOW THERE'S NO FORGIVING MY BREAKING A CONTRACT WITH THE EARL.
I DON'T CARE WHAT HAPPENS TO ME.
BUT AS A FELLOW MEMBER OF THE UNION...
...I ASK THAT YOU PLEASE AID LORD THEO!

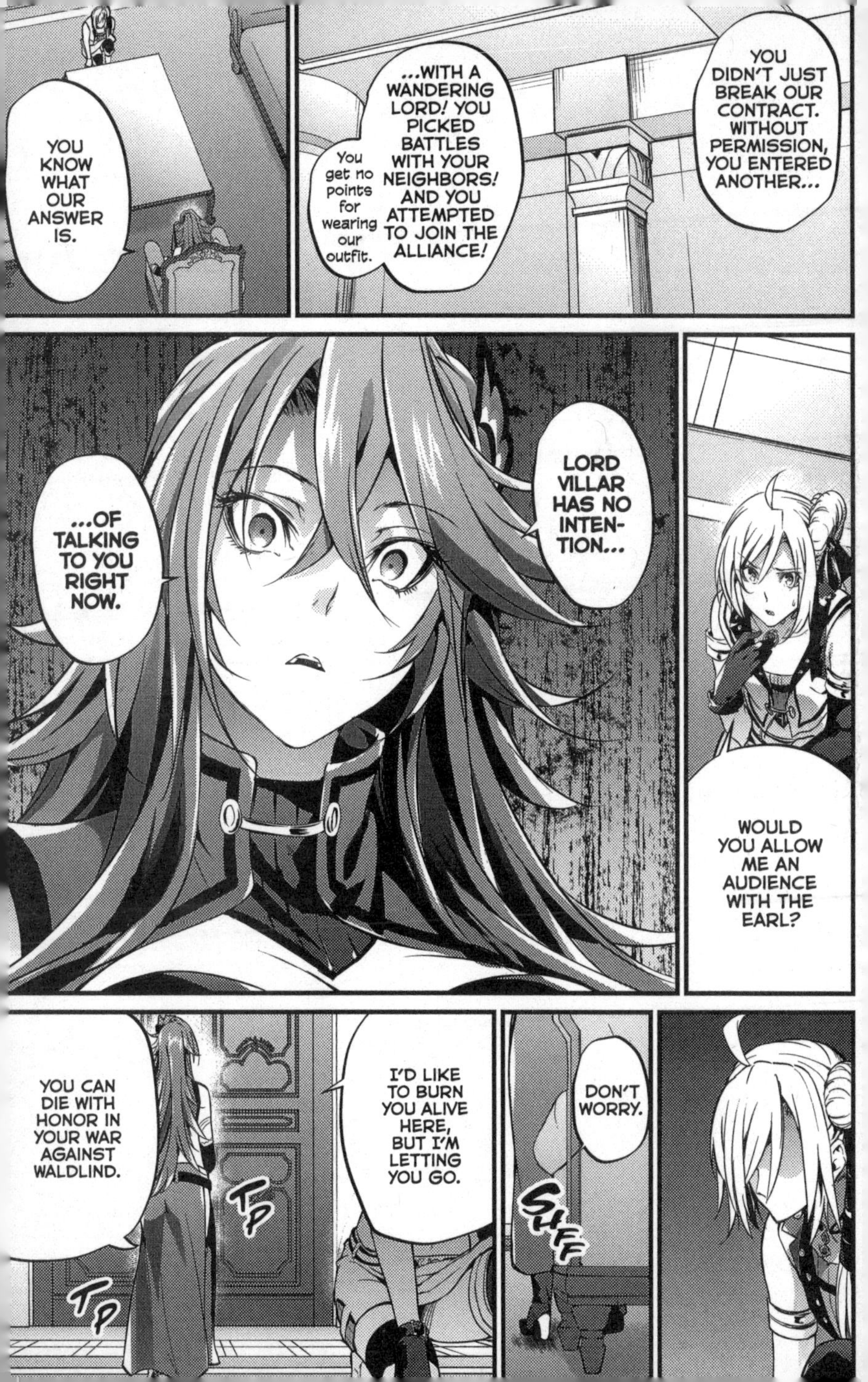
YOU DIDN'T JUST BREAK OUR CONTRACT. WITHOUT PERMISSION, YOU ENTERED ANOTHER...
...WITH A WANDERING LORD! YOU PICKED BATTLES WITH YOUR NEIGHBORS! AND YOU ATTEMPTED TO JOIN THE ALLIANCE!
You get no points for wearing our outfit.
YOU KNOW WHAT OUR ANSWER IS.
WOULD YOU ALLOW ME AN AUDIENCE WITH THE EARL?
LORD VILLAR HAS NO INTENTION...
...OF TALKING TO YOU RIGHT NOW.
DON'T WORRY.
SHFF
I'D LIKE TO BURN YOU ALIVE HERE, BUT I'M LETTING YOU GO.
TP
YOU CAN DIE WITH HONOR IN YOUR WAR AGAINST WALDLIND.
TP

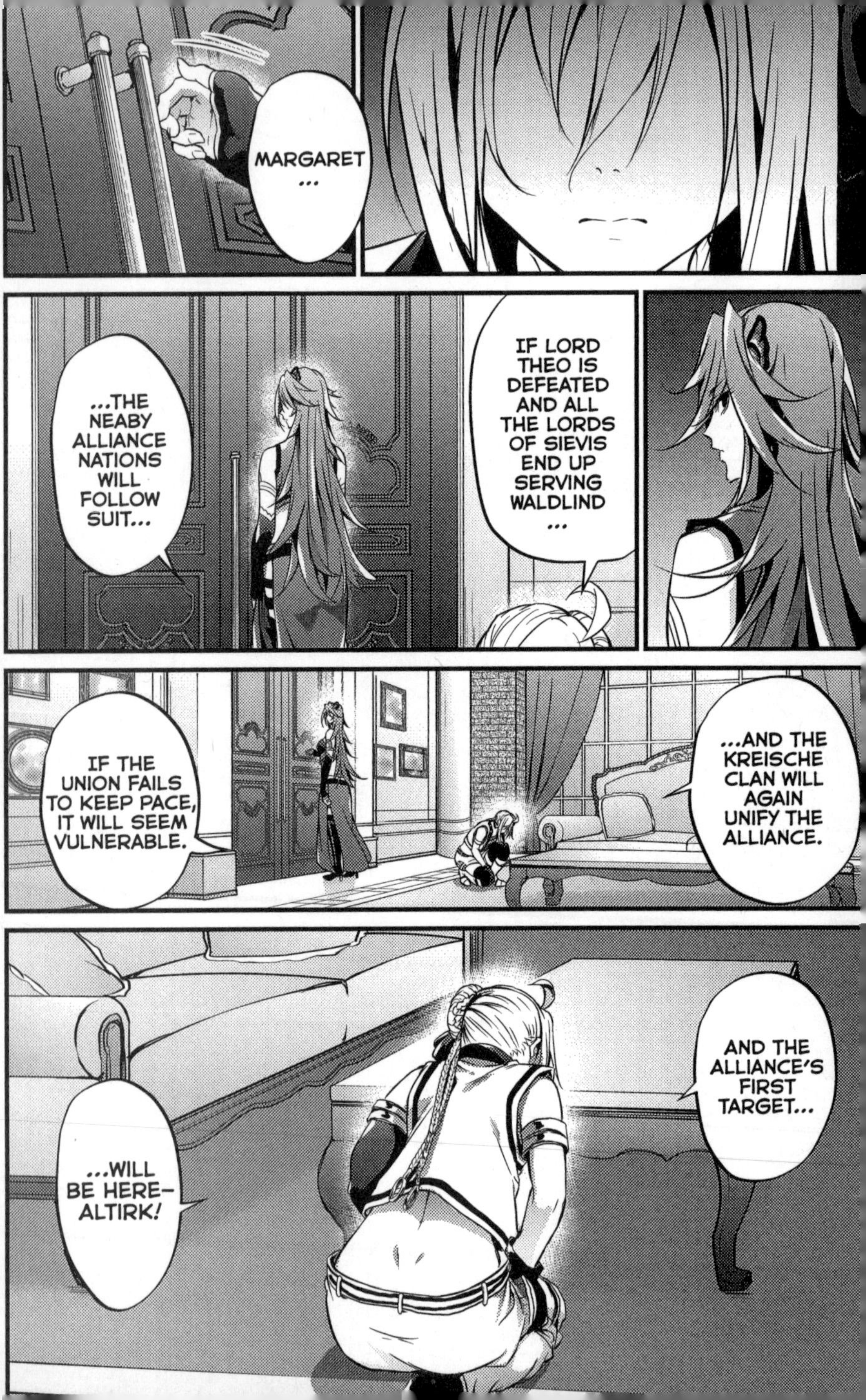
MARGARET ...
IF LORD THEO IS DEFEATED AND ALL THE LORDS OF SIEVIS END UP SERVING WALDLIND ...
...THE NEABY ALLIANCE NATIONS WILL FOLLOW SUIT...
...AND THE KREISCHE CLAN WILL AGAIN UNIFY THE ALLIANCE.
IF THE UNION FAILS TO KEEP PACE, IT WILL SEEM VULNERABLE.
AND THE ALLIANCE'S FIRST TARGET...
...WILL BE HERE—ALTIRK!

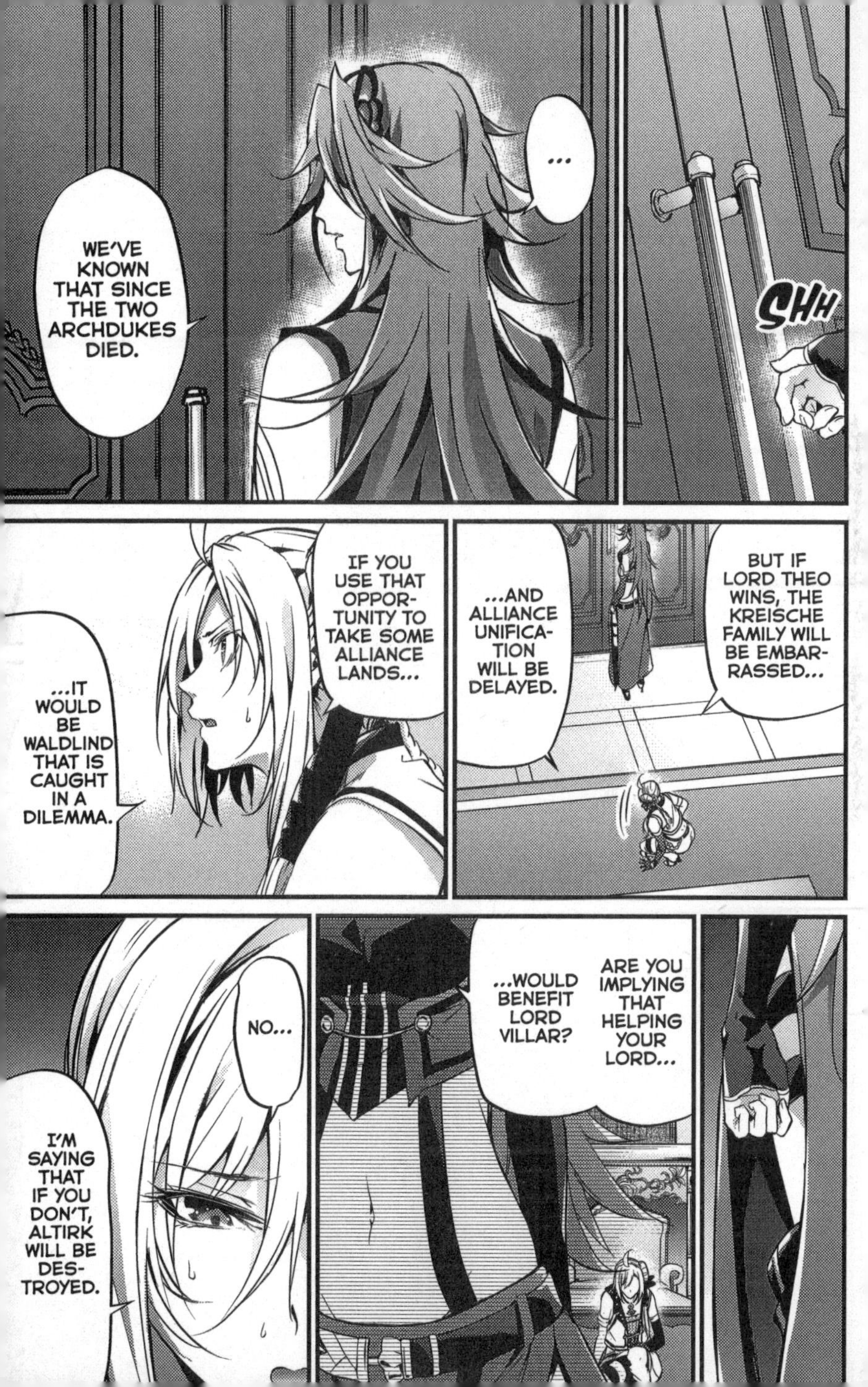
SHH
...
WE'VE KNOWN THAT SINCE THE TWO ARCHDUKES DIED.
BUT IF LORD THEO WINS, THE KREISCHE FAMILY WILL BE EMBARRASSED...
...AND ALLIANCE UNIFICATION WILL BE DELAYED.
IF YOU USE THAT OPPORTUNITY TO TAKE SOME ALLIANCE LANDS...
...IT WOULD BE WALDLIND THAT IS CAUGHT IN A DILEMMA.
ARE YOU IMPLYING THAT HELPING YOUR LORD...
...WOULD BENEFIT LORD VILLAR?
NO...
I'M SAYING THAT IF YOU DON'T, ALTIRK WILL BE DESTROYED.

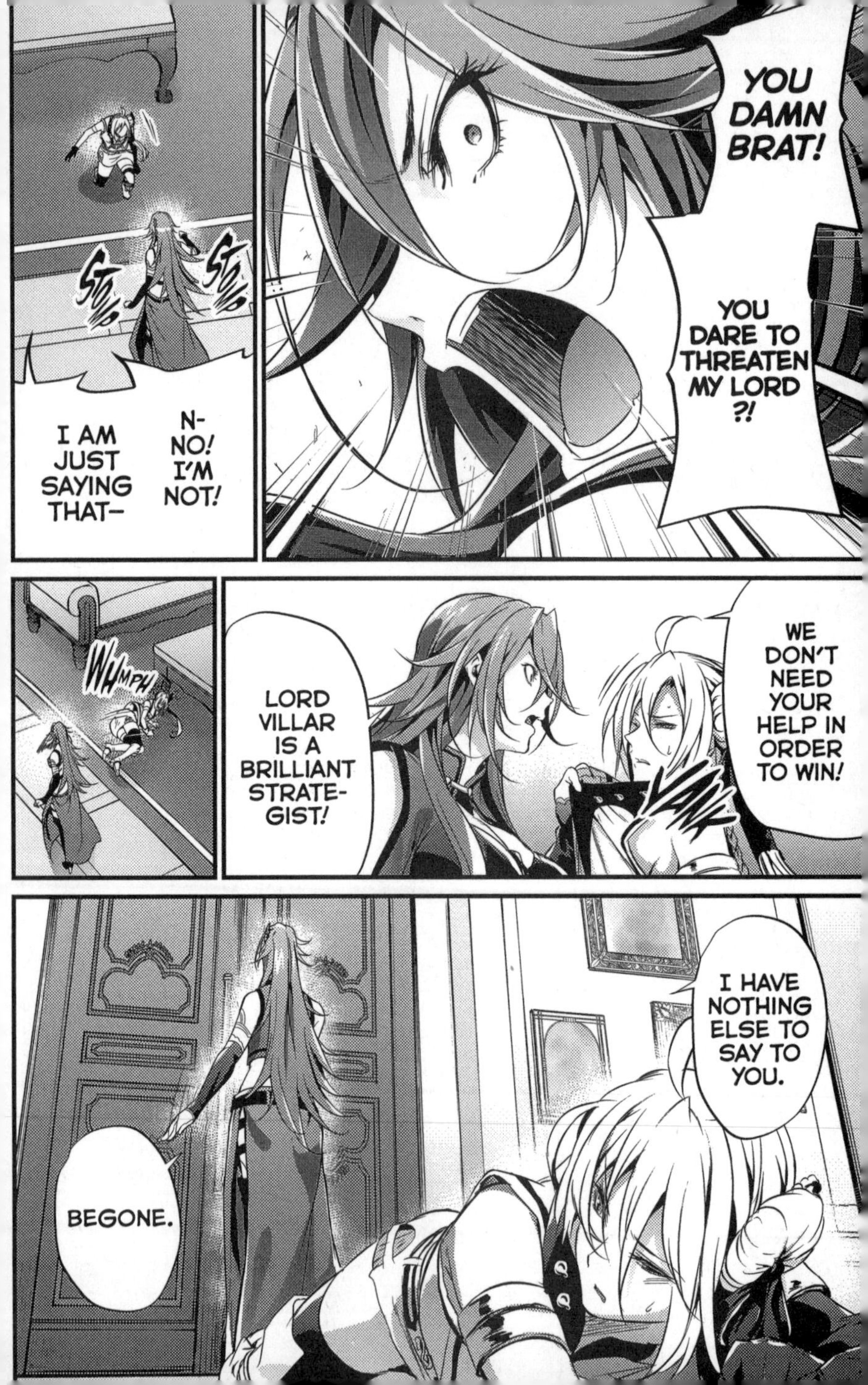
YOU DAMN BRAT!
YOU DARE TO THREATEN MY LORD ?!
STOMP
STOMP
N-NO! I'M NOT!
I AM JUST SAYING THAT—
WE DON'T NEED YOUR HELP IN ORDER TO WIN!
YANK
LORD VILLAR IS A BRILLIANT STRATE-GIST!
WHMPH
I HAVE NOTHING ELSE TO SAY TO YOU.
BEGONE.

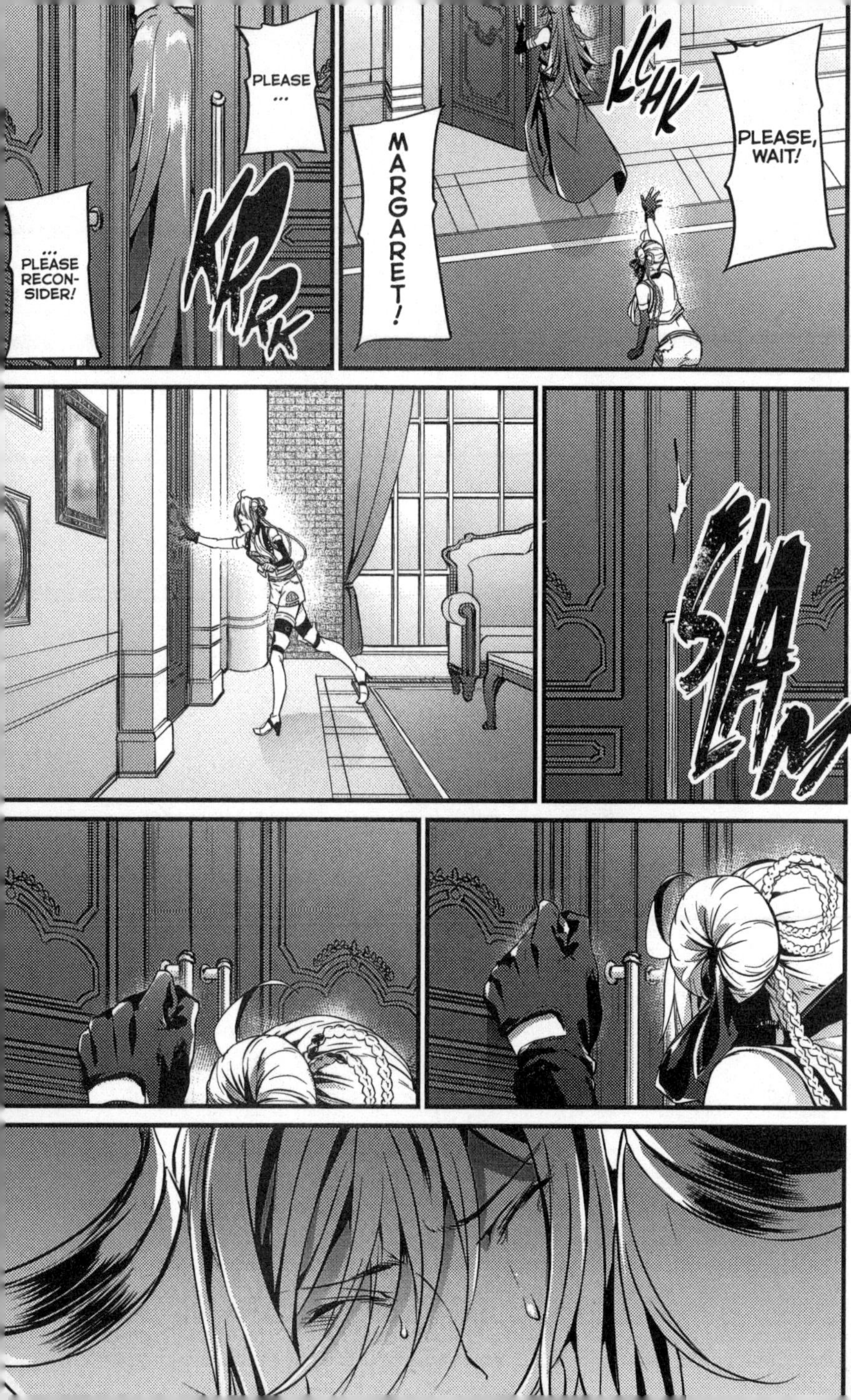
PLEASE, WAIT!
KCHK
MARGARET!
PLEASE ...
KRRK
... PLEASE RECONSIDER!
SLAM

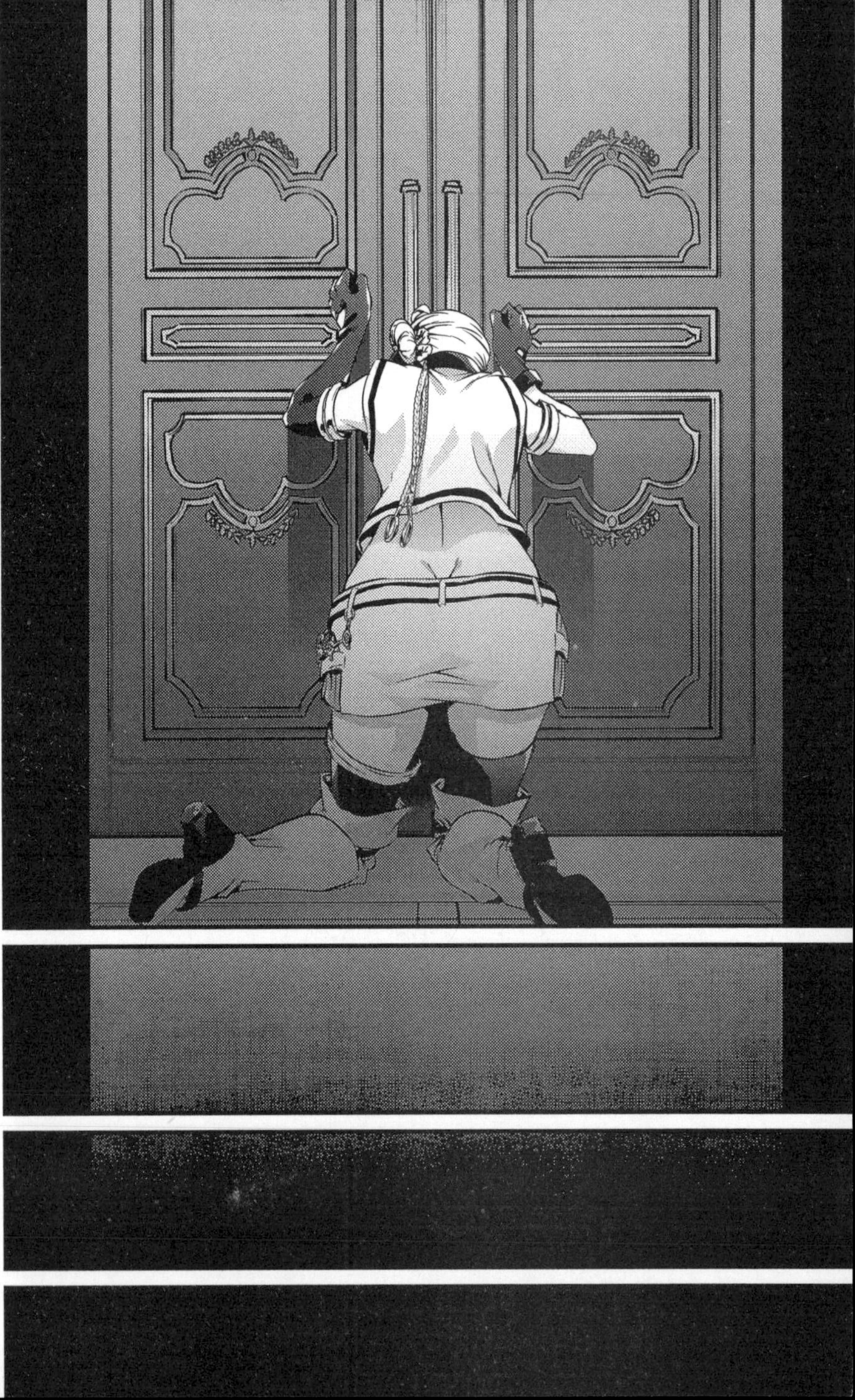

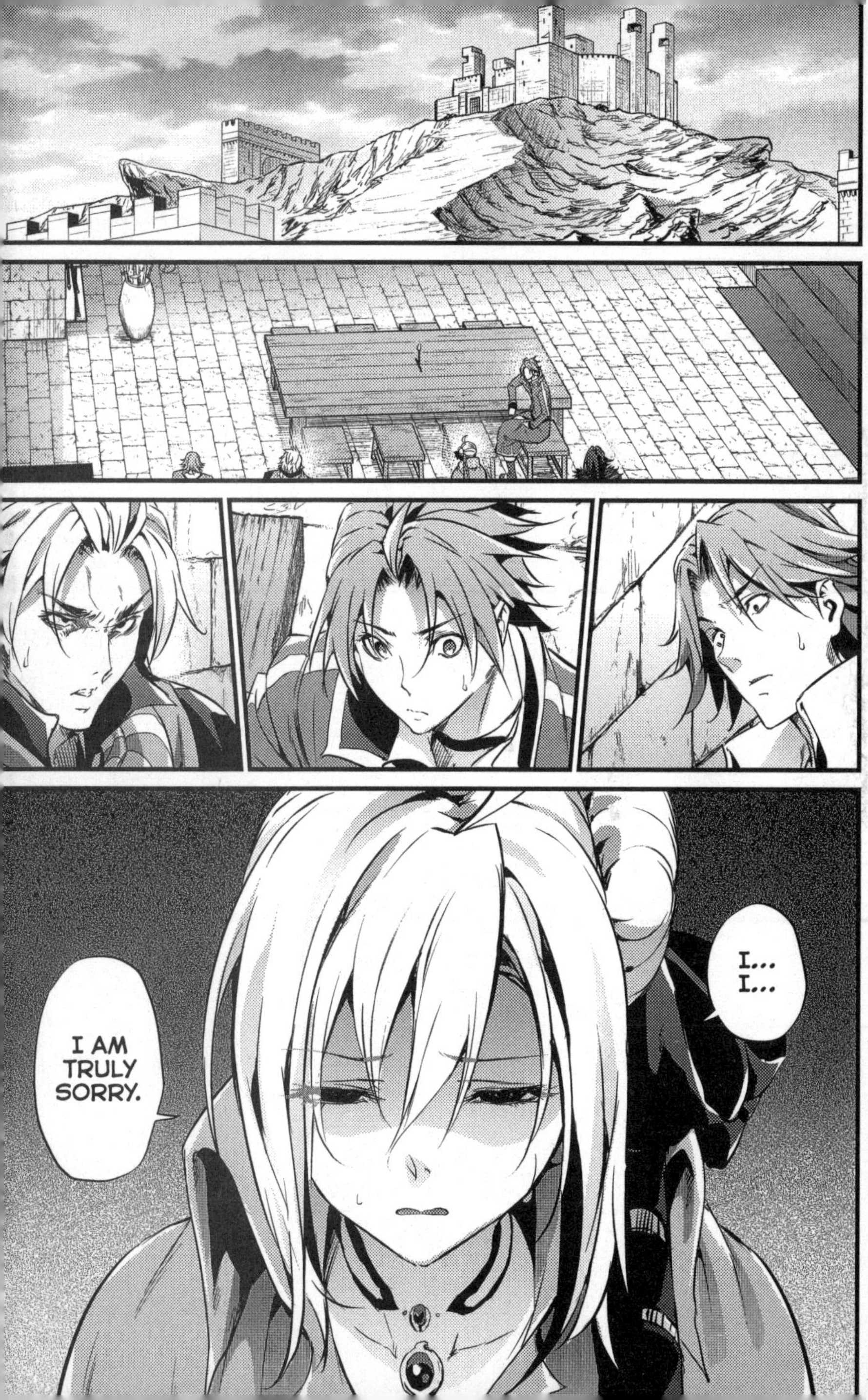
I... I...
I AM TRULY SORRY.

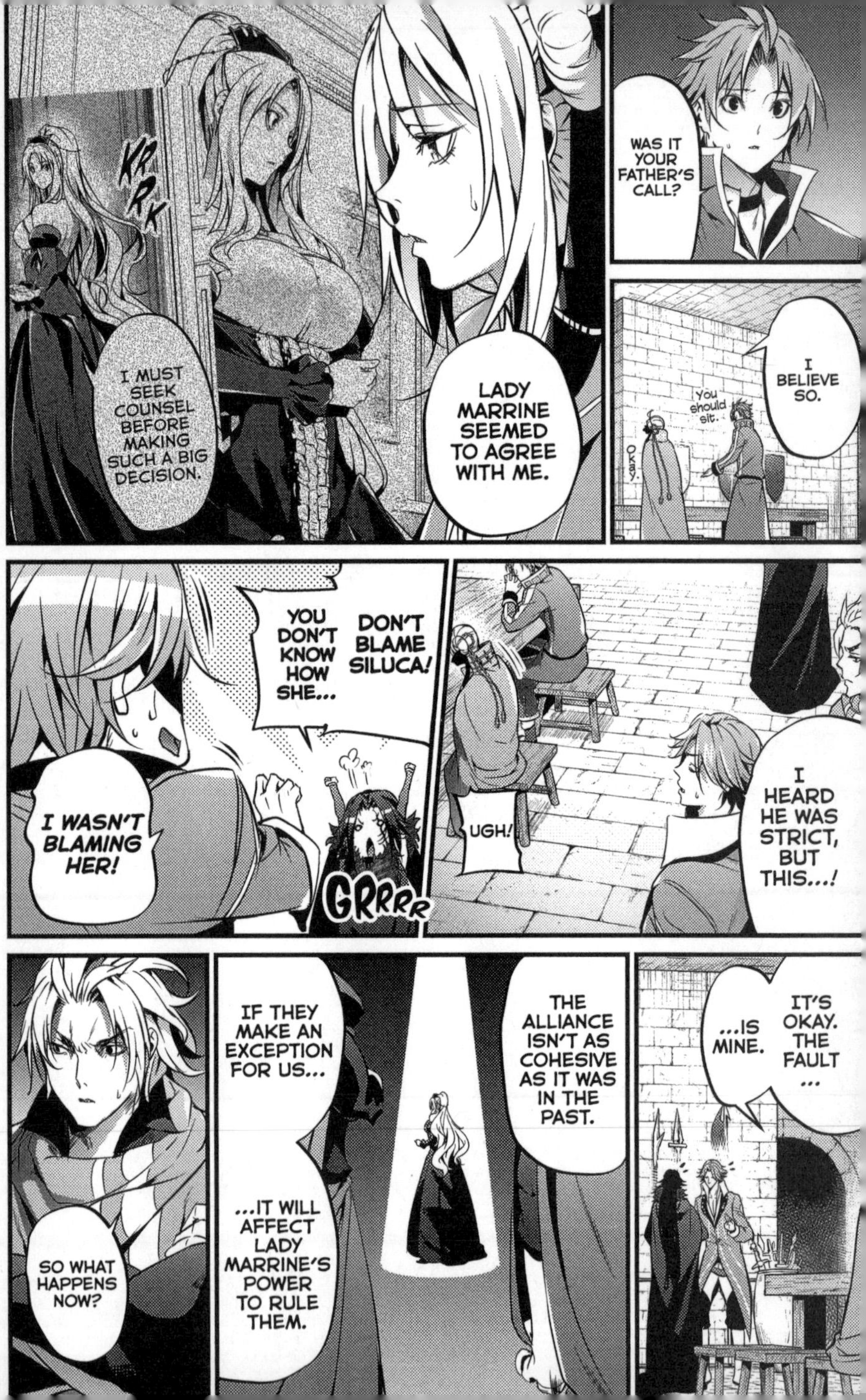
WAS IT YOUR FATHER'S CALL?
I BELIEVE SO.
You should sit.
Okay.
LADY MARRINE SEEMED TO AGREE WITH ME.
KRRK
I MUST SEEK COUNSEL BEFORE MAKING SUCH A BIG DECISION.
I HEARD HE WAS STRICT, BUT THIS...!
UGH!
DON'T BLAME SILUCA!
YOU DON'T KNOW HOW SHE...
I WASN'T BLAMING HER!
GRRRR
IT'S OKAY. THE FAULT...
...IS MINE.
THE ALLIANCE ISN'T AS COHESIVE AS IT WAS IN THE PAST.
IF THEY MAKE AN EXCEPTION FOR US...
...IT WILL AFFECT LADY MARRINE'S POWER TO RULE THEM.
SO WHAT HAPPENS NOW?

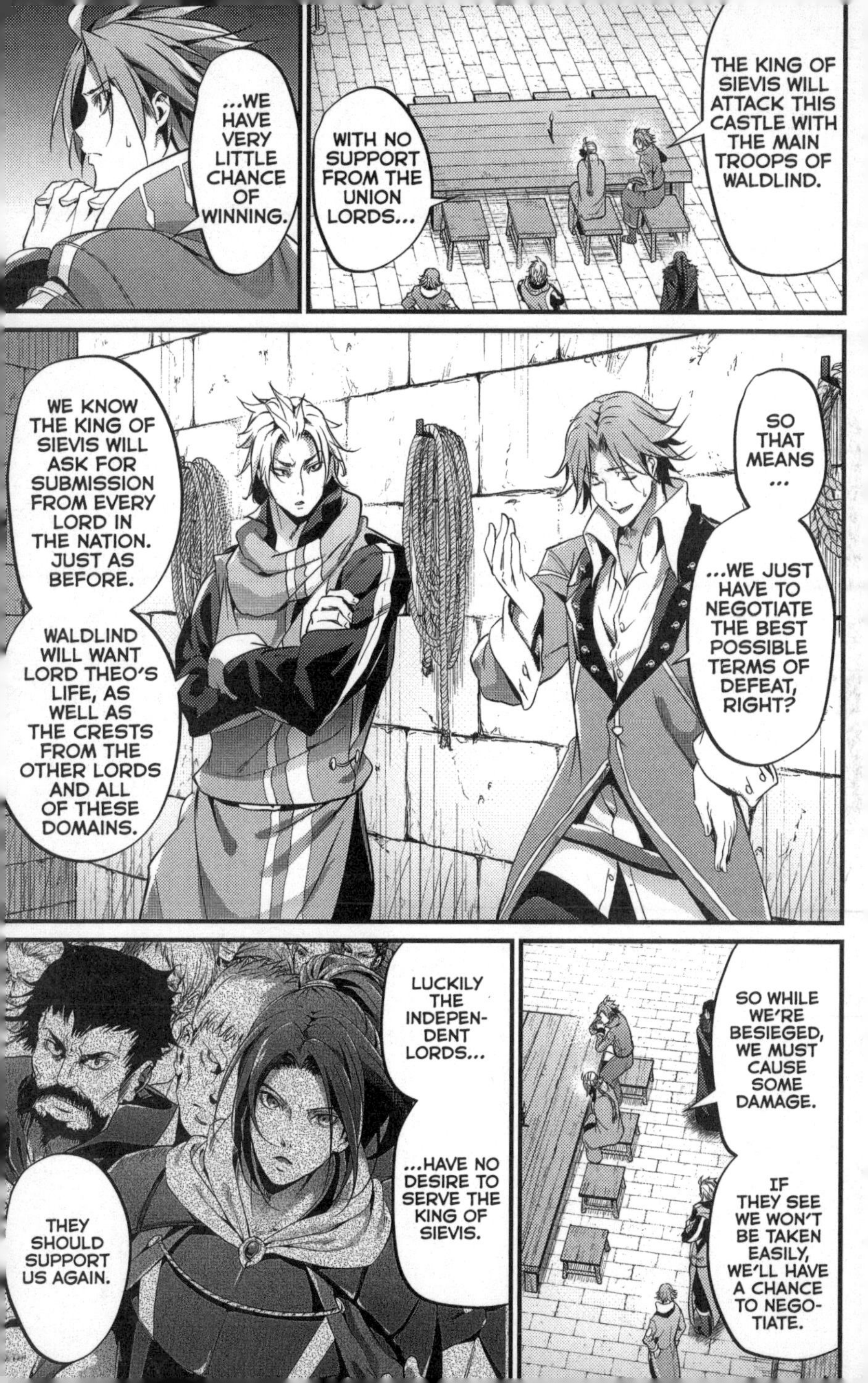
THE KING OF SIEVIS WILL ATTACK THIS CASTLE WITH THE MAIN TROOPS OF WALDLIND.
WITH NO SUPPORT FROM THE UNION LORDS...
...WE HAVE VERY LITTLE CHANCE OF WINNING.
SO THAT MEANS...
...WE JUST HAVE TO NEGOTIATE THE BEST POSSIBLE TERMS OF DEFEAT, RIGHT?
WE KNOW THE KING OF SIEVIS WILL ASK FOR SUBMISSION FROM EVERY LORD IN THE NATION. JUST AS BEFORE.
WALDLIND WILL WANT LORD THEO'S LIFE, AS WELL AS THE CRESTS FROM THE OTHER LORDS AND ALL OF THESE DOMAINS.
SO WHILE WE'RE BESIEGED, WE MUST CAUSE SOME DAMAGE.
IF THEY SEE WE WON'T BE TAKEN EASILY, WE'LL HAVE A CHANCE TO NEGOTIATE.
LUCKILY THE INDEPENDENT LORDS...
...HAVE NO DESIRE TO SERVE THE KING OF SIEVIS.
THEY SHOULD SUPPORT US AGAIN.

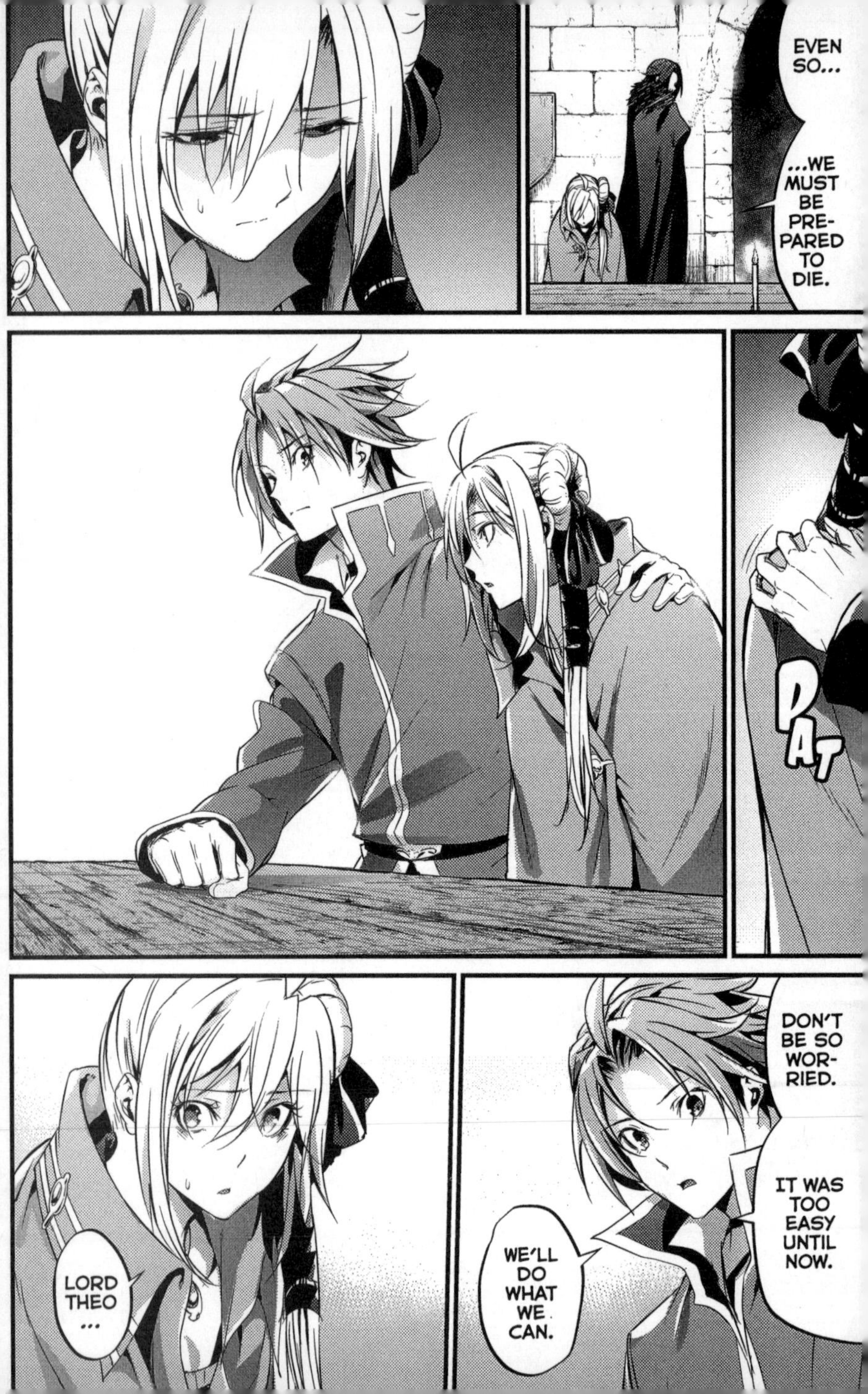
EVEN SO...
...WE MUST BE PRE-PARED TO DIE.
PAT
DON'T BE SO WOR-RIED.
IT WAS TOO EASY UNTIL NOW.
WE'LL DO WHAT WE CAN.
LORD THEO...

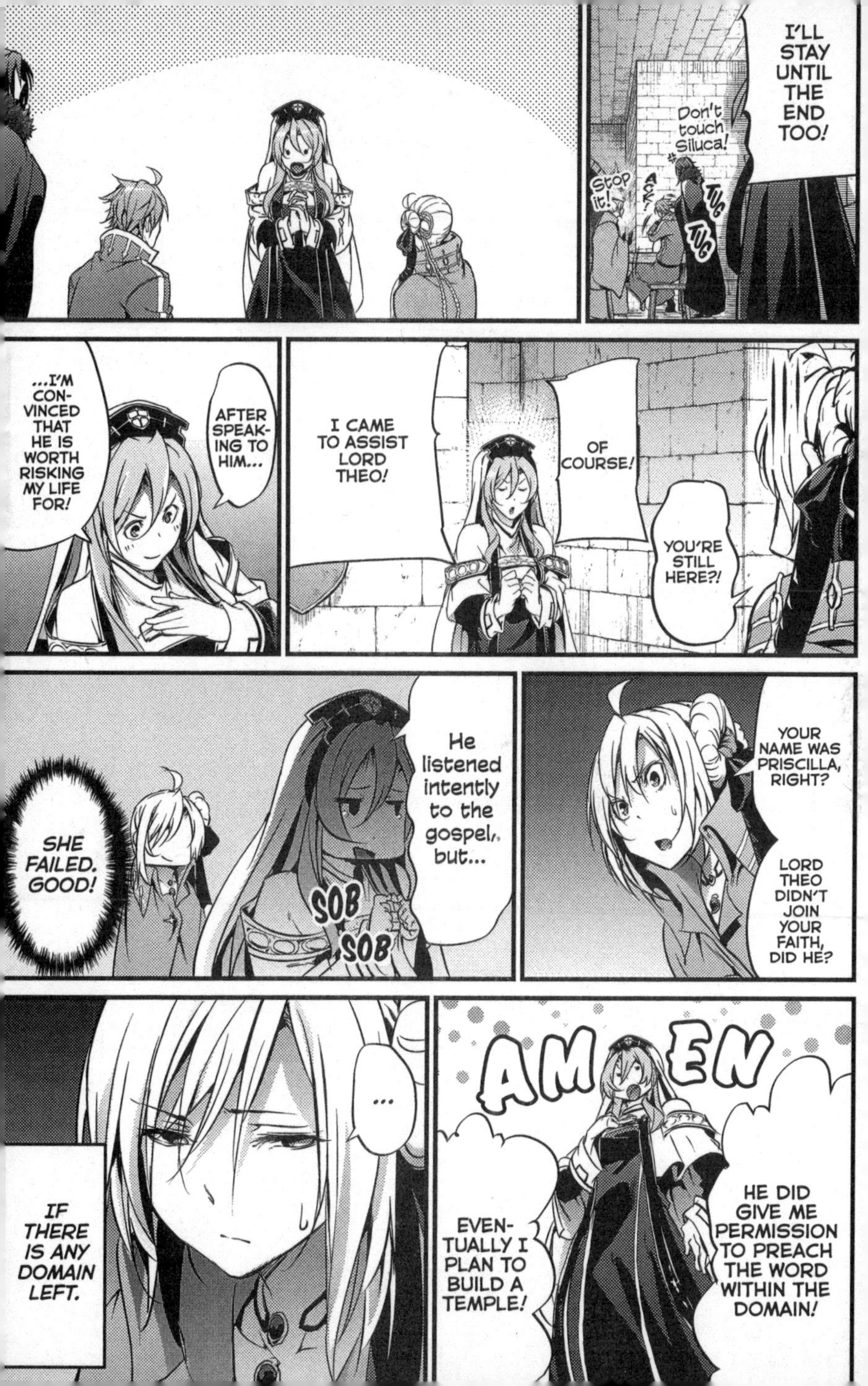
I'LL STAY UNTIL THE END TOO!
Don't touch Siluca!
TUG TUG
ACK!
Stop it!
OF COURSE!
YOU'RE STILL HERE?!
I CAME TO ASSIST LORD THEO!
AFTER SPEAKING TO HIM...
...I'M CONVINCED THAT HE IS WORTH RISKING MY LIFE FOR!
YOUR NAME WAS PRISCILLA, RIGHT?
LORD THEO DIDN'T JOIN YOUR FAITH, DID HE?
He listened intently to the gospel, but...
SOB SOB
SHE FAILED. GOOD!
AMEN
HE DID GIVE ME PERMISSION TO PREACH THE WORD WITHIN THE DOMAIN!
EVENTUALLY I PLAN TO BUILD A TEMPLE!
...
IF THERE IS ANY DOMAIN LEFT.

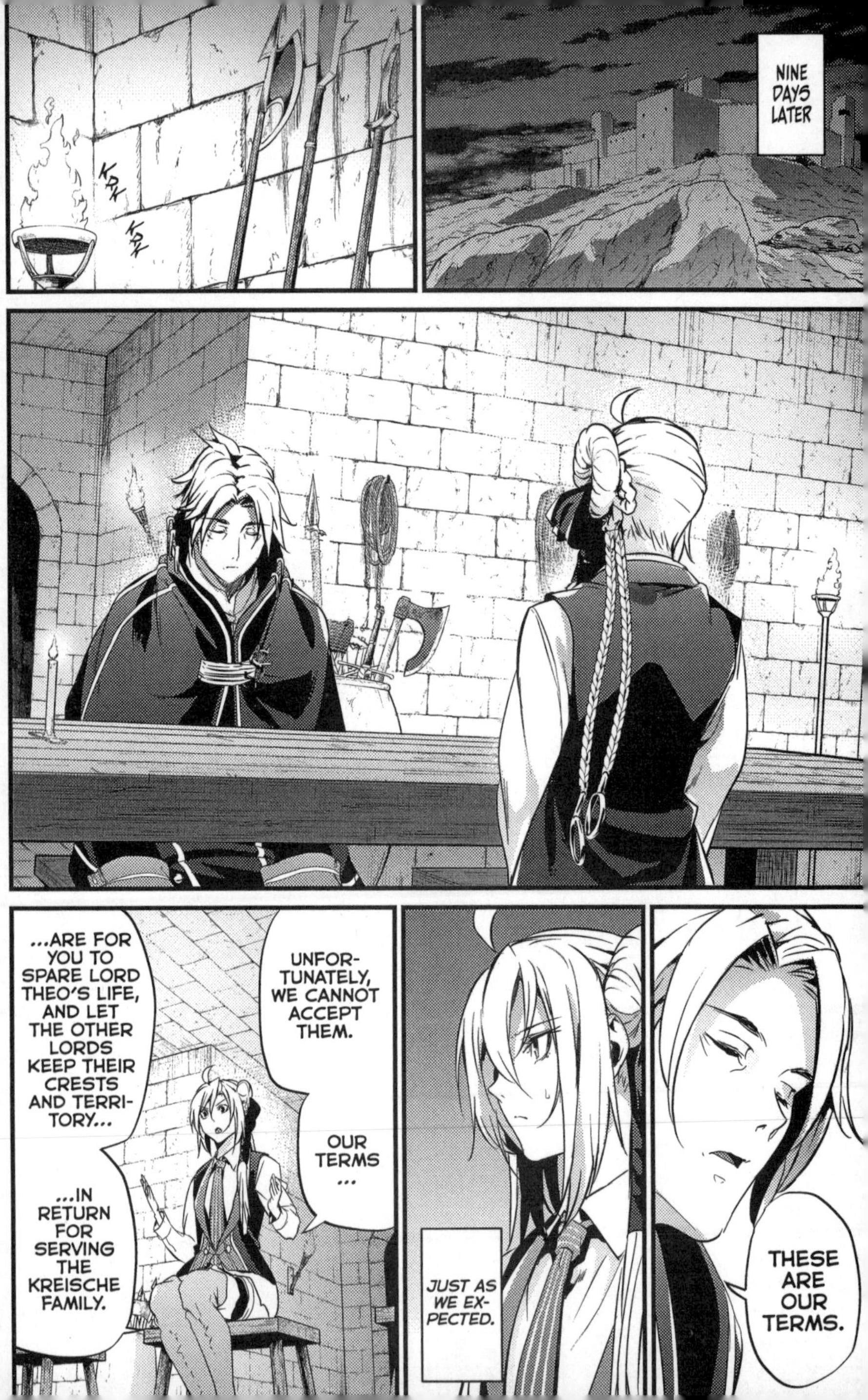
NINE DAYS LATER
KRK
KRK
THESE ARE OUR TERMS.
JUST AS WE EXPECTED.
UNFORTUNATELY, WE CANNOT ACCEPT THEM.
OUR TERMS...
...ARE FOR YOU TO SPARE LORD THEO'S LIFE, AND LET THE OTHER LORDS KEEP THEIR CRESTS AND TERRITORY...
...IN RETURN FOR SERVING THE KREISCHE FAMILY.

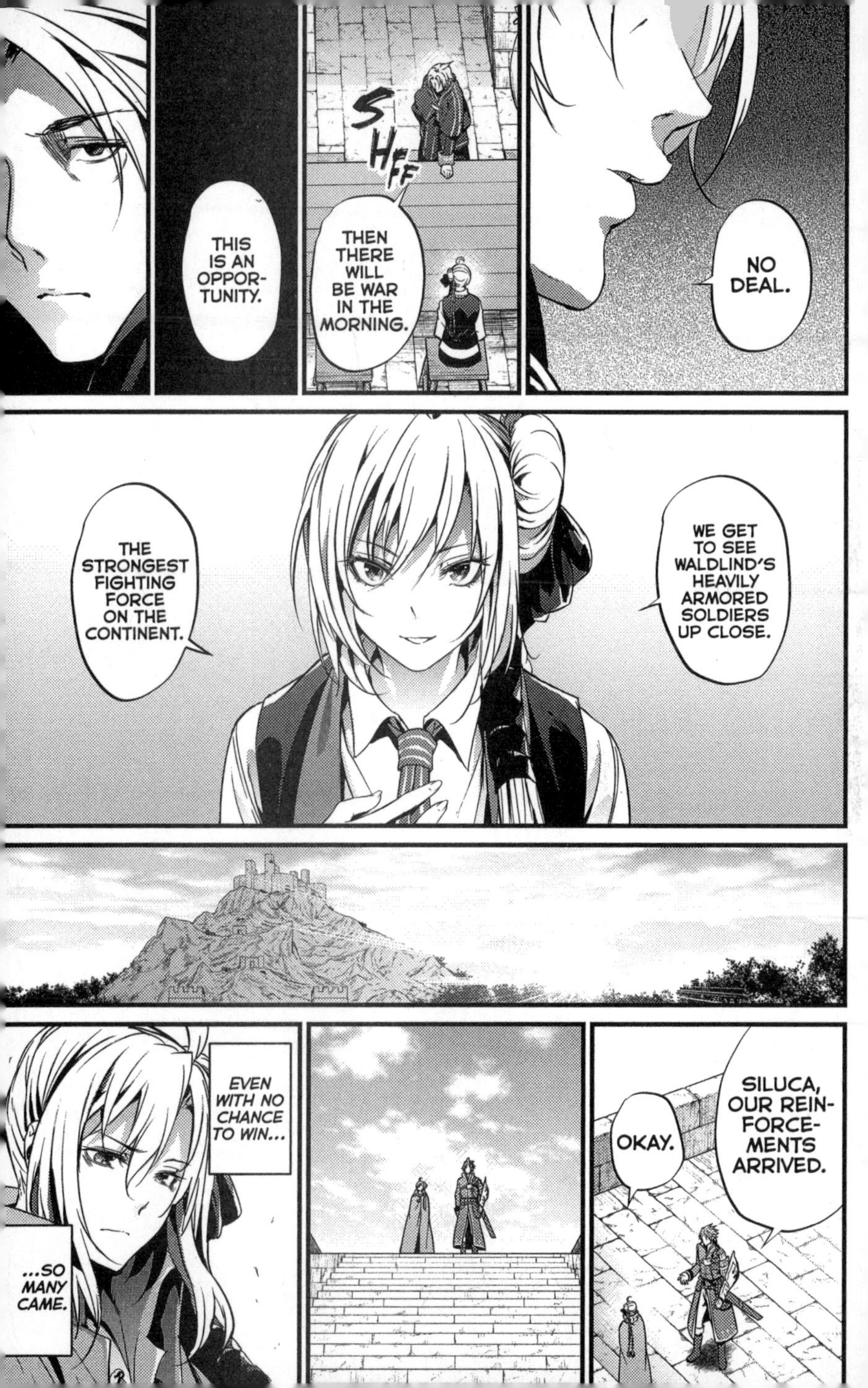
NO DEAL.
SHFF
THEN THERE WILL BE WAR IN THE MORNING.
THIS IS AN OPPORTUNITY.
WE GET TO SEE WALDLIND'S HEAVILY ARMORED SOLDIERS UP CLOSE.
THE STRONGEST FIGHTING FORCE ON THE CONTINENT.
SILUCA, OUR REINFORCEMENTS ARRIVED.
OKAY.
EVEN WITH NO CHANCE TO WIN...
...SO MANY CAME.

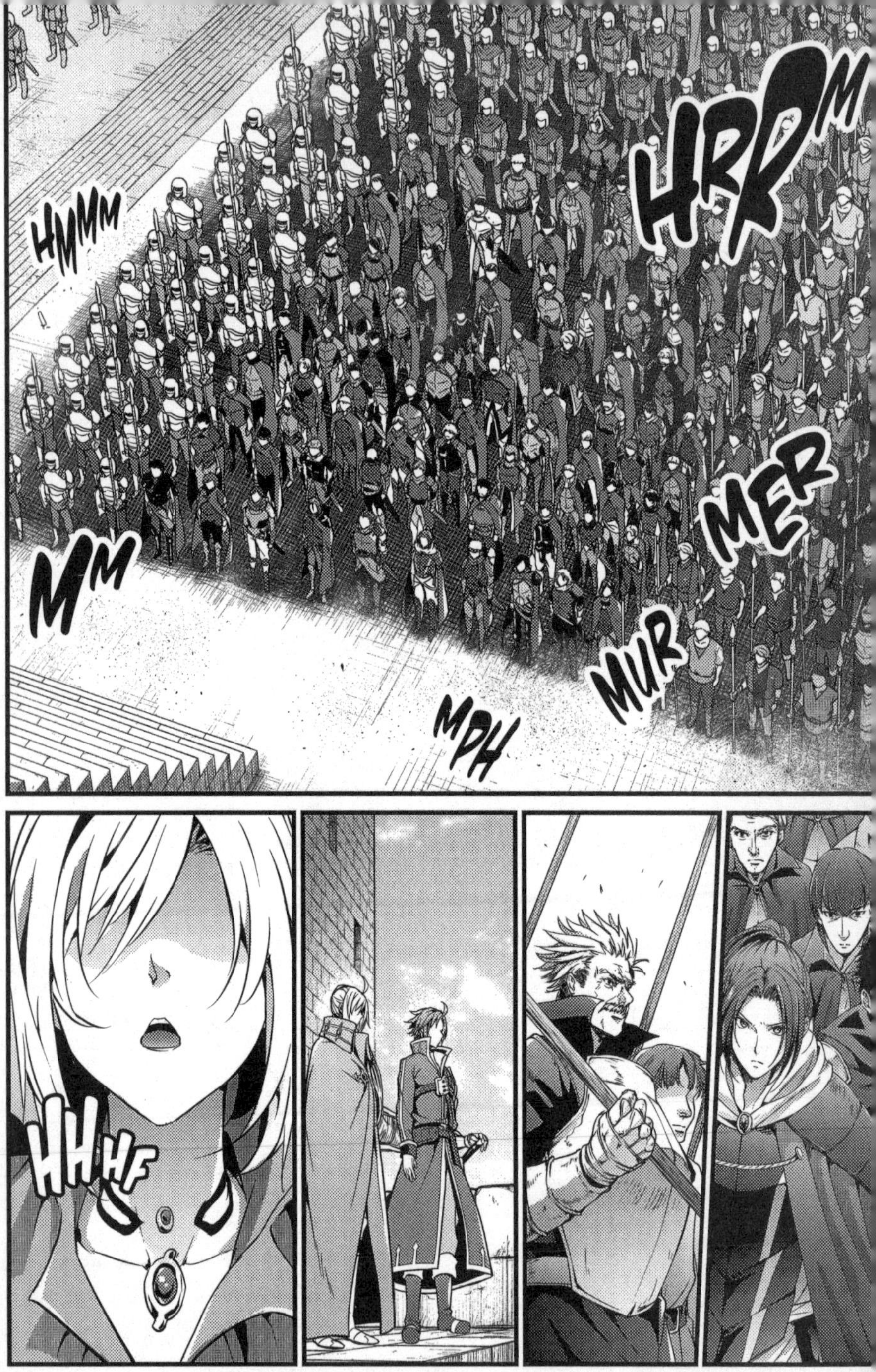
HRRM
MER
MUR
MPH
HMMM
MM
HHHF

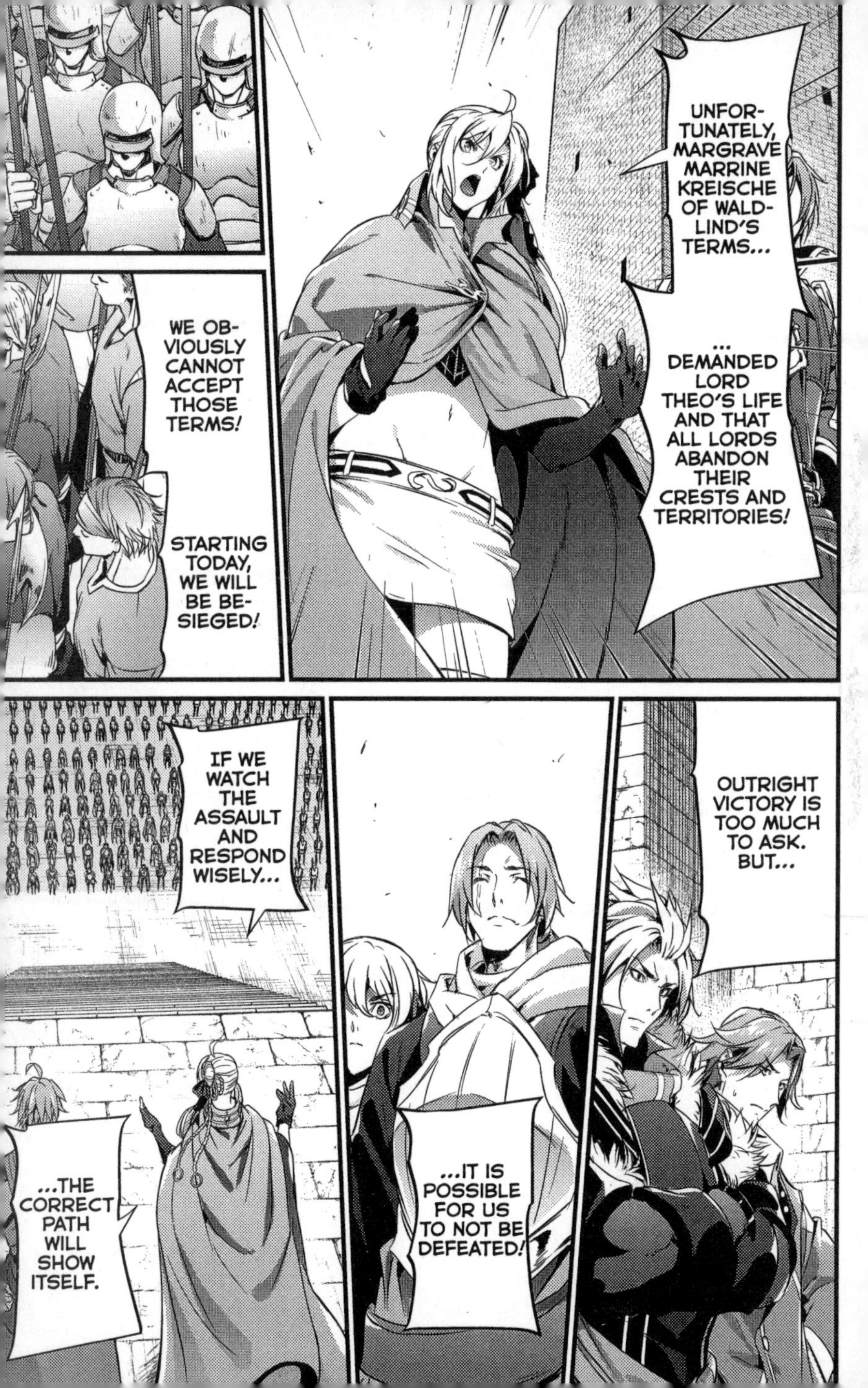
UNFOR-TUNATELY, MARGRAVE MARRINE KREISCHE OF WALD-LIND'S TERMS...
...DEMANDED LORD THEO'S LIFE AND THAT ALL LORDS ABANDON THEIR CRESTS AND TERRITORIES!
WE OB-VIOUSLY CANNOT ACCEPT THOSE TERMS!
STARTING TODAY, WE WILL BE BE-SIEGED!
OUTRIGHT VICTORY IS TOO MUCH TO ASK. BUT...
...IT IS POSSIBLE FOR US TO NOT BE DEFEATED!
IF WE WATCH THE ASSAULT AND RESPOND WISELY...
...THE CORRECT PATH WILL SHOW ITSELF.

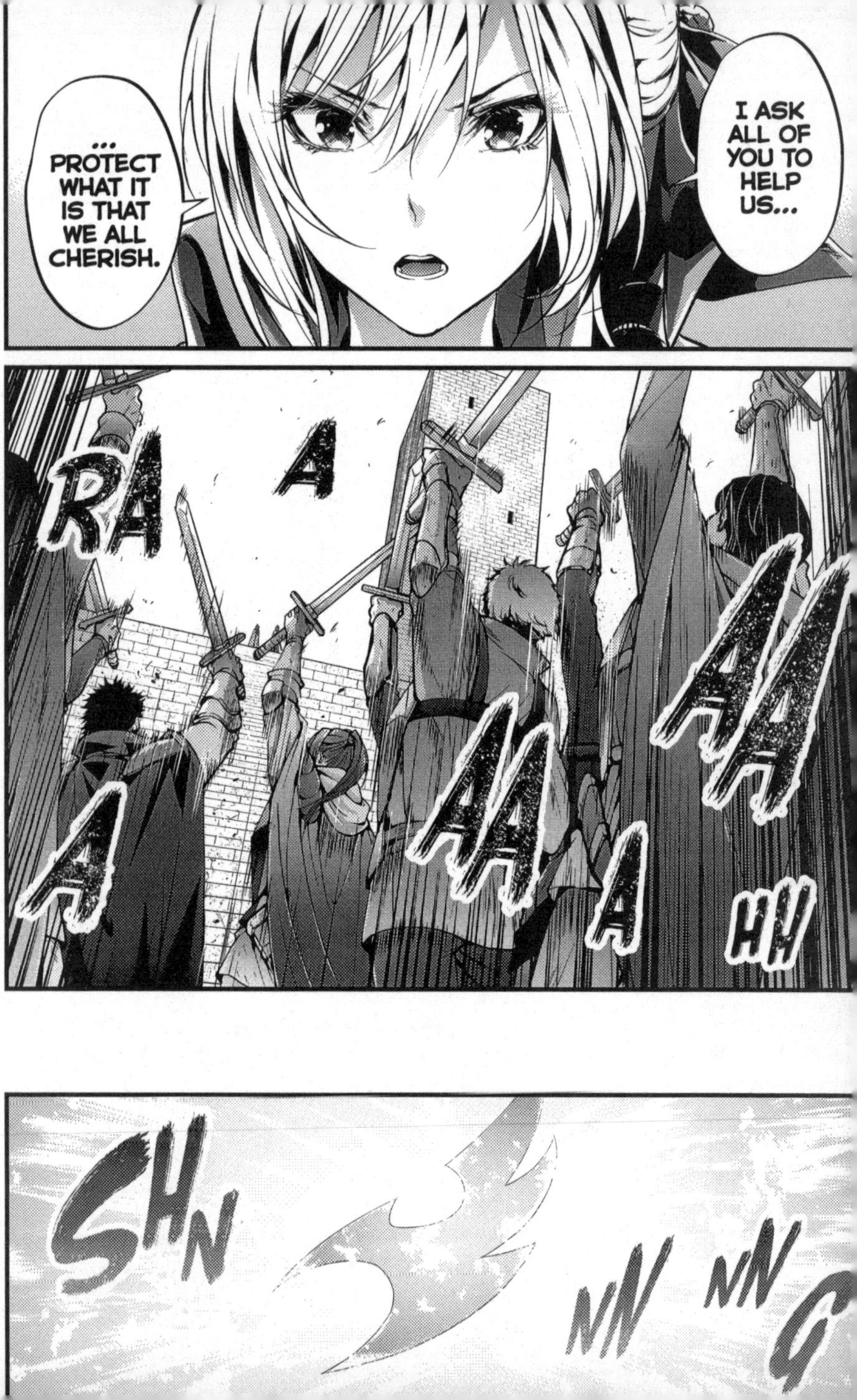
I ASK ALL OF YOU TO HELP US...
... PROTECT WHAT IT IS THAT WE ALL CHERISH.
RA A A AA AA A AA HH
SHNNNNNNG

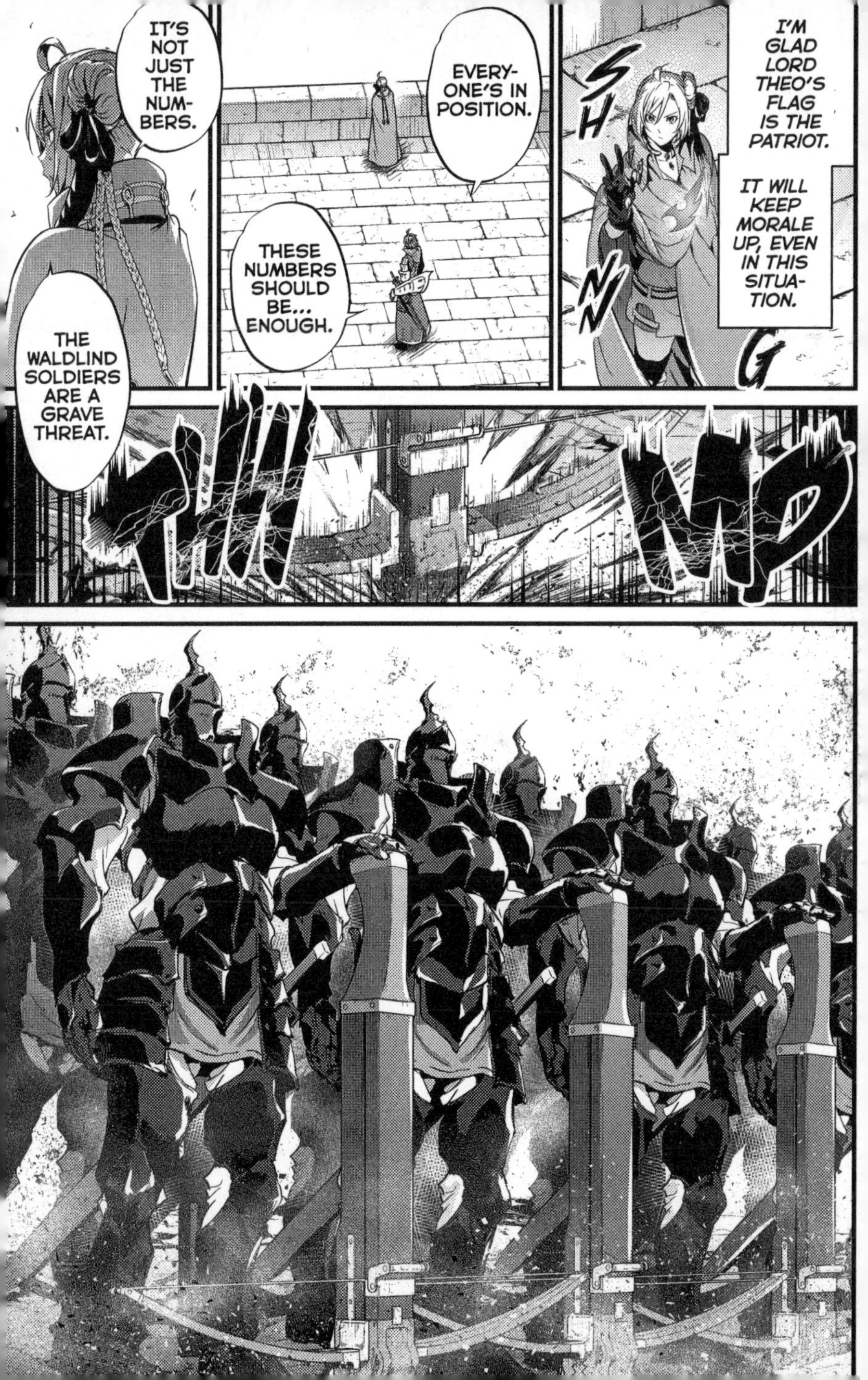
SHNNG
I'M GLAD LORD THEO'S FLAG IS THE PATRIOT.
IT WILL KEEP MORALE UP, EVEN IN THIS SITUATION.
EVERY-ONE'S IN POSITION.
THESE NUMBERS SHOULD BE... ENOUGH.
IT'S NOT JUST THE NUM-BERS.
THE WALDLIND SOLDIERS ARE A GRAVE THREAT.
THWMP

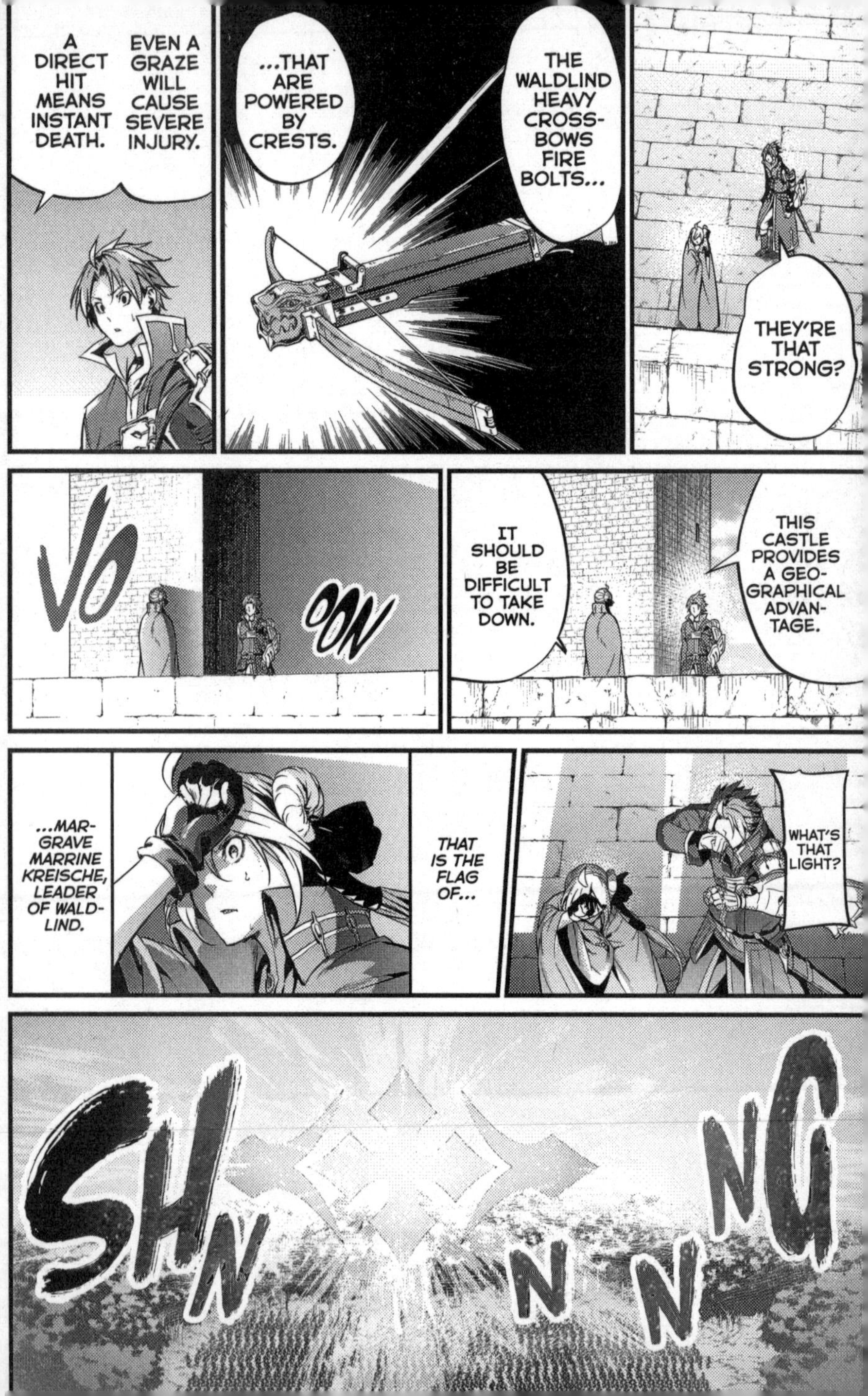
THEY'RE THAT STRONG?
THE WALDLIND HEAVY CROSSBOWS FIRE BOLTS...
...THAT ARE POWERED BY CRESTS.
EVEN A GRAZE WILL CAUSE SEVERE INJURY.
A DIRECT HIT MEANS INSTANT DEATH.
THIS CASTLE PROVIDES A GEOGRAPHICAL ADVANTAGE.
IT SHOULD BE DIFFICULT TO TAKE DOWN.
VOOON
WHAT'S THAT LIGHT?
THAT IS THE FLAG OF...
...MARGRAVE MARRINE KREISCHE, LEADER OF WALDLIND.
SHNNNNG

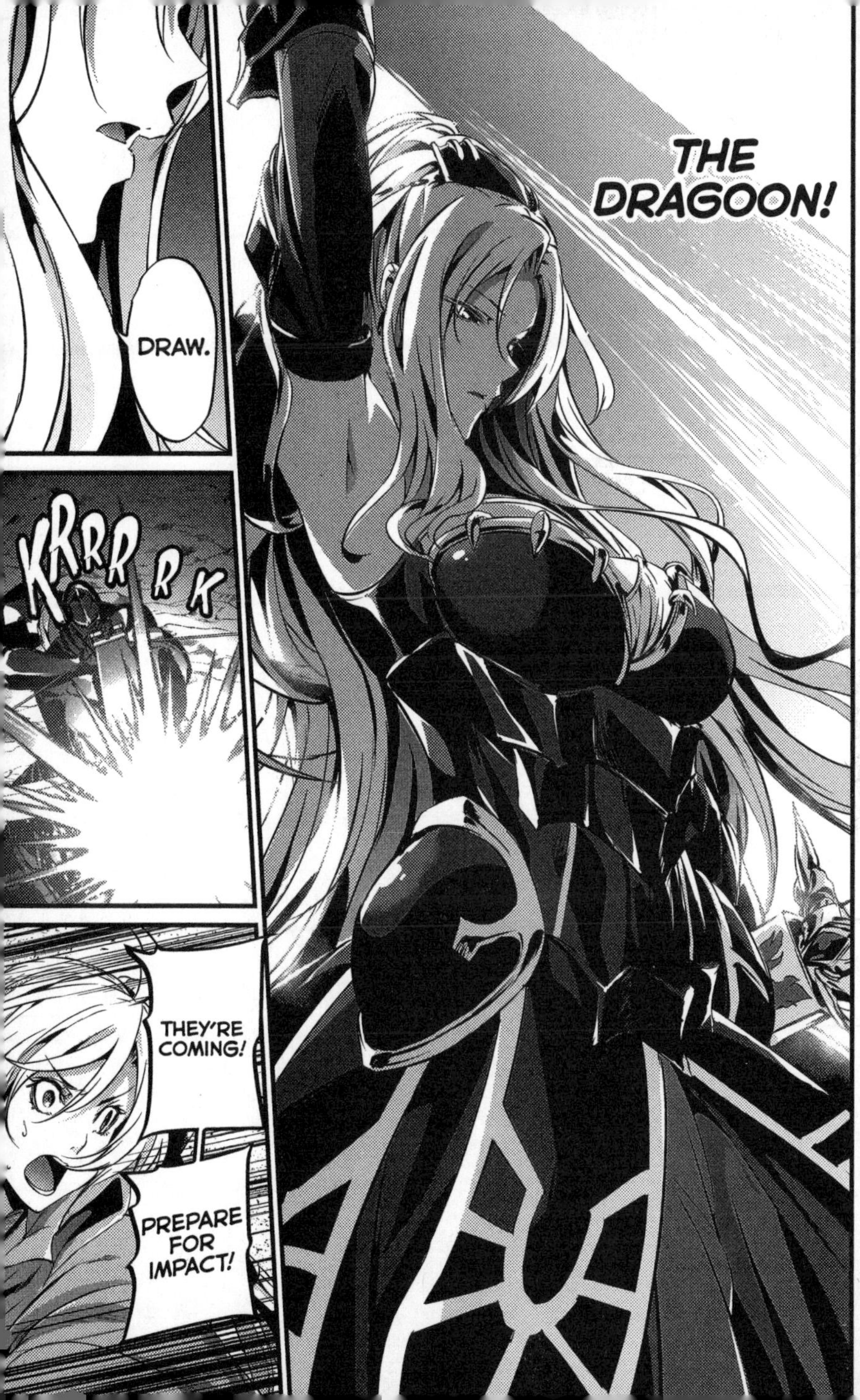
THE DRAGOON!
DRAW.
KRRRRRK
THEY'RE COMING!
PREPARE FOR IMPACT!

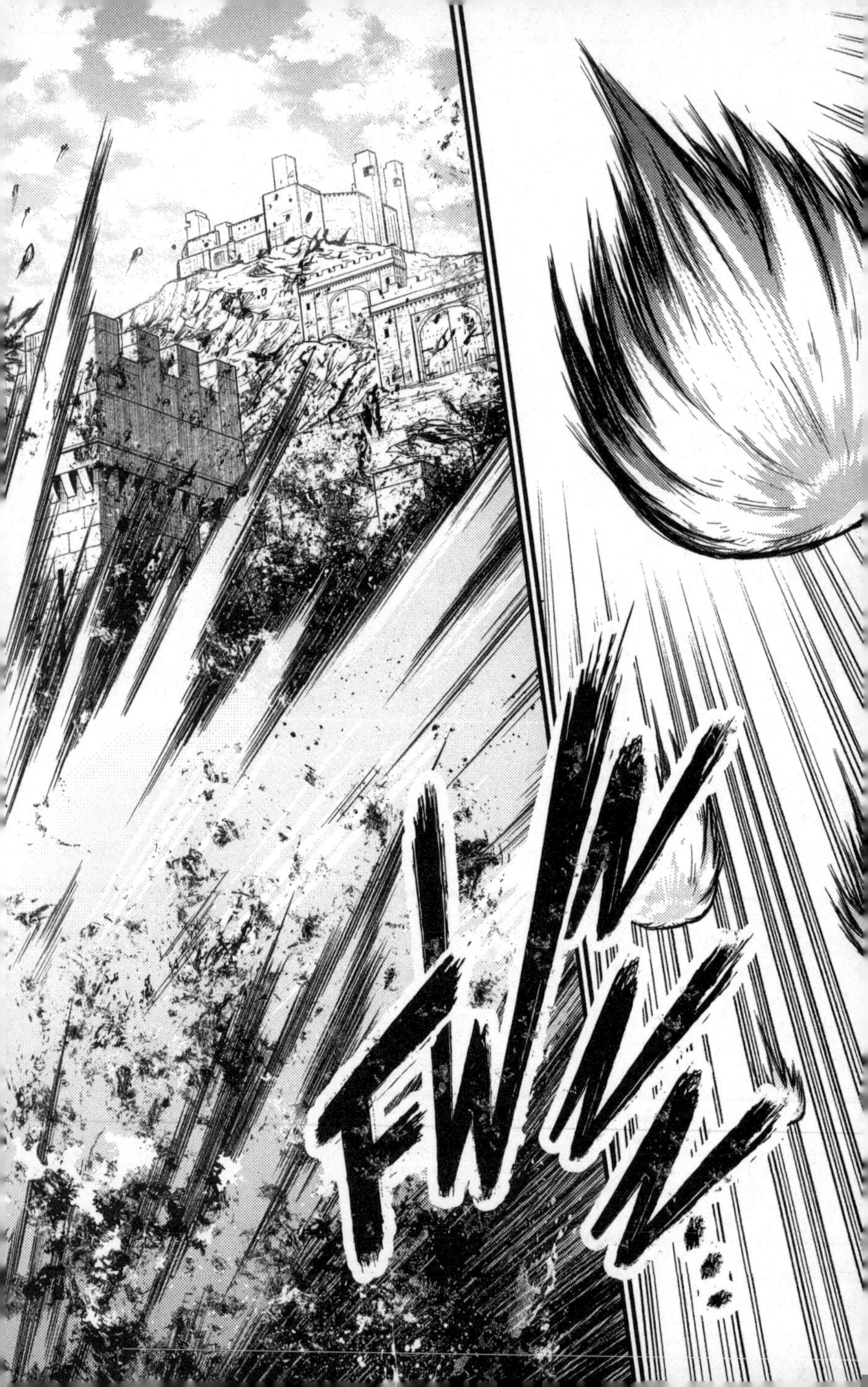
FWSH

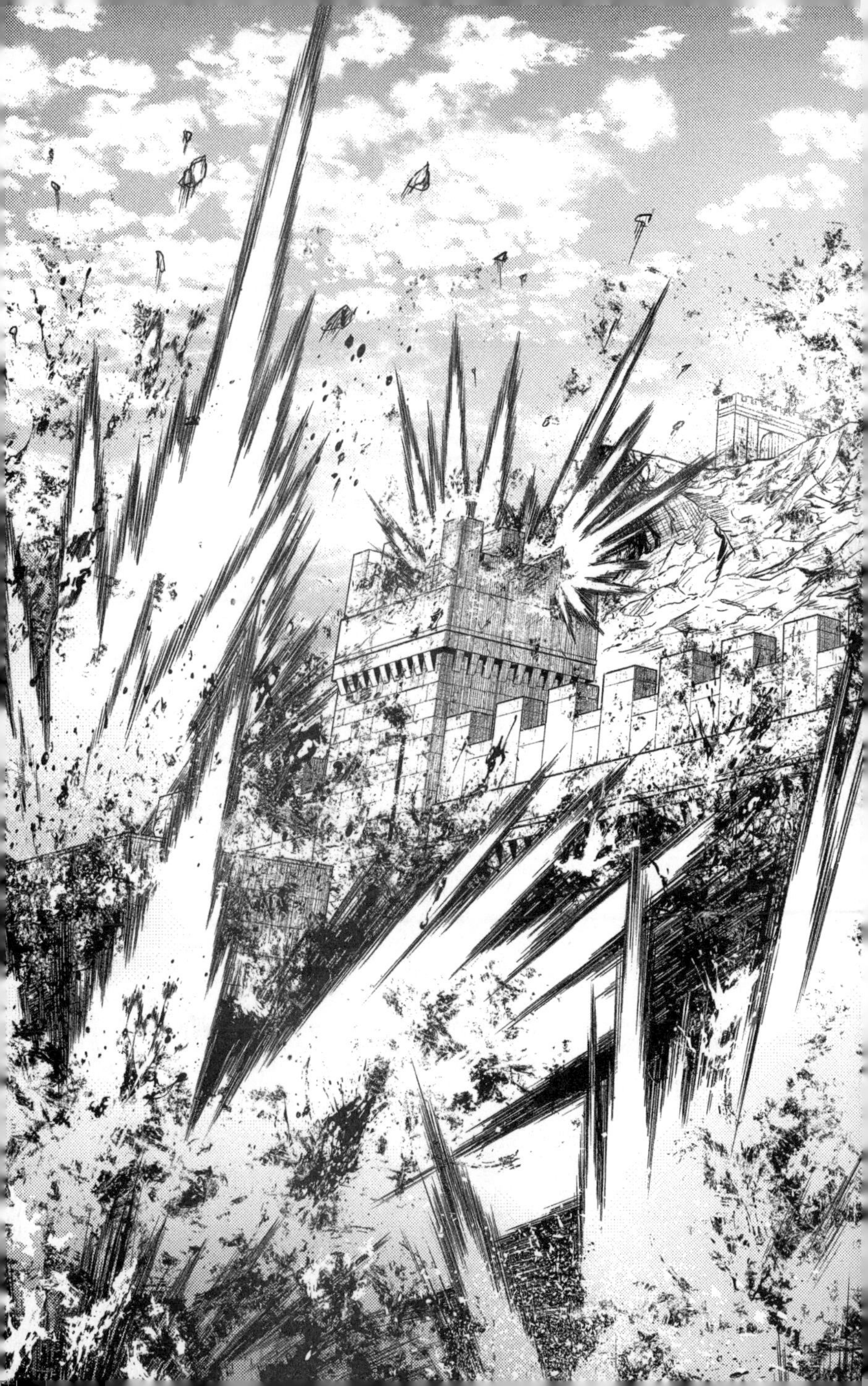

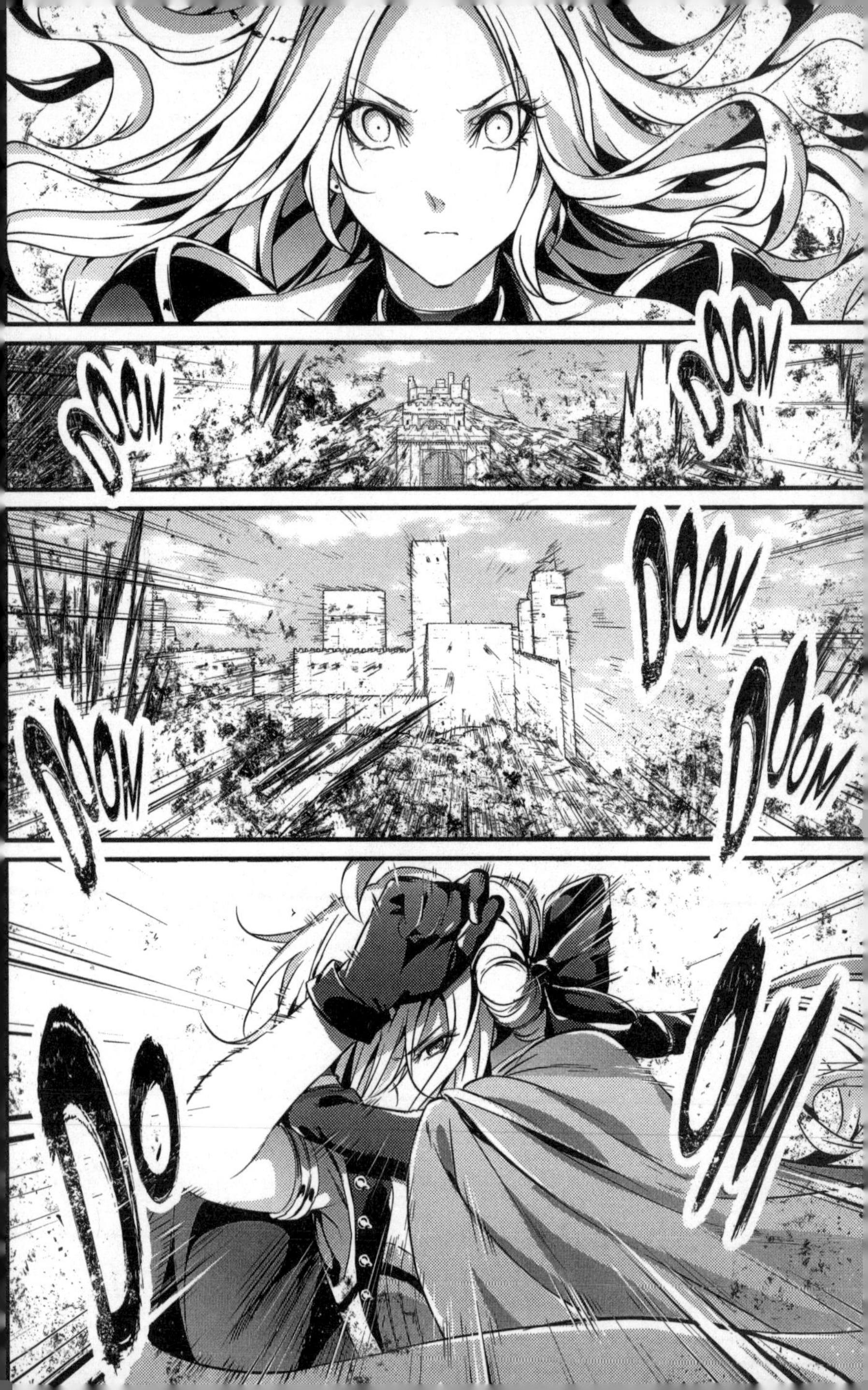
DOOM
DOOM
DOOM
DOOM
DOOM
DOOM

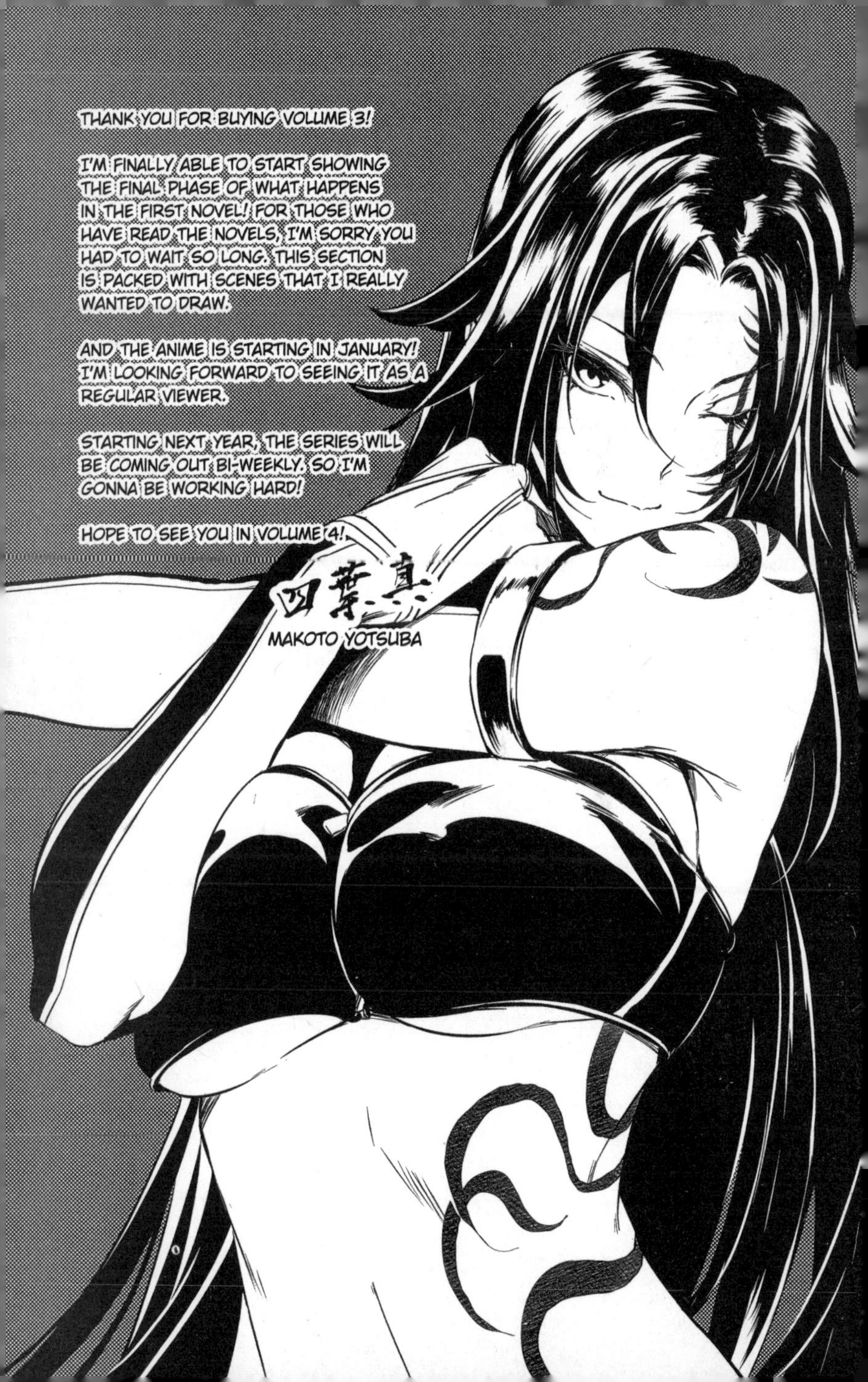
THANK YOU FOR BUYING VOLUME 3!
I'M FINALLY ABLE TO START SHOWING THE FINAL PHASE OF WHAT HAPPENS IN THE FIRST NOVEL! FOR THOSE WHO HAVE READ THE NOVELS, I'M SORRY YOU HAD TO WAIT SO LONG. THIS SECTION IS PACKED WITH SCENES THAT I REALLY WANTED TO DRAW.
AND THE ANIME IS STARTING IN JANUARY! I'M LOOKING FORWARD TO SEEING IT AS A REGULAR VIEWER.
STARTING NEXT YEAR, THE SERIES WILL BE COMING OUT BI-WEEKLY. SO I'M GONNA BE WORKING HARD!
HOPE TO SEE YOU IN VOLUME 4!
四葉真
MAKOTO YOTSUBA

RECORD OF
GRANCREST
—WAR—

VOLUME 3

Original Story by **Ryo Mizuno**
Story & Art by **Makoto Yotsuba**
Character Design by **Miyuu**

Translation: **Satsuki Yamashita**
Touch-Up Art & Lettering: **James Gaubatz**
English Adaptation: **Stan!**
Design: **Julian [JR] Robinson**
Editor: **David Brothers**

GRANCREST SENKI by Ryo Mizuno,
Makoto Yotsuba, Miyuu
© 2016 Ryo Mizuno • Miyuu / KADOKAWA
© Makoto Yotsuba 2018
All rights reserved.
First published in Japan in 2018 by
HAKUSENSHA, Inc., Tokyo.
English language translation rights arranged with
HAKUSENSHA, Inc., Tokyo.

Printed in the U.S.A.

Published by VIZ Media, LLC
P.O. Box 77010
San Francisco, CA 94107

10 9 8 7 6 5 4 3 2 1
First printing, May 2019

PARENTAL ADVISORY
RECORD OF GRANCREST WAR is rated M
for Mature and is recommended for Mature
readers. This volume contains graphic
violence and sexual themes.

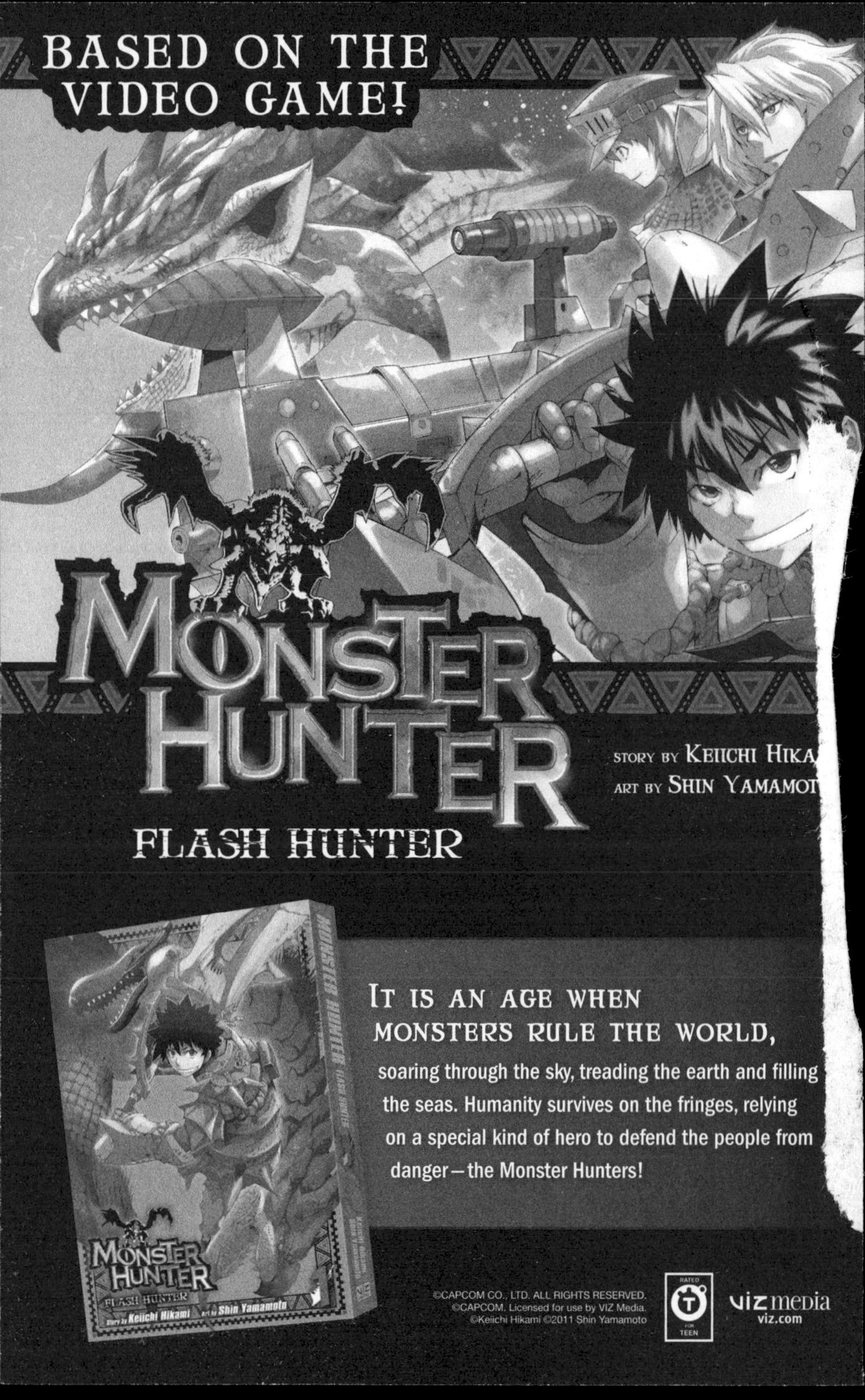

BASED ON THE VIDEO GAME!
MONSTER HUNTER
FLASH HUNTER
STORY BY KEIICHI HIKA
ART BY SHIN YAMAMOT
MONSTER HUNTER
FLASH HUNTER
Story by Keiichi Hikami Art by Shin Yamamoto
IT IS AN AGE WHEN MONSTERS RULE THE WORLD,
soaring through the sky, treading the earth and filling the seas. Humanity survives on the fringes, relying on a special kind of hero to defend the people from danger—the Monster Hunters!
©CAPCOM CO., LTD. ALL RIGHTS RESERVED.
©CAPCOM. Licensed for use by VIZ Media.
©Keiichi Hikami ©2011 Shin Yamamoto
RATED T FOR TEEN
viz media
viz.com

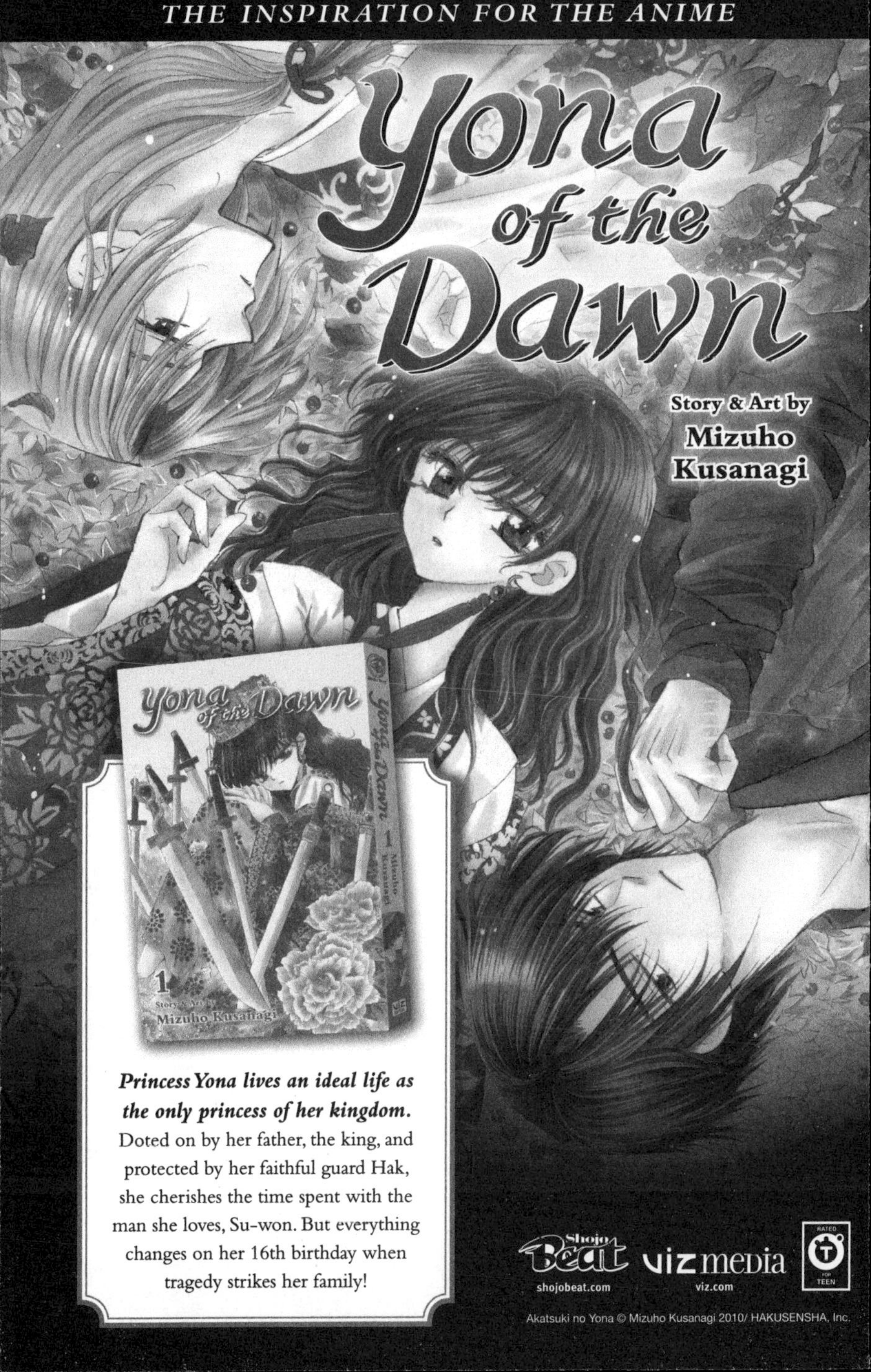
THE INSPIRATION FOR THE ANIME
Yona of the Dawn
Story & Art by
Mizuho Kusanagi
Yona of the Dawn
1
Story & Art by
Mizuho Kusanagi
Princess Yona lives an ideal life as the only princess of her kingdom.
Doted on by her father, the king, and protected by her faithful guard Hak, she cherishes the time spent with the man she loves, Su-won. But everything changes on her 16th birthday when tragedy strikes her family!
Shojo Beat
shojobeat.com
viz media
viz.com
RATED T FOR TEEN
Akatsuki no Yona © Mizuho Kusanagi 2010/ HAKUSENSHA, Inc.

YOU'RE READING THE WRONG WAY

Record of Grancrest War reads from right to left, starting in the upper-right corner. Japanese is read from right to left, meaning that action, sound effects, and word-balloon order are completely reversed from English order.

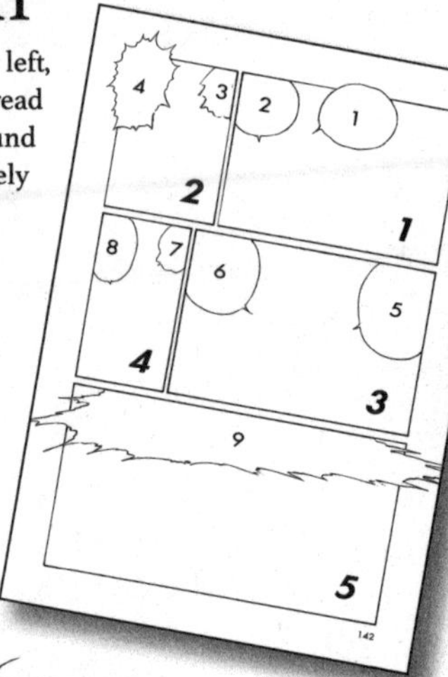

1
2
3
4
1
2
5
6
7
8
3
4
9
5
142

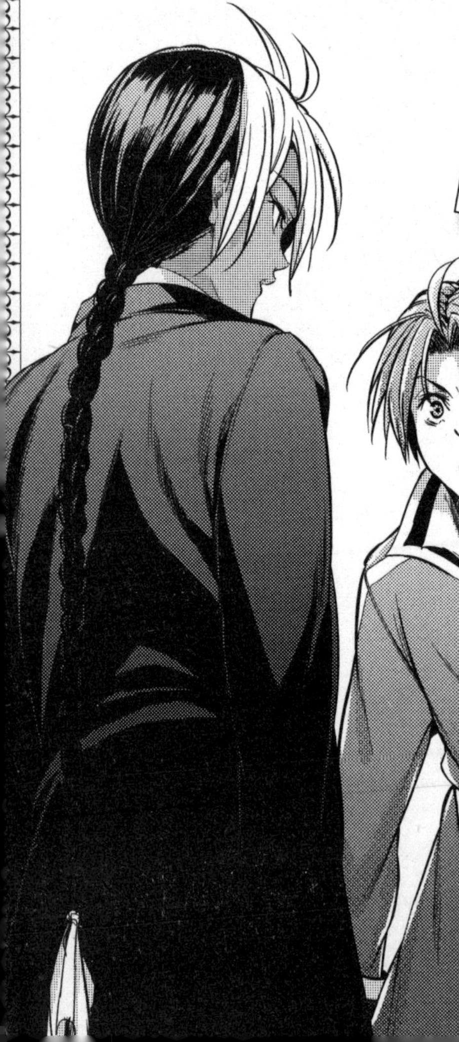
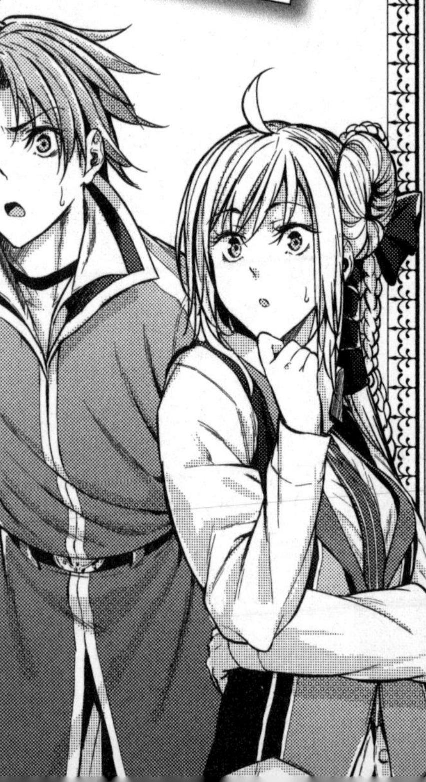

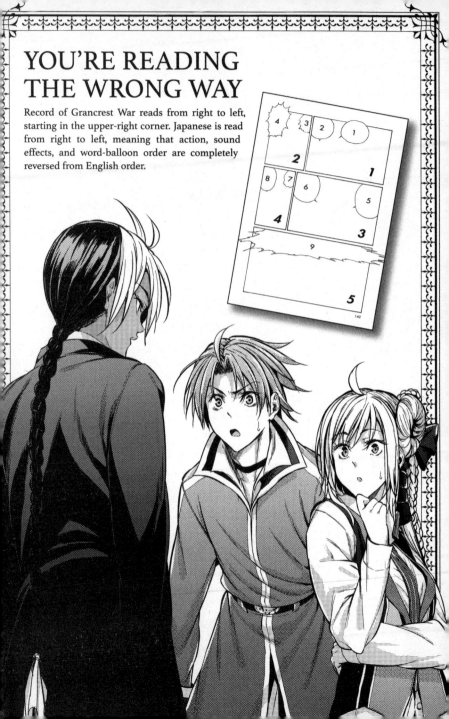